*Studies in Economic Transition*

*General Editors*: **Jens Hölscher**, Reader in Economics, University of Brighton; and **Horst Tomann**, Professor of Economics, Free University Berlin

This series has been established in response to a growing demand for a greater understanding of the transformation of economic systems. It brings together theoretical and empirical studies on economic transition and economic development. The post-communist transition from planned to market economies is one of the main areas of applied theory because in this field the most dramatic examples of change and economic dynamics can be found. The series aims to contribute to the understanding of specific major economic changes as well as to advance the theory of economic development. The implications of economic policy will be a major point of focus.

*Titles include:*

Lucian Cernat
EUROPEANIZATION, VARIETIES OF CAPITALISM AND ECONOMIC PERFORMANCE IN CENTRAL AND EASTERN EUROPE

Bruno Dallago and Ichiro Iwasaki (*editors*)
CORPORATE RESTRUCTURING AND GOVERNANCE IN TRANSITION ECONOMIES

Bruno Dallago (*editor*)
TRANSFORMATION AND EUROPEAN INTEGRATION
The Local Dimension

Hella Engerer
PRIVATIZATION AND ITS LIMITS IN CENTRAL AND EASTERN EUROPE
Property Rights in Transition

Saul Estrin, Grzegorz W. Kolodko and Milica Uvalic (*editors*)
TRANSITION AND BEYOND

Daniela Gabor
CENTRAL BANKING AND FINANCIALIZATION
A Romanian Account of how Eastern Europe became Subprime

Oleh Havrylyshyn
DIVERGENT PATHS IN POST-COMMUNIST TRANSFORMATION
Capitalism for All or Capitalism for the Few?

Iraj Hoshi, Paul J.J. Welfens and Anna Wziatek-Kubiak (*editors*)
INDUSTRIAL COMPETITIVENESS AND RESTRUCTURING IN ENLARGED EUROPE
How Accession Countries Catch Up and Integrate in the European Union

Mihaela Keleman and Monika Kostera (*editors*)
CRITICAL MANAGEMENT RESEARCH IN EASTERN EUROPE
Managing the Transition

David Lane (*editor*)
THE TRANSFORMATION OF STATE SOCIALISM
System Change, Capitalism, or Something Else?

David Lane and Martin Myant (*editors*)
VARIETIES OF CAPITALISM IN POST-COMMUNIST COUNTRIES

Jens Lowitzsch
FINANCIAL PARTICIPATION OF EMPLOYEES IN THE EU-27

Enrico Marelli and Marcello Signorelli (*editors*)
ECONOMIC GROWTH AND STRUCTURAL FEATURES OF TRANSITION

Tomasz Mickiewicz
ECONOMIC TRANSITION IN CENTRAL EUROPE AND THE COMMONWEALTH OF INDEPENDENT STATES

Tomasz Mickiewicz
ECONOMICS OF INSTITUTIONAL CHANGE SECOND EDITION
Central and Eastern Europe Revisited

Milan Nikolić
MONETARY POLICY IN TRANSITION
Inflation Nexus Money Supply in Postcommunist Russia

Julie Pellegrin
THE POLITICAL ECONOMY OF COMPETITIVENESS IN AN ENLARGED EUROPE

Stanislav Poloucek (*editor*)
REFORMING THE FINANCIAL SECTOR IN CENTRAL EUROPEAN COUNTRIES

Johannes Stephan (*editor*)
TECHNOLOGY TRANSFER VIA FOREIGN DIRECT INVESTMENT IN CENTRAL AND EASTERN EUROPE

Horst Tomann
MONETARY INTEGRATION IN EUROPE

Pasquale Tridico
INSTITUTIONS, HUMAN DEVELOPMENT AND ECONOMIC GROWTH IN TRANSITION ECONOMIES

Milica Uvalic
SERBIA'S TRANSITION
Towards a Better Future

Hans van Zon
RUSSIA'S DEVELOPMENT PROBLEM
The Cult of Power

The full list of titles available is on the website:
www.palgrave.com/economics/set.asp

**Studies in Economic Transition**
**Series Standing Order**
(*outside North America only*)

You can receive future titles in this series as they are published by placing a standing order. Please contact your bookseller or, in case of difficulty, write to us at the address below with your name and address, the title of the series and the ISBN quoted above.

Customer Services Department, Macmillan Distribution Ltd, Houndmills, Basingstoke, Hampshire RG21 6XS, England

# Institutions, Human Development and Economic Growth in Transition Economies

by

Pasquale Tridico

*University Roma Tre*

palgrave
macmillan

Softcover reprint of the hardcover 1st edition 2011 978-0-230-24068-1

First published 2011 by
PALGRAVE MACMILLAN

Palgrave Macmillan in the UK is an imprint of Macmillan Publishers Limited, registered in England, company number 785998, of Houndmills, Basingstoke, Hampshire RG21 6XS.

Palgrave Macmillan in the US is a division of St Martin's Press LLC, 175 Fifth Avenue, New York, NY 10010.

Palgrave Macmillan is the global academic imprint of the above companies and has companies and representatives throughout the world.

Palgrave® and Macmillan® are registered trademarks in the United States, the United Kingdom, Europe and other countries.

ISBN 978-1-349-31655-7 ISBN 978-0-230-31388-0 (eBook)
DOI 10.1057/9780230313880

This book is printed on paper suitable for recycling and made from fully managed and sustained forest sources. Logging, pulping and manufacturing processes are expected to conform to the environmental regulations of the country of origin.

A catalogue record for this book is available from the British Library.

A catalog record for this book is available from the Library of Congress.

10 9 8 7 6 5 4 3 2 1
20 19 18 17 16 15 14 13 12 11

*Dla Ani.*
*A mia Madre, e alla memoria di mio Padre.*

# Contents

# List of Tables

## Appendix

# List of Figures and Maps

## Figures

## Maps

# Acknowledgements

I started to work on transition economies in 2002 when I began writing my PhD thesis in Brighton at the University of Sussex. Since then I have worked extensively on this subject. This book is partly a product of my PhD thesis (Chapters 2–4) and partly a product of my post-doc and current research (the rest of the chapters). During this period of research I met many people to whom I am indebted. First of all, my supervisors Sebastiano Fadda at University Roma Tre and Alan Mayhew at the University of Sussex, where I was Marie Curie Fellow (2002–3), both of whom gave me initial inspiration and support. I am indebted also to Pasquale De Muro, the supervisor of my post-doc research fellowship, for his support, and for the comments to the human development parts. Empirical research in Poland contributed enormously to this book. I am grateful to Maria Lissowska (Warsaw School of Economics), Jan Jakub Michałek and Katarzyna Nicholson (Warsaw University), Jerzy Hausner (Cracow University of Economics) and Mirosława Klamut (Wrocław University of Economics) for comments and support during my research visits to Polish universities. Similarly, I wish to thank Bob Jessop, Paul Walsh and Frank Moulaert for their support and comments to my work during my research visit periods at Lancaster University (autumn 2005), Trinity College Dublin (autumn 2006) and Newcastle University (autumn 2007) respectively. Finally, my research activity benefited greatly from a research visit at the Center for European and Eurasian Studies at the University of Los Angeles in California (UCLA) in the autumn of 2009 and at the Center for European Studies at New York University (NYU) where I was Fulbright Scholar (2010–11). I greatly appreciate the comments from Ivan Berend (UCLA) and the support from Gail Kligman (UCLA) and Larry Wolff (NYU). Several chapters of this book, in preliminary versions, were presented at the Annual Conferences of the European Association for Evolutionary Political Economy (EAEPE) and at the European Association for Comparative Economic Studies (EACES). I wish to thank people at those conferences for their comments, in particular scholars of the EAEPE Research Area on 'Structural and Institutional Change in Eastern Europe' and 'Human Development and Institutions' (Bernard Chavance, Caroline Vincensini and Geoff Hodgson). I also wish to thank Antonella

Mennella and Giacomo Sbrana for their comments on the empirical part. Moreover, I wish to thank the Series Editor of Palgrave Macmillan, Jens Holsher, for his support and all the people at Palgrave Macmillan who assisted me during this project (Taiba Batool, Gemma Papageorgiou and Jon Lloyd). Last but not least, I wish to thank my family and my mother for their unconditional love, and Ania, my love and unique support. She was with me during all these years since Brighton where I met her. I enjoyed long conversations, her comments and extraordinary support. This book is dedicated to her, to the memory of my father and to my mother. All mistakes and omissions are obviously mine.

# Introduction

Transition economies in Central and Eastern European Countries (CEECs) and the former Union of Soviet Socialist Republics (USSR), currently known as the Commonwealth of Independent States (CIS), have undergone considerable transformation since 1989–91. After the recession of the early 1990s, some of these economies experienced GDP recovery at a different pace and with different outcomes in terms of economic growth and social performance (that is, human development, employment, poverty and inequality). Human development, defined as a process of enlarging people's choices that is achieved by expanding human capabilities and functioning (UNDP, 1990), has worsened in some transition economies. This has been largely ignored by the economic transition literature. The level of life expectancy, one of the most important features of the Human Development Index (HDI), worsened. Moreover, extreme diversity and fragility in the performance of the main economic variables such as GDP growth, public debt, trade balance and inflation are evident, although economic policies advised by international organisations and implemented by national authorities are quite similar.

The main questions that this book aims to answer are why transition economies had different levels of performance, why some of them grew faster than others, which model of capitalism they were aiming at, what are the roles of institutions and of institutional change on development, and what are the main determinants of a process of economic development, which includes both income and non-income dimensions (life expectancy and education levels in particular). Moreover, I will explore whether democracy, among transition economies, is conducive to economic development or whether the reverse applies. Finally, the relevance of social capital will be examined in detail, in order to test a relation of causality between social capital and development.

At the beginning of transition, the prevalent idea among economists and international economic organisations was very market-oriented. Reforms in many transition economies mainly followed the *Washington Consensus* (WC), which designed policies according to neoclassical theories, with adverse effects and poor results in many transition countries (Lin, 2005). The World Bank and the International Monetary Fund (IMF) advised very strict fiscal and monetary policies for all transition countries, whatever their circumstances. The results were high social costs and slow economic recovery. To some extent, economic recession was also attributed to the WC recipe (Kolodko and Nuti, 1997; Stiglitz, 1998; Chang, 2008). In fact, a state of *vacuum*, chaos and disorganisation in the economic framework was created. Oliver Blanchard (1997) refers to this period as a *systemic vacuum* and an economy of chaos. In many post-communist economies this vacuum favoured anti-social behaviour and perverse attitudes such as lobbying and corruption, increased egoism, threatened trust, increased inequality and favoured personal privileges, power groups and rent-seeking behaviour of oligarchs, with negative effects on social capital and development.

Nevertheless, the transformation of former communist countries has been unique. From one side it took place peacefully and it was an astonishingly fast process towards a Western mode of development, with some exceptions in the CIS. From another side it was characterised by deep economic troubles. As such, it is a process which involves successes and failures and which varies consistently among transition countries (Holscher and Gabrisch, 2006; Kornai, 2006; Ebert, 2007). The views of economists on the transformation policies and on their outcomes have been quite controversial and diverse (Sachs, 1991; Balcerowicz, 1993; Kolodko and Nuti, 1997; Åslund, 2001). During the 1990s, the debate among economists on the type of transformation and on the mistakes of policy makers was very intense. Briefly, some economists criticised the timing of implementation, others the intensity of policies and yet others the need and the appropriateness of the transformation. Many economists today would agree that an institutional and appropriate strategy focusing on institutions was missing, at least at the beginning of transition, in almost all Former Communist Economies (FCEs). Institutions, such as formal and informal rules affecting the behaviour of economic agents, were not considered important for development; public institutions were neither replaced nor created; international constraints were just accepted and implemented; culture, social capital, domestic norms and values were simply ignored; and path-dependency theory was not considered to be relevant (Kregel and Matzner, 1992; Murrel, 1992; Gomulka, 1995; De Vincenti, 1998; Nuti, 1999; Falcetti *et al.*, 2000; Beck and Laeven, 2006).

Today, a new consensus seems to be emerging, which claims that institutions matter and policy strategies are relevant for further development and for the building of an economic system.

I argue that, broadly speaking, the reasons for different levels of performance are first of all attributable to *institutions*, which include in a wide sense the different institutional policies and strategies implemented, the mistakes of policy makers, regulation, competition, international regimes, labour market institutions, monetary constraints, policies and incentives for human capital and innovation, agents' reactions to new policies, levels of trust and social capital, democratic political institutions, people's capabilities and opportunities, path dependency, control of corruption, participation and accountability of people and different initial conditions. All these variables identify a socio-economic model within the capitalist mode of production.

In fact, one can observe that institutions made the difference in Poland, Slovenia, Hungary, the Czech Republic and, to some extent, Estonia, which all have better political institutions indices (voice and accountability, democracy, freedom, political rights and civil liberties, and the rule of law) and socio-economic indicators (health and education in particular).[1] These are countries where, sooner or later, socially oriented reforms, institutional strategies, income distribution policies, conflict management institutions, social pacts and welfare support were introduced during the 1990s. In contrast, a clear institutional approach and a socially oriented strategy were missing in the CIS – and partly so in Bulgaria and Romania – countries which are affected by political troubles, corruption, lack of trust and lower levels of voice and accountability, democracy, freedom, political rights and civil liberties, and the rule of law. Similar stories can be found in most of the former Yugoslav countries, although these were also negatively affected by war.

In the CEECs, recession at the beginning of transition was from 20 to 40 per cent of GDP, whereas in the Former Soviet Republics (FSRs), it was worse and GDP fell in some cases by 65 per cent (Transition Report, 2001). At the same time, economic recovery was faster and more consistent in the CEECs than in the CIS. After ten years of transition, only a few economies reached or exceeded the 1989 level of GDP (Poland, Hungary, Slovakia and Slovenia). The rest of the CEECs and the CIS were still below that level. After 15 years, the Czech Republic, Estonia and

Albania joined this club. Interestingly enough, in the CIS, only Belarus, Uzbekistan and Turkmenistan had a GDP level equal to or higher than 100 in 2004 (with the level in 1989 being equal to 100). After 20 years of transition, the situation in most of the former communist countries does not seem to have stabilised. Moreover, the current economic crisis shows how vulnerable transition economies are with respect to external shocks. The average GDP level in 2008 was 117. Considering the slump caused by the current economic crisis, at the end of 2009 transition economies had an average GDP level much the same as in 1989, with several countries still below that level. Today, roughly only half of the CEECs and half of the CIS surpassed the GDP level that they had in 1989.

Although this was not the main objective of the book, I can say that the financial crisis of 2008–10 had very detrimental effects on all transition countries, which showed both political vulnerability and economic volatility. However, some countries managed their economies better during the crisis, and this can be attributed to the maturity of pre-crisis institutions and to a more developed domestic market (Transition Report, 2009). The case of Poland is very interesting, as it is one of the very few countries in the European Union (EU) and was one of the few transition economies not to experience recession during 2008–10, with a positive GDP growth in 2009 (+1.3 per cent). On the contrary, countries which adopted an extreme export-led model with an uncontrolled openness to foreign direct investment (FDI) (such as Estonia, Latvia and Lithuania) were the most hard-hit by the crisis (in the Baltic region and in some other countries, GDP fell by around 15 per cent). The CIS, Eastern Europe and the Caucasus suffered the recession more heavily, with a reduction in output in 2009 of nine per cent on average, in particular in Russia, Ukraine, Georgia and Armenia. The rest of the CIS, in Central Asia, managed relatively better during the crisis (+0.8 per cent on average) than the CEECs (where GDP fell by five per cent on average).

The 2008–10 economic crisis also brought about a resurgence of Keynesian policies (Krugman, 2008; Rodrik, 2008). A new policy consensus on heterodox policies, institutionally aware strategies, demand-side policies and fiscal stimulus also seems to emerge among transition economies. This can be an important lesson that could enable a better economic recovery and the prevention of further economic crises.

## The collapse of a system: finding reasons for the crash

Contrary to Marx's view, the first great experiment of communism was established in the feudal society of Russia, and not in the industrial societies of Western Europe, as foreseen in *Capital* (Marx, 1867) or in *The Communist Manifesto* (Marx, 1848). The capitalist crisis described by Marx, generated by lower and lower profits after capitalist expansion, did not come to pass. Neither did the internal contradictions of capitalism materialise. Capitalism was generated by the enlargement of a greater industrial reserve, which, although angry and desperate, did not assault the power of the bourgeoisie in most cases. On the contrary, working conditions in Western Europe improved consistently.

A few decades later, China was also a non-industrial society when the communists took power. Similar stories can be written about the Cuban Revolution, communism in Vietnam and North Korea, and many other African countries after independence, where some forms of a communist state were founded by revolutionary independents. At the end of the 1980s, about one-third of the world's population was living under more or less extended communist rules and planned economies.

No one at the beginning of 1989 could have imagined that the fall of communism in Central and Eastern Europe was very close. Ironically, only some accidental prophecies without scientific analysis, Nostradamus-type predictions and some satiric journals foresaw it, such as the prophecy of Levin (1993) or the satiric weekly *Il Male* in 1980 (see Nuti, 2009). However, economic crises and political troubles were already present in the 1980s in many former communist countries, and not only in the Poland of Solidarność (Nuti, 1984).

Before the 'Russia experience', industrialisation was a process which took place only where the feudal society was already defeated somehow. When it took place in Britain, royal governance had already been replaced by some extent of democracy. In France, the industrialisation process followed the French Revolution, which was led mainly by the bourgeoisie against the aristocracy. The USA and Canada are two good examples of fast development processes with no resistance or opposition by royalty or the aristocracy. On the contrary, the experience in Latin America shows different stories: aristocracy, landowners, renters and lords from Spanish and Portuguese motherlands impeded or did not favour an industrial transformation and therefore a sustained accumulation and development process.

Japan was able to start its development and modern industrialisation process only after the Second World War, when the previous oligarchs, ruling classes, their family structures and war generals were to some extent defeated (Lockwood, 1954). Finally, Africa is another example of resistance against modernisation opposed mainly by some organisation prone to defend the old cultural background, particular objectives, clan values and personal interests crystallised into dominant positions of some groups. A modern society, technological change and fast development would throw away all these particular advantages and therefore these processes are opposed by the people and power groups who enjoy these advantages. Consequently, if these groups are stronger, industrialisation becomes difficult to undertake, and norms and social values which inhibit economic growth prevail.

In Russia and then in all the FSRs, Leninism and Stalinism challenged the old paradigm of industrialisation and the Rostow (1960) theory of stages of development. However, in a way, state planning was an attempt to bring about a fast process of development using a forced action of industrialisation which took place in an astonishingly fast fashion. Real socialism proved that industrialisation should not have to be necessarily associated with capitalism. A transition towards a modern society was also possible under communism and planned economies. However, FCEs were not able to overcome the second transition: from modern and industrialised societies towards a 'knowledge-based economy'. This second transition should have started in the 1970s, when FCEs started to lag behind capitalist economies in Western Europe and North America. In the 1970s, a new revolution was needed against bureaucratic interests and ruling powers. A complex and articulated economic organisation was required in order to challenge the globalisation and the knowledge-based economy which was going to be consolidated during post-Fordism. Soviet planners were not able to do it. Interests were too rooted in the former system and in the old industrial sector, and therefore there was no place for new processes of production, technologies, interests, objectives and power groups. In fact, each technological change brings with it, as Schumpeter (1928) showed, new groups, new firms and new objectives which shape a new order, new powers and new domains. It is a selection process which favours some groups over others. The status quo will prevail if the current dominant group is stronger and able to resist the change. In the long run, however, if the change is really needed, the economy will decline in terms of competitiveness and wealth against other economies which adopted that change.

In the end, capitalism proved to be stronger against real socialism in Soviet-type societies; however, there was a period of time – which was quite long – at least during the 1950s and 1960s, which can be defined as a 'take-off stage' in Rostow (1960) terms, in which working-class conditions in communist countries were better off than working-class conditions in a capitalist society during their take-off stages. Moreover, when one considers the great advantage that colonial capitalism had enjoyed for many decades, then the Soviet development, from a purely economic point of view, during the 1950s and 1960s is more remarkable and the failure of communism in 1989 can be reconsidered.

However, such a reconsideration is not absolute and does not consider the political dimension and tragedies of the regime. It is only useful in order to better understand the main causes of the economic development until 1970 and to put forward an argument which would explain the causes of its collapse. As a starting point of this argument, I will list five features, which can be considered stylised facts, of Soviet-type societies:

1. Planned economies in the CEECs and in the FSRs were able to deliver better performance in physical terms, for instance, in tonnes of coal, in kWh of energies, in gold medals, etc. They were not able to calculate opportunity costs and therefore to start a virtuous process of selection with appropriate incentive mechanisms.
2. Beyond the Comecon or the Council for Mutual Economic Assistance (CMEA), the CEECs and the USSR were not able to diversify production, to exploit geographical advantages or to build appropriate institutions favouring openness and trade (even under the control of the state).
3. Most of the former communist planned economies focused too heavily on natural resources and tried to exploit competitive advantages coming from there; however, advantages in terms of natural resources can work as a trap, which embeds the economy in a vicious circle of limited production, with lower productivity gains in the long run and pollution problems. Moreover, the rate of investment required to improve output in a natural resource-oriented economy is very high and increases the capital-output ratio (**v**), reducing performance in terms of GDP growth (**g**) in the long run, for each saving rate **s** (in the traditional terminology of growth theory $\mathbf{g} = \mathbf{s}/\mathbf{v}$). As such, an economy of this kind would need more and more capital to obtain one unit of output, increasing instability and the inflationary process, since the *aggregate demand* would be constantly higher than the *supply*.
4. The communist ruling class was politically hostile towards the middle class and middle-income peasants. Such hostility did not allow for the creation of more democratic institutions and, consequently, for a further accumulation process, which would favour, via parallel and private channels, the development process. Development relied solely on the developmental role of the state.

5. There is a path dependency and an historical legacy in Tsarist Russia as far as hostility against the middle class and middle-income peasants is concerned. In Russia, both Peter the Great and the Empress Catherine II never favoured agriculture and industry. During this time, heavy industry was mainly developed by the aristocracy, and small firms and handcrafts were discouraged. Agriculture was left without an infrastructure to connect the vast Russian Empire with its main cities. The Soviet regime was mainly organised in the same way, with open hostility shown towards the Kulaks (middle-income peasants) and little attention given to the manufacturing industries. The CIS in general was more affected by these issues than the CEECs.

Paradoxically, the Soviet-type economies were able to produce output following the neoclassical mainstream argument based on a production function type $Y = F(L, K)$, as a 'sausage-making machine', which uses pigs (raw material) + sausage machine (capital) + labour (men) to get sausages in huge quantities, although within a planned framework of fixed wages, with no differentials for work effort and no profits (Dillon and Wykoff, 2002). In FCEs, output was very minimally differentiated and heavy industry created and run mainly by large state-owned enterprises (SOEs) was the main output, because it fit better into the planned economy model. Modern industry, complex manufacturing and technologically advanced products, which would eventually have a global demand, would have been more difficult to manage under a planned system, which would need a greater and faster circulation of information. Moreover, in this context, 'negative incentives' of production and obedience to the system were implemented, such as imprisonment, torture and state terror, while positive incentives were neglected.

A Fordist model of production, with mass consumption and mass production, repetitive behaviour and demand management, was also the main model used in the West. However, the West, unlike the FCEs, as Berend (2009) shows, was able to start an adjustment process towards a global economy, differentiated production and technological change in the 1970s when globalisation needed it.

## The ten straws that broke the camel's back

In FCEs during the 1970s and 1980s, the role of the developmental state decreased and the problems of the economy, listed above, emerged strongly. In particular, the capital-output ratio was very high, the marginal productivity of capital was very low and the economies were using more and more capital. In some FCEs such as Poland, Romania and several FSRs, this was done at the expense of a growing external debt (Dillon and Wykoff, 2002). Moreover, in the 1970s and 1980s, 'mother' Russia, a symbol and a model for all Soviet republics and Central and Eastern European satellites, showed more and more signs of weakness, which were exacerbated by the following ten events:

1. The end of Revolution enthusiasm and an increasing distance between second and third nomenclature generations and ordinary people.
2. The success of industrialisation created a society with different and more sophisticated needs and requirements than just the simpler ones of the post-Second World War era.
3. The impasse of the Afghanistan War which weakened both the Soviet Army and the Empire.
4. The improvement in education increased the level of criticism and contradictions in society.
5. The success of Japan, through a particular type of capitalism, convinced many Soviet satellites of the possibility of an 'own style' of development.
6. The Chernobyl disaster, which was a shock from an image point of view abroad and a negative turning point for the propaganda of triumphalism.
7. A more and more inefficient, cumbersome and corrupted bureaucracy.
8. The Reagan 'Star Wars' policy, which challenged the Russia technological system and showed the great gap between the USSR and the USA.
9. The income gap between West and East: the West of Europe was geographically too close for people to be able to hide the increasing income differentials and the relative impoverishment of the East in the 1980s.
10. Imbalances in the badly administered price system were too great, with too strong inflationary pressures.

When Gorbachev came to power, aware of these problems in the USSR and in Russia in particular, he focused mainly on the possibility of saving the hegemony of the USSR and Russia. Therefore, he left the CEECs to their destiny and accepted that these states were emancipated from USSR control. For the first time in history since the time of the Tsars, domestic affairs were more important to Russia than its foreign close-neighbouring policy (Gros and Steinherr, 1995). With Gorbachev's *Perestroika* in the middle of the 1980s, the Brezhnev Doctrine was abandoned.[2] Hence, the USSR tolerated Solidarność in Poland during the 1980s, accepted its first government in 1989, overlooked the market-oriented reforms introduced in Hungary in the 1980s, ignored the soft revolution in Czechoslovakia in the summer and autumn of 1989 and did nothing to prevent – and perhaps even accelerated – the fall of the Berlin Wall in November 1989, anticipated by mass demonstrations in Leipzig, Berlin and other cities in East Germany (GDR) throughout the autumn of 1989.

At the same time, however, within the USSR and in Russia in particular, the conflict between hardliners and party reformers became clearer. Opposition to Gorbachev's reforms became stronger and culminated with the August Coup in 1991, which was an attempted coup d'état against Gorbachev by hardline Communist Party members and the KGB. After the coup failed, Yeltsin, who had publicly opposed it, came out as a hero while Gorbachev's power was effectively ended. After the coup, the USSR became extremely weak and the Soviet republics accelerated their process towards independence, declaring their sovereignty one by one and establishing the CIS in December 1991, which is a mere confederation of independent states (Yavlinsky *et al.*, 1991).

In Central and Eastern Europe, the sources of the fall of communism in 1989, which anticipated the dissolution of the USSR in 1991, have similar roots of those in the FSRs. In fact, the stylised facts listed above, plus some of the ten events which anticipated the collapse of the USSR, apply to Central and Eastern Europe too. Moreover, in the CEECs the fall of communism was anticipated by a latent-turned-open hostility towards Russian hegemony. Several countries such as Poland, Czechoslovakia, Hungary, Romania and the Baltic states had continually been the victims of Russian interference throughout history. Poland in particular was for several centuries under Russian occupation. The Baltic countries were fully integrated after the Second World War into the USSR. In addition, the Warsaw Pact sent the Red Army into Hungary and Czechoslovakia in 1956 and 1968 respectively to repress the winds of reformism in those countries.

As far as religion is concerned, most of the CEECs belong to the Christian Catholic Church, while Russia is predominantly Russian Orthodox. Such a difference became clearer and perhaps more problematic with the election of the Polish Cardinal Karol Wojtyla as Pope John Paul II in 1978. The influence of John Paul II's election was strong for Polish emancipation, and for the success of the Solidarność revolution, although nobody could really imagine in the 1980s that Solidarność would lead the country from communism to capitalism. In the best-case scenario, Solidarność was perceived as an important social force that could result in some economic reforms to improve the living conditions of workers. However, in the late 1980s, they started to question the one-party system, the prevalence of the Polish Communist Party and also asked for political reforms, pluralism and democratisation. The *Round Table* in February–April 1989 was appointed in order to reach a compromise between Solidarność and communist requirements for the future development of the political and economic systems in Poland.

To sum up, the industrialisation effort in former communist countries on the one hand reached the objective of setting up industrial society in the East of Europe, but on the other hand did not achieve the objective of overcoming the living standards of Western society. In the long run, industries in the East lost competitiveness towards the West and productivity decreased steadily. Labour productivity was in general lower in the East and economic growth slowed down. Industrial investment became more and more inappropriate and inefficient in increasing productivity considerably. Hence, the gap between East and West increased. It is interesting to observe, from an historical perspective, that some countries like Poland, Hungary, Czechoslovakia and on average the USSR had, in 1950, a GDP per capita higher than Portugal, Greece and Spain, and a very similar one to those of Italy, Ireland and Austria. On the eve of the fall of the Berlin Wall in 1989, the situation was reversed. All the Western economies had higher GDP per capita figures than those countries.

In particular, the income gap increased during the 1970s and 1980s. Finally, the transition recession in the 1990s significantly increased the gap. The reasons for this can be traced back to the 1970s when communist economies lost 'an encompassing national interest' (Olson, 1992) and missed the opportunity to embark on an innovation process (Berend, 2009), because institutions and incentives were no longer appropriate.

## Institutional change and development

One of the initial questions economists should pose in addressing development issues is what kind of 'development' exactly is being discussed or explored to begin with?

In the widely quoted book *Economics of Development*, Perkins *et al.* (2006) stress the difference between 'economic growth' (referring to the rate of growth in goods and services produced) and the broader concept of 'development' – one that involves the combination of economic growth and changes in human development variables, such as life

*Table 1* Levels and growth of GDP in some FCEs and old EU Member States (1950–90)

| Countries | GDP in $ | | GDP 1950 = 100 | Average GDP growth (in %) | | | |
|---|---|---|---|---|---|---|---|
| | 1950 | 1989 | 1990 | 1950–60 | 1960–70 | 1970–80 | 1980–90 |
| Czechoslovakia | 3,501 | 8,768 | 250 | 3.9 | 2.9 | 2.1 | 1.2 |
| USSR | 2,841 | 7,098 | 250 | 3.4 | 3.6 | 2.2 | 0.9 |
| Poland | 2,447 | 5,684 | 232 | 2.4 | 3.2 | 3.4 | −0.4 |
| Hungary | 2,480 | 6,903 | 278 | 4 | 3.8 | 2.1 | 1 |
| Average for the socialist countries (4) | 2,819 | 7,013 | 239 | 3.3 | 3.5 | 2.3 | 0.8 |
| Austria | 3,706 | 16,369 | 442 | 6.3 | 4.2 | 3.9 | 2 |
| Belgium | 5,462 | 16,744 | 307 | 2.4 | 4.2 | 3.3 | 1.9 |
| Denmark | 6,943 | 18,261 | 263 | 2.9 | 3.8 | 2 | 1.8 |
| Finland | 4,253 | 16,946 | 398 | 3.3 | 4.4 | 3.3 | 3.2 |
| France | 5,271 | 17,730 | 336 | 3.7 | 4.6 | 3 | 1.7 |
| Greece | 1,915 | 10,086 | 527 | 5 | 6.6 | 4.4 | 1.3 |
| Ireland | 3,453 | 10,880 | 315 | 1.7 | 4.2 | 3.2 | 2.7 |
| Italy | 3,502 | 15,969 | 456 | 5.6 | 5.4 | 2.9 | 2.3 |
| The Netherlands | 5,996 | 16,695 | 278 | 2.8 | 4 | 2.5 | 1.3 |
| Portugal | 2,086 | 10,372 | 497 | 3.1 | 6 | 4.5 | 3 |
| Spain | 2,189 | 11,582 | 529 | 3.5 | 7.1 | 4.2 | 2.5 |
| Sweden | 6,739 | 17,593 | 261 | 2.5 | 3.8 | 2 | 1.8 |
| United Kingdom | 6,939 | 16,414 | 237 | 1.7 | 2.5 | 2.2 | 2.2 |
| Average for the EU countries (13) | 4,688 | 15,519 | 337 | 3.2 | 4.3 | 2.9 | 2.1 |

*Source*: Kornai, 2006

expectancy, infant mortality and education, and other factors, such as environment sustainability, political democracy, income distribution, participation, access to resources, etc. Cypher and Dietz (2004) also make such a differentiation between economic growth and 'development'. The latter 'encompasses a wide range of social and human goals that, while including the level of income and economic growth, goes well beyond this as well' (Cypher and Dietz, 2004: 29). Another interesting differentiation is the one discussed among institutional economists[3] who perceive economic growth as a static phenomenon and economic development as a wider notion of development that includes structural and institutional change, social dynamics and cultural change (Myrdal, 1974). These two perspectives of development, one put forward by Perkins *et al.* (2006) and Cypher and Dietz (2004) and the other put forward by Myrdal (1974), seem likely to converge in the end because, as Myrdal (1974: 729) himself states, economic development arguably and ideally brings about improvements in health, education and other collective goods.

Development according to the IMF and the World Bank is not just about economic growth in general but a particular kind of economic growth, identified by the words 'high-quality growth' (HQG), which the IMF and the World Bank claim to promote (IMF, 1995). In particular, the IMF defines HQG as 'growth that is sustainable, brings lasting gains in employment and living standards and reduces poverty'. The IMF claims that HQG should promote greater equity and equality of opportunity, respect human freedom and protect the environment – it should 'bear the primary responsibility for care, nutrition, and education'. As such, according to this institution, HQG 'depends, therefore, not only on pursuing sound economic policies, but also on implementing a broad range of social policies' (IMF, 1995: 286). Hence, great emphasis is placed on the reduction of poverty and inequality, together with the pursuit of social goals, such as improved health and education, which are expected to increase accordingly during the process of economic growth.

This definition is important to understand as it is commonly accepted that *development* does not mean only economic growth. In this book I use a classification of two levels of 'development':[4]

1. The first one is *economic growth*, which involves only the GDP dimension (development as GDP growth).
2. The second level is *human development*, which is drawn from Sen's concept of capability (Sen, 1985) and is strongly linked to people participation and democracy. Human development is a consequence

of an expansion of people's capabilities that allows individuals to directly improve their condition and standard of living. Human development involves the improvement of two fundamental variables, i.e., life expectancy and education levels, along with GDP and other social goals such as equality, poverty eradication, access to resources, etc. It includes a process of institutional change (development as shown by higher levels of life expectancy and education plus institutional change). It is synthesised by the HDI, which consists of the life expectancy index, the education index and per capita GDP, taking into account purchasing power parity (development as higher HDI, with more capabilities and democracy).

There are substantial differences between the first and the second definitions. However, sometimes I will refer to *economic development* (or simply *development*) as a broader and general concept of human progress and living standard improvements.

Transition economies are countries which need to boost a process of development. However, most importantly, they are countries where a process of institutional change, generally speaking, has taken place. In fact, they are experiencing, in different measures, a transformation which involves formal institutions, such as laws, organisations and state institutions, and informal institutions, i.e., social rules and uncodified laws that structure social interactions (Knight, 1992; Hodgson, 2006) and affect both the economic behaviour of agents and their choices in several ways (Nugent and Lin, 1995).

In order to be socially sustainable and macro-economically stable, the incumbent process of institutional change has to be consistent; the change occurring in the formal sphere of the institutional framework should move coherently with that in informal institutions. Moreover, and most importantly, the change has to guarantee equal gains to people who would otherwise resist the transformation. Inertia towards a new institutional framework occurs when the social benefits of transformation are not universal and where during the transformation many people become losers in terms of unemployment, purchasing power, education, etc. (Beck and Laeven, 2006; Tridico, 2006). A stable and sustainable development process needs a radical transformation that involves coherent social norms and formal rules, as well as relationships between the various powers, values and lobbies (Mabogunje, 1989).

Following this approach, development is a process that involves institutional change (Toye, 1995) along with social, cultural and political change. As Kuznets put it when referring to developing countries

(1965: 30): 'the transformation of an underdeveloped into a developed country is not merely the mechanical addition of a stock of physical capital: it is a thoroughgoing revolution in the patterns of life and a cardinal change in the relative powers and positions of various groups in the population'. The process of institutional change has to guarantee two important factors: first, a breaking with previous institutions, routines and norms in order to overcome 'the resistance of a whole complex of established interests and values' that previously impeded economic growth (Kuznets, 1965: 30); secondly, it has to guarantee the distribution of growth and the social benefits of development. Therefore, it is crucial to know how to change institutions and how to enforce a new institutional deal which will bring about economic development, i.e., improving both living conditions, in terms of income and distribution, and quality of life, in terms of health and education. As such, institutional policies and the active role of the state are needed during such a transformation in order to guarantee stable and sustainable economic development.

I maintain that the type of development will not be the same among transition economies, in the sense that formal institutions and strategies for development can be different. Informal institutions are also different. Moreover, if the formal economic institutions are neglected, informal institutions and processes of spontaneous forces will prevail (Pejovich, 1999). These forces fill the *power vacuum* of the system. Consequently, the transformation favours better organised groups, elites, the better educated and groups in a dominant position (Gil *et al.*, 1998; Szélenyi, 2009). Simultaneously, it causes disadvantages to less organised groups, the unskilled, the poor and the less well educated. As a consequence, economic growth, if it occurs, will not be distributed, inequality will rise and poverty will not be defeated. Development would therefore be uneven, opportunities and *capabilities* for many people would decrease, and there would be many more losers than winners. Thus, such uncontrolled transformation strongly favours the emergence of organised crime, corrupted bureaucracy, informal economies, negative informal economic networks, rent-seeking, illegal lobbies, etc.

To characterise institutions and institutional reforms is a very difficult task. Recently, more and more economists have started to take into account the role of institutions for economic growth and development (Jones, 1981; North, 1990; Knack and Keefer, 1995; Mauro, 1995 and 2000; Olson *et al.*, 1998; Nugent and Lin, 1995; Acemouglu *et al.*, 2001; Bardhan, 2005; Rodrik and Rigobon, 2005). According to Rodrik and Rigobon (2005), income gaps between countries are mainly explained by democracy and the rule of law. Olson *et al.* (1998) show that better governance and quality of institutions are the main sources of economic growth and determine the differences between the output of the various countries. Along the same lines, Jones and Hall (1999) find that 'social infrastructure' and governmental policies explain the different levels of residual productivity among countries which, in turn, is based on their GDP levels. However, very often the main problem with this analysis is a reliable estimate of the impact of institutions on economic performance. Usually, rich countries have better institutions. The difficulty is in obtaining an instrumental and exogenous variable to compare with income. Acemouglu *et al.* (2001) estimate in a cross-country section that institutions, expressed instrumentally by settler mortality rates, have a significant effect on economic growth.

## The structure of the book

The book is divided into three parts. In Part I ('Transformation, Decline and Unstable Growth'), I will compare transition economies and explore differences in terms of transformation strategies and economic performance.

The main political economy strategies and policies of transition such as shock therapy, gradualism and institutionalism will be analysed (Chapter 1). Some historical narratives about the background of transition and the technological gap between the East and the West are briefly examined. The core idea of this part of the book is that there is no general recipe for transition economies, and macro-economic policies are context-dependent, that is, they depend on the country or region where they are implemented and their success or failure depends on several factors which are strictly connected with agent behaviour and with the reaction to implemented policies within the given social and cultural context.

Chapter 2 will detail a complete analysis of recession and recovery in transition economies during the past 20 years of transformation. International constraints will also be examined. As far as the new Member States of the EU are concerned, this chapter will analyse the conditionality and compliance of the candidates. Recession was severe both in the CEECs and in the FSRs at the time of transformation. However, I argue that during transformation and the economic recovery, the CEECs were, to some extent, favoured by EU conditionality, while the FSRs were not interested in this process. Most of the CEECs in fact benefited from EU membership from 2004 onwards, and this was probably a positive conditionality and a source of financial aid that did not apply in the CIS. However, EU membership does not seem to be the crucial factor for the relatively faster economic development of the CEECs, since one can also observe very different speeds of development among the CEECs.

Part II of this book ('Institutional Change and Varieties of Capitalism in Transition Economies') analyses transition from the point of view of institutional change and will give a detailed definition of an *institution* (Chapter 3). Transition economics provide a very interesting case of institutional change. Variation in terms of institutional policies and socio-economic performance are evident. Such variation is very useful for testing whether and in what way institutions, human development and economic growth are related (Ranis *et al.*, 2000). Many economists agree that institutional transformation lies at the heart of post-communist transition. However, different concepts of what an institution is create different interpretations of that transformation. In transition economies, the change was very significant, and both economic and institutional frameworks were modified considerably. In the CEECs and the CIS today, there are guarantees relating to private property, new banks, new economic and administrative organisations, and other formal institutions exogenously imposed in a short time by political decisions. However, the behavioural rules have not completely changed. Economic agents often continue to think in terms of a previous economic logic. Consequently, in order to change institutions, the prevalent social rules also need to be changed. In transition economies, informal economic institutions (that is, uncodified and prevalent social rules) are far from a complete adaptation.

Given the concept of institutions, including both formal and informal institutions, it is no longer sufficient to change formal institutions in order to achieve another system. What is more important is to 'change the mentality' of economic agents. Both prevailing rules and the mentality of agents can be considered in the sense of Veblen's shared 'habits of thought' (Veblen, 1919: 273). As Murrel (1992: 51) puts it, 'even old, inefficient institutions may be better than ones that are planned but which do not yet exist'. Economic agents feel more secure and protected within an old institutional framework. Therefore, a self-reinforcing process exists, which allows for the path dependency of institutions. Moreover, interaction between new formal rules and old social customs will affect the evolutionary path of institutions. Indeed, in transition economies, certain institutions survive even if they appear inefficient, whereas others disappear. This is because each society has its own history, path of development, habits and behavioural rules – in other words, its own values (North, 1990).

Therefore, in Part II, I will argue that transition from a planned economy towards a market economy cannot be realised simply through the introduction of reforms and that development cannot be achieved easily. In order to initiate a development process, transition economies need to undergo radical transformation, which involves social norms and informal institutions, and a change in the power relations and the values of dominant groups. Hence, development might be defined as a process of economic growth through institutional change. During this process, it is necessary to have institutional policies and an active role taken by the state in order to foster development. By contrast, the role of institutions and of the state, in particular at the beginning of the transition process, have been largely under-estimated or ignored.

In Chapter 4, I will also try to give a clear idea about the problems related to institutional change and to the inertia and conflicts between old and new institutions. All the institutional aspects related to transition will be explored: the formal change in rules and institutions; the transformation of informal institutions; the institutional costs of this change; the inertia which occurred during institutional transformation; and the conflicts between groups, main actors, the former ruling classes, lobbies, new elites, foreign investors, old industries, emerging industrial sectors, elderly people, younger people, etc. The main idea here is that institutional instability and the lack of consistency in the new institutional framework are the main reasons for poor economic performance. The behaviour of economic agents is affected not only by formal institutions such as law, new constitutions and organisations, but also by informal institutions (social norms, old values and habits). I would argue, developing a so-called *dichotomy thesis*, that in transition economies there has been little consistency between formal and informal institutions since the new institutions were built on the dichotomy between old rules (the *old ethos*) and new formal rules, and on the groups supporting each set of these rules. The inconsistency between both seems to affect economic performance, increasing transaction costs and other institutional costs, which I will call *the extra cost of transaction*. Moreover, accession to the EU, at least for the CEECs, and the significant increase in FDI has had a significant impact on development paths and on institutional change in those economies.

Finally, in Chapter 5, I will classify transition economies according to their socio-economic models and I will test whether the type of system has an impact on the development of the country, considering both economic growth and some socio-economic indicators. Following the varieties of capitalism literature (Jessop, 2002; Amable, 2003; Amoroso, 2003; Brenner, 2005; Lane and Myant, 2007; Myant and Drahokoupil, 2010), countries will be classified according to their main macro-economic characteristics and institutional variables drawn from the European Bank for Reconstruction and Development (EBRD), such as enterprise and privatisation, market and competition, trade and openness, financial system, wage nexus and social investments. Following this classification, I found five types of socio-economic model among FCEs: the *competitive capitalist model*, the *corporative capitalist model*, the *dirigiste model*, the *hybrid model* and the *state capitalist model*. Using a factor analysis, I found out that GDP may be affected depending on the type of model used. Moreover, I found out that the corporative capitalist model is better able to combine freedom and social rights. In fact, countries using the corporative capitalist model always show better socio-economic variables, such as inequality, poverty, voice and accountability, freedom index, life expectancy and the HDI. By contrast, countries following the dirigiste model show worse variables.

In Part III ('The Capability Approach, Social Capital and Human Development in Transition Economies'), after having briefly illustrated some of the main traditional growth theories (Chapter 6), I will examine the new trajectories of development theories which are relevant for my analysis. These new trajectories form the basis of my model, which I will test using ordinary least squares (OLS) cross-country regressions. In this model, economic development is seen as a complex process comprising the interaction between capabilities and institutions. This interaction brings about human development, which in turn leads to economic growth. However, in the end, the very foundation of this process, as I will show in Chapter 8, has to be found in the social capital endowment of countries.

This part will also clarify that GDP growth does not necessarily correspond to human development, and it is the latter that is highly preferable for countries. In fact, human development involves the improvement of other crucial variables in people's lives, such as education and life expectancy, alongside an improvement in GDP. A great deal of empirical evidence shows that in both developing and developed economies, some countries have relatively high GDP per capita but very low indicators of development such as literacy, access to drinking water, infant mortality rates, life expectancy, education, etc. (UNDP, 2001). This is in part due to the fact that wealth is unequally distributed. Conversely, there are cases of relatively low GDP per capita and high indicators of development in countries where income is more equally distributed (Ray, 1998).

The foregoing analysis pinpoints that macro-economic stabilisation, although necessary, is not a sufficient condition for economic development. Moreover, there is also little evidence so far that growth reduces income poverty, something which increased dramatically in all FSRs and in some of the CEECs too. Most transition economies that experienced fast growth during the mid-1990s did not see a reduction in income poverty (Golinowska, 1996). By contrast, the results seem to suggest that human development (without the income dimension) stimulated by a better institutional framework is a sufficient condition for economic growth.

A better institutional framework has to be identified within a situation where relevant political, institutional and social variables interact with each other and provide people with opportunities and therefore capabilities for doing and being. These variables are: health and education expenditure, voice and accountability, and freedom. A country that enjoys greater democracy, freedom, political and social rights would extend capabilities to its people more easily than a country where these rights were restricted. It is important to consider that these variables were found to be better in the corporative capitalist model. It will be shown, first, that these variables increase the level of human development (without the income dimension) and then that human development causes GDP growth (Chapter 7).

However, I will show that two fundamental factors are at the basis of this process of development: social capital and a strong middle class (Chapter 8). I used OLS cross-country regressions to test these models. 2SLS methods and IV approaches were also used in both Chapters 7 and 8 in order to check for endogeneity problems.

Social capital was measured with the variable 'trust' (from the World Values Survey). My idea is that democratic institutions, which are crucial for the building of an appropriate institutional framework, come from a middle class and social capital (first hypothesis), before a democratic society endowed with high levels of social capital and a consistent middle class generates both higher levels of HDI features and economic growth. In this second hypothesis, education and human capital play a crucial role. Democracy helps to distribute growth and therefore to further human development.

The formation of a middle class in my approach has two origins. The first one has to be traced back into the structural change of the economy: the post-industrial society brought about a third group, between the elites and the working class, forming a distinct political actor. The second feature which shapes the formation of the middle class is social capital, which is the bearer of particular values such as trust, cooperation, civil society involvement in public affairs, respect of rules, social networks, reputation, anti-corruption social norms, etc. All these values characterise the institutional framework of a society and promote and set up institutions beneficial for the whole community. Thus, a middle class is not identified simply by a certain level of income but, most importantly, by a level of social capital and civil society involvement which are present first and establish institutions capable of spinning off the process of development.

The comparative analysis among the CEECs and the FSRs shows that the former performed better in terms of HDI features because they have a better endowment of social capital and also because, during transformation, they implemented policies better able to boost democracy, to reinforce the middle class, to reduce the influence of oligarchs and to fill the initial systemic vacuum. Democratic institutions, which as I will show are favoured by public investments in health and education and by a better control of corruption, are more developed in the CEECs than in the FSRs. The FSRs not only tend to be poorer but also to be dominated by authoritarian regimes: in transition economies, higher HDI features are always associated with democratic and semi-democratic regimes rather than authoritarian ones.

In the end we can generally state that many shadows darken the balance of the transition process, and above all FSRs neither reached the levels of wealth dreamed about on the eve of the transformation nor reached the kind of democratic society for which they fought.

# Appendix A: The Countries

The countries which are analysed in this book are as follows (see the maps below).

- *Fifteen countries of the former Soviet Union*: Armenia, Azerbaijan, Belarus, Estonia, Georgia, Kazakhstan, Kyrgyzstan, Latvia, Lithuania, the Republic of Moldova, the Russian Federation, Tajikistan, Turkmenistan, Ukraine and Uzbekistan.
- *Six countries of Central Europe and the South-Eastern Balkans*: Albania, Bulgaria, Czechoslovakia, Hungary, Poland and Romania.
- *Five Republics of the former Yugoslavia Federation*: Bosnia and Herzegovina, Croatia, the Former Yugoslav Republic of Macedonia, Serbia and Montenegro, and Slovenia.

However, since 1989, the political and geographical situation of several of these countries has changed. Some of them split and became independent states (the Czech Republic and Slovakia, formerly Czechoslovakia, split in 1993). The former Yugoslavia Federation collapsed between 1991 and 1994. Montenegro and Serbia split in 2006 and in 2008 Kosovo, a former region of Serbia, unilaterally declared its independence. Hence, from the former Yugoslavia Federation there are today seven countries, one of which, Bosnia and Herzegovina, is a complex combination of several governments: 1) the federation of Bosnia and Herzegovina; 2) Republika Srpska; and 3) the Brěko District, which is a neutral, self-governing administrative unit, under the sovereignty of Bosnia and Herzegovina. Only in one case among the FCEs has there been a unification process, that is, in Germany. The former GDR dissolved naturally into the Federal Republic of Germany in 1990. That is the reason why in my sample of FCEs, the GDR is not analysed and does not appear as a country. Finally, a brief note on Mongolia. Mongolia used to be a country with strong links with the USSR and it featured a form of planned economy until the early 1990s. However, it was never formally part of the USSR and it experienced a very different path of transition, so it is not included in the analysis of this book.

In the book I use the following terminology for the 28 transition economies considered:

- *Central and Eastern European Countries (CEECs)*: Bulgaria, the Czech Republic, Estonia, Hungary, Latvia, Lithuania, Poland, Romania, Slovakia and Slovenia (*ten countries*). All these countries have in common the fact that between 2004 and 2007 they became members of the EU.
- *Commonwealth of Independent States (CIS) or Former Soviet Republics (FSRs)*: Armenia, Azerbaijan, Belarus, Georgia, Kazakhstan, Kyrgyzstan, the Republic of Moldova, the Russian Federation, Tajikistan, Turkmenistan, Ukraine and Uzbekistan (*12 countries*). In this case I have obviously excluded the three Baltic countries. All these countries are full members (ten countries), associate members (Turkmenistan) or participating countries (Ukraine) of the CIS, which is a very loose association of states established in 1991 from the ashes of the USSR.
- *Balkans*: Albania, Bosnia and Herzegovina, Croatia, the former Yugoslav Republic of Macedonia, Montenegro and Serbia (*six countries*). Kosovo is included in the analysis of Serbia. I am aware that this classification can be geographically questioned. However, in this context, the classification is politically neutral. It is just useful to aggregate countries which, at first instance, appear to experience similar transition processes and directions of change. Very often, however, throughout the book I consider the CEECs and the Balkans together, while the CIS is always considered separately.

## The geography of the CEECs and the USSR

*Map 1* Central and Eastern European Countries (CEECs)
© The Regional Environment Center for Central and Easter Europe, www.rec.org

*Map 2* The former USSR

# Part I

# Transformation, Decline and Unstable Growth

# 1
# Transition to Market: A Long and Undefined Journey

## 1.1 Introduction

The transition from a planned to a market economy has been described using several metaphors. One of the most interesting described the transition as a jump from one side of a swamp to another, which needed to be done at once in order to avoid the impasse of being sucked into the marsh. This chapter will examine different perspectives, therapies and trajectories of this jump called 'transition'.

However, this book considers transition as a complex issue from a development perspective which also involves people as agents. In fact, the transformation of an economy is above all a transformation of a society which has hopes and dreams. Obviously, reality can differ greatly from hopes and this is what citizens living in former communist countries today know well. Nevertheless, at the beginning of transition, the approach was very different. In a survey of the early transition period, people were asked which country they would like to emulate. The table below shows their wishes.

Today, transition economies are very far from the countries they wanted to emulate, both from economic and social points of view. Transition involves many failures and some success, the latter in particular being the case among Central European countries and, to be more precise, among some of the new EU Member States such as the Czech Republic, Estonia, Hungary, Poland and Slovenia. The reasons for this are various and include initial conditions as well as policies and institutions implemented during transition, and a relatively better endowment of some important intangible sources of capital such as trust, civil society involvement and social capital. All this forms the core of this book and the milestone of the interpretation of transition in our approach.

*Table 1.1* The countries Central Europeans wanted to emulate

| | Czechoslovakia (%) | Hungary (%) | Poland (%) | Avg (%) |
|---|---|---|---|---|
| Germany | 31 | 38 | 37 | 35 |
| Sweden | 32 | 34 | 21 | 29 |
| USA | 14 | 10 | 30 | 18 |
| Italy | 9 | 9 | 0 | 6 |
| France | 5 | 2 | 7 | 5 |
| Britain | 3 | 3 | 3 | 3 |
| Other | 6 | 3 | 2 | 3 |
| Soviet Union | 0 | 1 | 0 | 0.3 |

*Source*: Rose, 2009: 15

## 1.2 The background of transition: from the oil crises until the fall of the Berlin Wall

The fall of the Berlin Wall, although unforeseen in the literature of the 1970s and 1980s, had origins stretching back a long time. There was a clear difference between the speed and steps of development before and after the 1970s in almost all FCEs. Rates of growth in GDP show this cleavage. Fast growth and industrialisation lasted for almost 30 years after the Second World War; stagnation, inefficiencies, corruption, loss of enthusiasm and increasing criticism became the dominant factors from the mid-1970s onwards.

Berend's main argument, in a very recent book (2009), is to explain why income gaps between East and West accelerated in particular from the 1970s and the different responses that the two macro-European regions were able to give to the oil crises and international crises of the 1970s, and to the beginning of globalisation, which was anticipated by structural change and post-industrialisation. In fact, taking the Organization of the Petroleum Exporting Countries (OPEC) oil crisis of 1973 as his starting point, Berend charts the gradual unravelling of state socialism in Central and Eastern Europe and the FSRs, its ultimate collapse in the revolutions of 1989 and the economic restructuring and lasting changes in income, employment, welfare, education and social structure which followed. After 1973, the West was able to adjust, using structural change, to the new challenges brought by globalisation, while the East remained backward and technologically focused in the heavy industrial sector. Even if the economic performances of the West after the 1970s in general were not as good as they were during the three decades after the Second World War, they were still superior compared to those of the East during the same period. On the one hand, FCEs had an advantage because they were not so greatly affected by the oil crises. On the other hand, they could not embark on a structural change towards more technologically advanced post-industrial sectors because apparently this was not necessary: raw materials were abundant and were still relatively cheaper than in the West.

In the end, technology in the FCEs became obsolete and economies relied almost exclusively on heavy industries. In the 1980s energy intensity in the Central Eastern Europe industrial triangle region (made up of East Germany, Czechoslovakia and south Poland) was nearly eight times higher than that of the EU (Berend, 2009: 21). The Soviet Union had similarly bad technological performance and it was calculated that it had 2.5 times higher levels of pollution than the USA during the 1970s. Czechoslovakia and Bulgaria, which were the most environmentally devastated countries in Europe, were ranked among the top ten biggest producers of sulphur dioxide emissions (Carter and Turnok, 2002). When pollution was calculated in relation to GDP per capita, a comparison between the West and East of Europe put the East in an even more dramatically low position. Poland had the sixth highest levels of air pollution in Europe.

This situation highlights an old-fashioned technology which, Berend (2009) argues, made the necessary structural change in the East of Europe much more difficult than in the West of Europe, where better technological levels and a greater investment levels in research and development (R&D) made the job easier.

During the 1950s, the 1960s and the first part of the 1970s, the former communist countries were able to perform better and to deliver better living conditions to their working classes (see also Gros and Steinherr, 1995). Planned economies, in a way, work better in circumstances where fast growth and catching up is required. Therefore, initially at least, economic growth and living conditions were sustained. Consequently, the one-party political system was relatively accepted, stable and successful.

Later, extensive growth was no longer possible. The agricultural sector, as a source of cheap labour in transition to the industrial sector, was becoming exhausted. Sustained economic development could only have been possible through new forms of technological organisation and intensive growth policy.

The attempt in Czechoslovakia to reform the economy in 1967–8, introducing market prices in some areas, able to improve efficiency and to compete with international prices, along the same lines as what was done in Yugoslavia in 1965 and in Hungary in 1968, failed because of the Soviet-led Warsaw Pact invasion.

Kornai (2006) is of the same opinion, arguing that for political reasons, the system which had acquired stability during the previous two to three decades was unable to reform itself, and therefore remained economically unchanged and did not adjust to the world technological changes that were required in the 1970s. This was the reason for another one or two decades of longevity and, in the end, the root cause of its collapse.

The figures below on electricity consumption and telephone lines give an idea of the technological gap between Eastern and Western Europe.

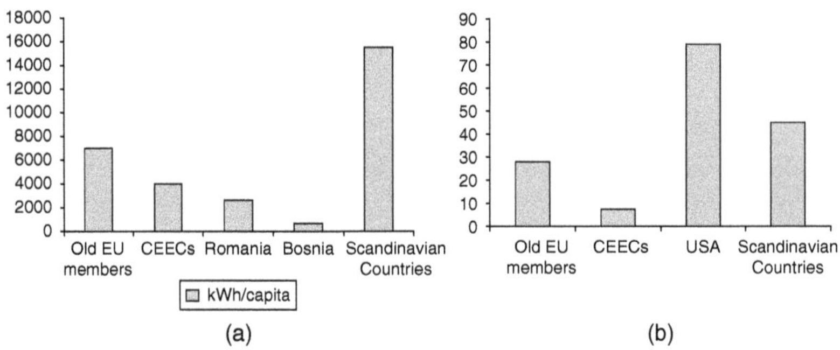


*Figure 1.1* (a) Consumption of electricity, 1990 (b) Telephone lines/100 inhabitants, 1980
*Source*: Berend, 2009

The figures for the first computers and fax machines were similar – both arrived later in former communist countries and ownership in the 1980s stood at only ten per cent of Western levels.

Why then did former communist countries allow such a gap in technological terms to build up? The answer can be found in Schumpeter (1928), who was the first economist to consider technology and innovation extensively as a first cause for growth. In his view, technology and innovation need a competitive and efficient environment, guided by appropriate incentives and institutions. Entrepreneurs in a market economy or state managers in a planned economy need to cope with the difficulties of changing practices, adapting to new situations, creating new products and processes, and destroying the older and inefficient ones. New technology and innovation are embodied in new firms, in new goods, in new methods of production and in new practices and combinations of knowledge, which find *sui generis* solutions for new tasks. Soviet-type economies were too stationary to follow these technological guidelines, their incentives too perverse and distorted and their management tasks much too focused on physical objectives. Moreover, technology was mainly perceived as a force which would destroy jobs, neglecting the subsequent job creation caused by an innovation wave. It was not in the interests of SOE managers to introduce innovation, because they were very interested in job-creation objectives in order to increase their personal awards (see also the appendix to this chapter) rather than in technology which would cut jobs.

Western European economies, and not necessarily competitive capitalist economies like the USA, were able to implement these guidelines and to reach respectable levels of innovation and technology, especially the social-democratic economies of Scandinavia. In the Scandinavian economies, managerial firms, under public control, were able to create modern firms and increase efficiency and competitiveness. In the USA, private entrepreneurs were able to do this job. In old EU Member States, a combination of both private and public firms created new and modern firms who were bearers of efficiency and competitiveness. In the FCEs, managerial bureaucracy, under the control of politics and party patronage, operated under different conditions and institutions, with corruption, misleading objectives and no positive incentives. Simultaneously, while R&D in the West started to become a big sector in the 1970s, strictly linked with industry and services, this was not the case in the East. In the FCEs, state research activity was mainly oriented towards defence and, again, heavy industry, and not really geared towards civil innovation, business services, high technology and the newest information and communications technology (ICT) sector.

Such a background created conditions for the obsolescence of traditional industry, for the inefficiency of the economy and for the attrition of politics. Political opposition arose and independent trade unions started to emerge and to question communist governments, first of all in Central Europe and particularly in Poland. In fact, the fall of the Berlin Wall marked the beginning of the transformation of former communist countries from a planned economy model towards a market economy model. However, other important events took place in 1989 in Central Europe. The first was the 'Round Table' Talks in Poland in the spring of 1989. This brought together communist and Solidarność leaders in order to broker an agreement about the future of Poland and to explore the possibility of starting a reform process that would lead the country towards greater freedom and political pluralism. The 'semi-free' elections which took place in June 1989 were a direct outcome of the Round Table Agreement and were indeed a most significant political event. It paved the way for further systemic change first in Central and Eastern Europe and then in the FSRs.

At the semi-free elections, 40 per cent of seats in the Lower House of the Parliament were freely contested and 60 per cent were reserved for the communists and their allies. All the free seats were won by the Solidarność coalition. In the Senate, all the seats were freely contested and 99 out of 100 were won by the Solidarność coalition. After this election, it was clear to everybody in Poland, the Soviet Empire and the West that the communists had lost their consensus. It was likely that they did not command a majority in the countries where they constituted the ruling government. Therefore, such semi-free elections represented a symbol marking the collapse of the communist system in Central and Eastern Europe. At the same time in the USSR, it also had a significant effect on the attempts of Gorbachev's *Perestroika* policy to lead the Soviet Federation towards a higher level of transparency, democracy and pluralism. In all likelihood, there was a mutual and positive interaction between *Perestroika* and Solidarność with the common aim of reforming the political system in former communist countries. Moreover, the role of Gorbachev was crucial to the avoidance of intervention by the Warsaw Pact's Army first in Poland and later in East Germany and in other CEECs.

The first non-communist government in the Warsaw Pact countries was established in September 1989 in Poland and was led by Mazowiecki. In the autumn of 1989, the economic and political policies of the new government in Poland were not yet clear. Among Solidarność, one could characterise at least three different approaches towards the process of reform:

1. A type of transformation oriented towards social democracy modelled on the Scandinavian socio-economic example. Therefore, this approach aimed at transforming the country politically, introducing pluralism and democratic rules on the one hand and an economic model on the other hand which would be characterised by a strong role for trade unions and workers in the economy, which would be similar to the European social-democratic model.
2. The second approach was supported by the liberal economists and technicians of Mazowiecki's government, such as Leszek Balcerowicz,

and foreign advisers, such as Jeffrey Sachs, who wanted to transform the economy radically by following the Anglo-Saxon socio-economic model, towards the so-called 'Reaganomics', which combined the Reagan and Thatcher programmes of reform implemented in the USA and the UK during the 1980s. By the end of the 1980s, Reaganomics was about to be 'internationalised' and introduced in Latin America, along with other developing countries, and in former communist countries. It became known as the Washington Consensus (WC).

3. The third approach proposed to follow the continental European model, as found in Germany and France. The idea was to transform the country in a gradual manner, introducing private property rights while retaining some state control over the economy.

These three models were also perceived as potential options among those former communist countries that were about to experience a radical transformation between 1989 and 1990. However, in the end, most of these countries embraced the second model, supported by the IMF, the World Bank and by many international economists who immediately became prime advisers in many former communist countries. The IMF and the World Bank offered financial and technical assistance to transition economies during transformation on the condition that they adopted the recommended strategies and policies. The first option did not materialise in any of the former communist countries, while the third approach, i.e., gradual transformation towards a European continental model, was adopted to some extent by Hungary and Slovenia.

## 1.3 Transformation therapies and growth strategies

The transition from a planned economy towards a market economy is a difficult task which, during the past 20 years, has been well described by many metaphors. These illustrate a transition as a journey to an undefined place or as a jump into the unknown. Working out the best way to proceed is a difficult task. First of all, this is because economists and social scientists in general, unlike engineers, who can build and test a concrete or iron bridge following precise mechanical and physical rules and principles, can rely only on a set of theoretical assumptions that are valid under specific simple stylised facts. Therefore, transition, when perceived as a precise policy prescription which allows for the passage through a metaphorical bridge from plans to markets, is a misleading concept. It neglects many complex social facts and will most likely lead to failures. In fact, societies, markets and economic and political systems are too complex to be transformed following standard formulae drawn from theoretical assumptions based on very simple and few stylised facts. Moreover, transition is a relatively new field of study and research. No models had been tested on this subject before and no policies had been implemented before in countries to allow for such a complex transformation. Markets were created in capitalist countries over a very long period of time, with a combination of public and private institutions, in an environment of genuine attempts towards better living conditions. After the Second World War in particular, these attempts were inspired by Keynesian policies, within a specific institutional framework that was oriented towards social policies and welfare, rather than an environment of cultural and ideological adversity towards the collective good and social policies such as the one prevailing after the fall of the Berlin Wall in many FCEs.

In most of the transition economies, no attention was paid to institutions and governance, particularly in the beginning: institutions and rules were not considered important for development. Public institutions were neither replaced nor created; international constraints were merely accepted and implemented; culture, social capital, domestic norms and values were simply ignored; and path-dependency theory was not considered to be relevant (cf. Kregel and Matzner, 1992; Murrel, 1992). Financial institutions were, and still are, very weak and oligarchs took control over many former SOEs, enjoying private forms of monopoly.

The prevalent idea among economists and international economic organisations was very market-oriented (Popov, 2007). Reforms in many transition economies mainly followed the WC, which designed policies according to neoclassical theories with adverse effects and poor results in many countries (Lin, 2005). The transformation paradigm, at least in the form of dominant and radical shock therapy, was inspired by following the simple assumption: *transition = liberalisation + privatisation* (Lipton and Sachs, 1990; Balcerowicz, 1995; Boycko *et al.*, 1995). An alternative strategy was paradigmatically inspired by the principle of introducing a gradual institutionally-driven transformation in a market economy, where the state could still play a role and market and non-market transaction costs could coexist (Dewatripont and Roland, 1992; Murrel, 1992; Pitelis, 1996; Wei, 1997). The table below shows the main characteristics of both strategies.

*Table 1.2* Shock therapy and gradual therapy

| | **Shock therapy/cold turkey**[1] | **Gradual therapy** |
|---|---|---|
| Paradigm | Transition = liberalisation + privatisation as soon as possible. No institutions. The only institution is the market which gets indications through prices | Gradual and institutionally-driven transformation towards a market economy |
| State and market relationship | Fast privatisation and immediate withdrawing of the state from the economy; reduction of public expenditure; total price liberalisation; elimination of subsidies to SOEs; closing down of obsolete SOEs | Market transactions and control of the state; full employment objectives; crisis prevention through public authorities; market and non-market transactions admitted; guarantee of existence and subsidies to SOEs which, although obsolete, still have added value |
| Macro-stabilisation | Structural adjustment: zero or small public deficit and reduction of public debt; fast disinflation | Gradual disinflation; control of long-term public debt; guarantee of public safety net |
| International regime | Immediate convertibility, devaluation and liberalisation of exchange rate; liberalisation of FDI; adjustment towards international competition and integration into the global economy with adherence to IMF, World Trade Organization (WTO) and World Bank disciplines | Integration into the EU and acceptance of EU conditionality (as regard European countries); integration into the global economy with protection of strategic industries |
| Wages | Flexible wages and prices, and anti-inflation anchors | Minimum wages; social dialogue over collective wage agreements |
| Property rights | Certainty and reinforcement of property rights | Control of contracts; guarantee and equilibrium between two principles: *restitution* to previous owners and *continuity* of use to current owners |

*Table 1.2* (Continued)

| | **Shock therapy/cold turkey**[1] | **Gradual therapy** |
|---|---|---|
| Social institutions | Individual-based social institutions (development of private pension funds, private insurance, private education, private healthcare, etc.) | Collective actions: conflict management of institutions, development of public goods and the significant role played by public social institutions (education, health, etc.) |

The World Bank and the IMF advised very strict fiscal and monetary policies for all transition countries indifferently. The result was a significant recession. Furthermore, a state of systemic vacuum, chaos and disorganisation in the economic framework was created. Oliver Blanchard (1997: 10) refers to this period as a *systemic vacuum* and as an economy of chaos.

The WC became the dominant paradigm in transition economies, being implemented in order to 'adjust, stabilize and privatize' the economies using a 'Structural Adjustment' programme, often uncritically implemented as a universal formula (Stiglitz, 1998). The WC referred to a *decalogue* of policies advised by Washington-based international financial institutions and marked the end of *Keynesianism* as the dominant policy paradigm, both in developing and in developed countries. The phrase 'Washington Consensus', originally coined by John Williamson in 1990, became a synonym for neoliberal policies and was initially implemented in Latin America. The WC policies, influenced by the so-called 'Reaganomics', mainly included the implementation of *monetarist* policies such as monetary strength, anti-inflation policies, minimal deficit policies, the privatisation of state assets and the complete liberalisation of prices, hence the official end of post-Keynesian policies. Reaganomics also meant the withdrawal of the state from strategic industries such as coal, steel, telecommunications and energy, as had happened in the UK during Margaret Thatcher's administration, and as it was in other European countries at the beginning of the 1990s.

The aims of these policies were essentially the reduction of inflation and domestic debt. Because high debt and high inflation rates would curb economic performance, soft monetary policies such as credit, monetary expansion and exchange rate devaluation would allow for an inflation spiral. Moreover, annual deficits, caused by state interventionism, generous welfare and demand subsidies, and inefficient bureaucracy would increase the total debt and the credibility of the economy, with negative effects on FDI, the business environment and trust. Hence, the targets became macro-economic stabilisation (reduction of inflation and debt) and structural adjustment through the liberalisation of prices and sectors, the privatisation of state assets, and deregulation, i.e., the withdrawal of the state from the economy.

## 1.4 From the Washington Consensus to the Augmented Washington Consensus

After 15 years, 'this (Washington) consensus has by now largely dissipated' (Rodrik, 2004: 1). In fact, since the mid-1990s, recurrent

*Table 1.3* The Washington and Augmented Washington Consensuses

| WASHINGTON CONSENSUS (1989) | AUGMENTED WASHINGTON CONSENSUS (2000) |
|---|---|
| 1) Fiscal discipline | 11) Corporate governance |
| 2) Reorientation and reduction of public expenditure | 12) Anti-corruption |
| 3) Tax reform (no or little progressive rate) | 13) Flexible labour market |
| 4) Financial and interest rate liberalisation | 14) Adherence to WTO disciplines |
| 5) Unified and competitive exchange rate | 15) Adherence to international financial codes and standards |
| 6) Trade liberalisation | 16) 'Prudent' capital account opening |
| 7) Openness to FDI | 17) Non-intermediate exchange rate regime |
| 8) Privatisation (state industries are inefficient) | 18) Independent central banks/inflation targeting |
| 9) Deregulation (excessive regulation causes corruption) | 19) Social safety nets |
| 10) Secure property rights | 20) Targeted poverty reduction |

*Source*: Williamson, 1990; Rodrik, 2004

economic crises in some countries such as Mexico, Russia and Argentina, champions of the IMF programme, have shown the poor economic performance yielded by orthodox WC policies.[2] The reforms of the 1980s and 1990s produced disappointing results (Rodrik, 2004). Moreover, the consensus among economists on those policies dissolved. Finally, civil society became more critical and organised against the consequences of neoliberal policies, i.e., globalisation and no state intervention. International financial institutions recognised some failures (Stiglitz, 1998) and as a result the so-called 'Augmented Washington Consensus' (or 'Post-Washington Consensus') was proposed. The new programme proposed an additional set of policy prescriptions circulating, along with the previous policies, within the 'renewed' Washington-based international financial institutions at the end of the 1990s.

The theoretical justification of the Augmented Washington Consensus seems to be tautological because it claims that the reasons for the poor results of the WC policies are due to a lack of effectiveness and corruption (Rodrik, 2004). Hence, the condition for the countries to develop is to set up some important institutions.[3] Although there are important innovations, this approach seems quite naïve and does not take into consideration crucial elements such as the specificity of the countries, the varieties of possible policies and the different ways of reaching similar objectives. Moreover, the apparent importance that the Augmented Washington Consensus gives to the role of institutions is based on the approach of 'the more the better', rather than on a deep institutional analysis of the country where these policies should be implemented. No importance is given to economic complexity and social dynamics in order to explain policy failures. Instead, policy failures are explained in terms of a lack of capacity for the implementation and effectiveness of WC policies.

Empirical evidence shows that the most successful countries in terms of growth performance during the 1980s and 1990s followed heterodox policies (McMillan and Naughton, 1992; Kolodko and Nuti, 1997; Rodrik, 2004). China, India and Vietnam, as well as the 'New Asian Tigers', i.e., Indonesia, Malaysia and Thailand, along with the 'Four Old Asian Tigers' (South Korea, Singapore, Taiwan and Hong Kong), adopted heterodox policies or did not follow the WC orthodoxy completely. In those countries, one can observe simultaneously mixed policies of trade protectionism and FDI openness; state interventionism and strong protection of property rights and enforcement of contracts; family capitalism and international investors; planned economy sectors and market-oriented zones; government-controlled banking and financial systems within the international competition system, etc. On the contrary, in Latin America, Sub-Saharan Africa and the FSRs, where IMF-based programmes were more strictly implemented, economic performance was much worse (cf. Bosworth *et al.*, 2003).

Rodrik (2004) claims that there are some limited objectives which can be considered to be common or similar for the majority of the countries. Nevertheless, the means used to reach those aims can be very heterogeneous. The objectives are: 1) macro-economic stability; 2) integration into the world economy; and 3) property rights and contract enforcement. Regarding the first objective, macro-economic instability does not come only from inflation and debt but also from an excessively deregulated financial system, uncontrolled FDI flows and trade liberalisation. Hence, the means used to reach macro-economic stability must be taken into consideration along with these problems – they must be context-dependent (Mundell, 1997). The second objective refers to integration into the world economy. International openness does not lead to economic development *per se*. Domestic and heterogeneous institutions are necessary to manage social conflicts, protect weak economies and assist in managing them. Finally, property rights and contract enforcement systems should be clear, with efficient incentives and transparent rule of law (Serguey and Yavlinsky, 2000). However, institutional arrangements should decide what type of property rights are the most appropriate in each context/sector/region, be it private, public or cooperative. What type of sanction and enforceable system? What type or degree of state interventionism? What type of legal regime?

In general, it is necessary to have particular means for specific aims. This should be the rule to follow, with particular attention to social cohesion, management of conflicts, inequality, unemployment and political stability (Summers, 2003).

## 1.5 A closer comparison between Eastern and Western Europe

In Eastern Europe, the success of Western societies is perceived mainly as a consequence of private property and competitive capitalism. This view is obviously wrong. Western societies, particularly in Continental and Mediterranean Europe and the Scandinavian countries, have a model consisting of a mix of state and private partnership, public and private institutions, welfare support and social institutions, public good and public companies, Keynesian policies and welfare states (Collier *et al.*, 1999). Moreover, this framework was built over a long period of time, during which a Fordist mode of production, development and regulation was dominant, with extensive economic programming. This prevailing model of development had three characteristics: first, the Fordist/Taylorist form of labour organisation, centred around a semi-skilled workforce within a framework of particular industrial relations; secondly, a regime of accumulation which allowed for the sharing of productivity gain between workers and firm owners; and, thirdly, the Keynesian welfare state, which on the one hand provided unemployment benefits, allowing people who were even excluded from the Fordist organisation to consume, and on the other hand allowed a high level of aggregate demand. All this was included in a framework of particular institutional forms and policies, as the table below shows (Boyer and Saillard, 2002).

In other words, the Fordist system had, on the one hand, mass production and mass consumption aims and, on the other, demand-side policies and demand management, full employment aims and welfare state institutions. These two dimensions went well together and allowed, in Western Europe as well as in the USA, a long wave of stability and growth with a coherent model of development (Tridico, 2006; Chang, 2008).

Hence, the key to the successful development in Western Europe was a creation of a good economic environment, supported by public institutions, with the state playing a major role, particularly after the Second World War (Boyer and Saillard, 2002; Berend, 2006). It is hard to imagine a working and functional economy without the state playing an important role in providing facilities in Western Europe. This includes legality, a good business environment, improvements in the collective good, education, state-provided welfare support, social institutions mitigating conflicts, the rule of law, property right reinforcement, income distribution policies, social cohesion policies, anti-corruption policies, anti-trust policies, anti-monopoly policies, infrastructures, a health system, firm subsidies and unemployment benefits, technology, R&D, etc.

Therefore, all these should be taken into consideration when attempting to implement transformation policies and institutions in FCEs. Moreover, *time* should also be a factor. Price liberalisation, trade liberalisation, capital account liberalisation and currency convertibility in particular cannot be introduced by a stroke of a pen from one day to another. Unfortunately, at the beginning of transformation, many transition economies did as Western advisors were saying, followed 'Bad

*Table 1.4* Fordism and post-Fordism in Western Europe: a comparison

| | Institutional forms | | | | | Policies | |
|---|---|---|---|---|---|---|---|
| | **Wage relations** | **Form of competition** | **Monetary regime** | **Relationship between state and economy** | **International regime** | **Macro-economic policy** | **Social policy** |
| Fordism | Sharing productivity gains. Collective bargaining; promotion of norms of mass consumption; full employment aims | Monopolistic and oligopolistic forms of competition | Soft money constraints; public credit management and credit; state control over money | Protection of strategic sectors; management of international economic relations; state interventionism in economy | National competition; strategic protectionism; frequent devaluation of exchange rate | Anti-cyclical policy; demand-side policy; state interventionism; promotion of economies of scale and mass production; R&D and productivity growth incentives | Income redistribution, progressive taxation; protection of welfare rights and social needs; strong welfare state |

*Table 1.4* (Continued)

| | Institutional forms | | | | | Policies | |
|---|---|---|---|---|---|---|---|
| | **Wage relations** | **Form of competition** | **Monetary regime** | **Relationship between state and economy** | **International regime** | **Macro-economic policy** | **Social policy** |
| Post-Fordism | No general agreements on sharing productivity gains; national and international wage pressure; flexible wage system; wage polarisation (skilled/ unskilled); labour market submitted to competition policy | National and international competition based on cost reduction | Hard money constraints; credit rationing; strict anti-inflationist anchors; promotion of international movement of financial capital; reduction of national financial sovereignty | Withdrawal of the state from the economy: privatisation and residual public sector market orientation | Internationalisation of competition; globalisation of trade and of financial flows | Supply-side policy; competitiveness aims; flexible innovation policy; economy of scope | Cost-saving social policy; reduction and deregulation of the welfare state; increasing private supply of public services |

*Source*: derived from Boyer and Saillard, 2002

Samaritans'[4] and then faced many negative consequences in terms of social costs, unemployment, institutional inconsistencies, transaction costs, overshooting and a reduction in output, beyond what was optimistically foreseen. The table below lists the main dimensions involved in the transition, with some specification of problems, based on the Western experience, which the East should have taken into consideration in order to avoid the huge social costs and the recessions which most transition economies experienced during the 1990s.

The political economy dimension of the transformation, which was almost completely neglected at the beginning of transition, should

*Table 1.5* Transition: what was needed?

| **Variables** | **Problems and issues** | **Possible solutions and appropriate strategies of transformation – Western European perspective** |
|---|---|---|
| Price liberalisation | 1. Loss of purchasing power for people<br>2. Housing problem and affordability of rent<br>3. Energy prices: problem with basic needs such as heating | 1. Control over a basket of food and basic good prices in order to avoid impoverishment of people<br>2. Creating opportunities to buy houses at reasonable prices<br>3. Creating opportunities to buy basic energy services |
| Trade liberalisation | 1. Loss of competitiveness within globalisation<br>2. Closing down of many firms facing global competition<br>3. Uncompetitive disadvantage: inexperience with import-export trade | 1. Some protectionism required<br>2. Unnecessary closing down of firms that are still productive, even if inefficient<br>3. Training and education required |

*Table 1.5* (Continued)

| Variables | Problems and issues | Possible solutions and appropriate strategies of transformation – Western European perspective |
|---|---|---|
| Capital account liberalisation | Capital movement | Instrumental in ensuring macro-economic stability |
| Exchange rate | Currency convertibility and exchange rate regime | Using exchange rate as a key policy tool in order to avoid imbalances, overshooting and deficits, through, for instance, an intermediate regime with a dual exchange rate system combining a free and a fixed regime |
| Property rights privatisation | Introducing new property rights from scratch | Effective; enforceable; clear prevalence of rule of law; guarantees for foreign investors; rule of law and anti-corruption institutions |
| Privatisation | Transformation of public assets into private assets | Guarantees for public good; state ownership for strategic assets and resources; private-state partnerships in different fields, such as telecommunication, education, infrastructure and technology; avoidance of private monopolies and oligarchies; equitable solutions for conflicts between previous owners (before communist nationalisation) and current users (during communism) |

| | | |
|---|---|---|
| Role of government | 1. Withdrawal of the state from the economy<br>2. Prevalence of an anti-state ideology | Developmental state; strategic investments; capital and credit; sound mix of policies able to manage aggregate demand and competitive supply (combination of subsidies to competitive firms and low wages); building of a welfare state; fiscal system and appropriate/progressive taxation; anti-cyclical monetary and fiscal policy not aiming solely to beat inflation rapidly; transparency and anti-corruption tools |

have aimed at implementing policies and introducing institutions according to social constraints, not only macro-economic stability (Roland, 1994; Roland, 2002; O'Brien and Williams, 2007). Paradoxically, social cohesion is needed more in transition economies than in advanced economies, since changes can otherwise incur dangerous levels of opposition and inertia (Van Zon, 1994; Uvalic, 2010). Moreover, new and emerging institutions need to be channelled according to the preferred direction of changes. Therefore, property rights and privatisation in particular need to be driven and supported by an appropriate political economy. Finally, the state should have acted as one of the most important actors of the economy. Its role is crucial and was crucial in the Western European, US, Japanese and other Asian economies during the initial stages of their development processes.

## 1.6 Initial conditions and finishing points: are there any obstacles?

At the beginning of transition, it was practically impossible to implement an institutionally-driven transformation strategy featuring an important role for the state and a strong institutional framework in transition economies, since economics was mainly led by a particular uncritical and perhaps ideological consensus which identified transition as the sum of privatisation and liberalisation (De Vincenti, 2002).[5] Political economy discourses were dominated by a very ideologically biased doctrine (Jessop and Sum, 2005). Transition was imagined merely as a journey from plan A to market B, where the B point was recognised as an ideal economy, an ideal Anglo-Saxon economy, better than those of the USA and the UK, which would have followed religiously all the free-market economy principles, such as the ones students find in neoclassical textbooks. Such an economy does not exist in reality. As Coase (1960) stated, it exists only in textbooks and is an abstraction which can be defined as 'the blackboard economy', i.e., an economy which works when one has perfect competition, perfect markets, perfect information and an atomistic system of agents similar to a physical model rather than to an economy embedded in a society filled with institutions, social relations, complex institutions, political economy games, irrational behaviour, bounded information, and different and multiform agents and organisation.

Once this is taken into consideration, a transition from A to B does not exist. Several different multidimensional and multispeed transitions or, to put it better, *transformations* from a planned economy to a market economy exist; therefore, many different transformation strategies, according to a specific context or country, should have been put forward by policy makers.

Countries were different in 1989 when they started the transformation towards a market economy (1991 for the FSRs). Countries are different today after 20 years of transformation and were also different during the period of transition (Giannaros, 2008). Each of them has some advantages and some disadvantages, particular characteristics, weaknesses and strengths. The transition marked, revealed and exposed these differences to world economy competition and pressure. The following table tries to trace, for each of the 28 transition economies analysed in this book, relevant problems and advantages and to summarise them in the column (−/+). However, the table does not aim to provide a rank on the basis of these features, first of all because each positive or negative score may be weighted differently.

This table is a classification on the basis of a wider, although approximate, analysis of institutional characteristics and socio-economic considerations such as initial conditions, EU membership, degree of recession and political institutions. What is interesting regarding this classification of transition economies is the general

*Table 1.6* Country-by-country characteristics: main problems and advantages

| Countries | Problems/ advantages | Characteristics | −/+ |
|---|---|---|---|
| 1. Slovenia | Main problems | Initial fragmentation problems due to split with the former Yugoslavia | −1 |
| | Main advantages | Better initial conditions in terms of GDP per capita and infrastructure; advanced industrial sector and better technology; very good geographical position; experience of market-oriented reform and private economy model during communism; EU membership; membership of the eurozone | +8 |
| 2. Czech Republic | Main problems | Little experience with private economy during communism; initial fragmentation problem due to split with Slovakia; high levels of pollution | −3 |
| | Main advantages | Better initial conditions in terms of GDP per capita and infrastructure; advanced industrial sector; very good geographical position, being in the centre of Central Europe; attractive for both FDI and tourists; EU membership | +7 |
| 3. Hungary | Main problems | Relatively high debt; more exposed to international financial crises; minority problems and tensions | −3 |
| | Main advantages | Experience of market-oriented reform and private economy model during communism; important tradition of economic school of thought; relatively well-functioning agricultural sector and economic structure better adjusted towards modern development; EU membership | +6 |

*Table 1.6* (Continued)

| Countries | Problems/ advantages | Characteristics | −/+ |
|---|---|---|---|
| 4. Croatia | Main problems | War; fragmentation from and tensions with former Yugoslavian republics (in particular Serbia); minority problems; huge war and transformation recession | −4 |
| | Main advantages | Better initial conditions in terms of GDP per capita and infrastructure; advanced industrial sector; experience of market-oriented reform and private economy model during communism; attractive for both FDI and tourists; concrete prospect of EU membership | +7 |
| 5. Estonia | Main problems | Inexperienced state apparatus; strong dependency on foreign demand; presence of Russian assets and minority problems and tensions with Russia | −4 |
| | Main advantages | Positive externalities with North European and Baltic countries; competitive economy; advanced tertiary sector; attractive for (mainly Scandinavian) FDI; EU membership | +5 |
| 6. Poland | Main problems | Large agricultural and heavy industry sectors; inconsistencies and irrational economic policies; problematic adaptive chance; bad infrastructure; East-West dualism; possible tensions with Germany due to past issues; huge migration | −7 |
| | Main advantages | Large domestic market; closeness to the centre of Europe; possibility of an important role in the EU; high level of education; attractive for FDI; EU membership; remittance from migrants | +7 |

| | | | |
|---|---|---|---|
| 7. Slovakia | Main problems | Inexperienced state apparatus; strong dependency on foreign demand and Czech policies; concentration of military industry during communism; high levels of pollution | −5 |
| | Main advantages | Closeness to city-region of Vienna; geographical externalities; EU membership; membership of the eurozone | +3 |
| 8. Latvia | Main problems | Inexperienced state apparatus and strong dependency on foreign demand; minority problems and tensions with Russia; large agricultural sector and backward economy; exposed to international financial crises; huge transformation recession | −5 |
| | Main advantages | Positive externalities with North European and Baltic countries; EU membership | +2 |
| 9. Lithuania | Main problems | Inexperienced state apparatus and strong dependency on foreign demand; minority problems and tensions with Russia; large agricultural sector and backward economy; exposed to international financial crises; huge transformation recession | −5 |
| | Main advantages | Positive externalities with North European and Baltic countries; EU membership | +2 |
| 10. Bulgaria | Main problems | Corruption; high levels of pollution; backward economy; political fragmentation; peripheral geographical position; huge transformation recession | −6 |
| | Main advantages | Tourism (in particular from Eastern Europe); EU membership | +2 |

*Table 1.6* (Continued)

| Countries | Problems/ advantages | Characteristics | −/+ |
|---|---|---|---|
| 11. Macedonia | Main problems | Fragmentation from and tensions with former Yugoslavian republics; minority problems; huge transformation recession; crime; corruption; less effective rule of law; political fragmentation | −7 |
| | Main advantages | Experience of market-oriented reform during communism; attractive for FDI; concrete prospect of EU membership | +3 |
| 12. Serbia | Main problems | War; fragmentation and tensions with former Yugoslavian republics; minority problems; corruption; crime; less effective rule of law; political fragmentation; huge war and transformation recession | −8 |
| | Main advantages | Advanced industrial sector; experience of market-oriented reform during communism; attractive for FDI and tourism from Russia | +4 |
| 13. Montenegro | Main problems | Political troubles; corruption; crime; less effective rule of law; political fragmentation; currency problems; strict dependency on foreign demand and Serbian economy in particular; huge transformation recession | −7 |
| | Main advantages | Experience of market-oriented reform during communism; attractive for FDI and tourism from Russia | +3 |

| | | | |
|---|---|---|---|
| 14. Russia | Main problems | Oligarchic economy; corruption; crime; less effective rule of law, political and geographical fragmentation; minority problems; political troubles and crisis; high levels of pollution; inequality and poverty; inertia and problematic adaptive change; huge transformation recession; heavy industry and large military industrial sector that is difficult to restructure | −15 |
| | Main advantages | Large domestic market; oil and energy relevance; relatively better initial conditions in terms of GDP and infrastructure; capital endowment; high level of education; important tradition of economic school of thought and universities | +10 |
| 15. Albania | Main problems | Crime; lower rule of law; political fragmentation; backward economy; huge migration; peripheral geographical position; high levels of pollution; huge transformation recession | −8 |
| | Main advantages | Huge remittance from migrants; high education; attractive for FDI (mainly Italians) | +3 |
| 16. Romania | Main problems | Crime; less effective rule of law; corruption; high levels of pollution; backward economy; peripheral geographical position; huge migration; minority problems; huge transformation recession | −9 |
| | Main advantages | Attractive for FDI (mainly Italians); EU membership; huge remittance from migrants | +3 |
| 17. Kazakhstan | Main problems | Political fragmentation and instability; less effective rule of law; political troubles; inequality and poverty; huge transformation recession; bad infrastructure; corruption | −9 |
| | Main advantages | Strategic position; abundant natural resources and energy; oil-driven economy | +3 |

*Table 1.6* (Continued)

| Countries | Problems/ advantages | Characteristics | −/+ |
|---|---|---|---|
| 18. Azerbaijan | Main problems | Political fragmentation and instability; less effective rule of law; political troubles; inequality and poverty; huge transformation recession; bad infrastructure; corruption | −9 |
| | Main advantages | Strategic position; abundant natural resources and energy; oil-driven economy | +3 |
| 19. Belarus | Main problems | Mainly a command economy; 'presidential-monarchy'; low political pluralism and low level of democracy; low income; very poor country; politically and economically dependent on Russia; inefficiency and corruption | −8 |
| | Main advantages | Minor recession at the beginning of transition | +1 |
| 20. Ukraine | Main problems | Crime; less effective rule of law; corruption; political fragmentation; political instability; high levels of pollution; backward economy; huge transformation recession; economically dependent on Russia; strong political tensions | −9 |
| | Main advantages | Large domestic market; Polish support for EU membership | +2 |
| 21. Bosnia and Herzegovina | Main problems | War; fragmentation and tensions with former Yugoslavian republics; minority and religious problems; crime; less effective rule of law; political fragmentation; backward economy; huge war and transformation recession | −9 |
| | Main advantages | International support and aid | +1 |

| | | | |
|---|---|---|---|
| 22. Armenia | Main problems | Corruption; political fragmentation; political instability; geographical fragmentation; minority problems; political troubles; inequality and poverty; huge transformation recession; bad infrastructure | −11 |
| | Main advantages | Strategic position, support and empathy from EU | +2 |
| 23. Georgia | Main problems | Corruption; political fragmentation; political instability; geographical fragmentation; minority problems; political troubles; inequality and poverty; huge transformation recession; bad infrastructure | −11 |
| | Main advantages | Strategic position; support from EU and USA | +2 |
| 24. Turkmenistan | Main problems | Mainly a command economy; 'presidential-monarchy'; low levels of political pluralism and democracy; low income; very poor country; politically and economically dependent on Russia; corruption; political troubles | −11 |
| | Main advantages | Minor recession at the beginning of transition | +1 |
| 25. Uzbekistan | Main problems | Mainly a command economy; 'presidential-monarchy'; low levels of political pluralism and democracy; low income; very poor country; politically and economically dependent on Russia; corruption; political troubles | −11 |
| | Main advantages | Minor recession at the beginning of transition | +1 |

*Table 1.6* (Continued)

| Countries | Problems/ advantages | Characteristics | −/+ |
|---|---|---|---|
| 26. Kyrgikistan | Main problems | Low levels of political pluralism and democracy; less effective rule of law; low income; poor country; extreme poverty; politically and economically dependent on Russia; bad infrastructure; corruption; political troubles | −12 |
| | Main advantages | Strategic position and natural resources | +1 |
| 27. Tajikistan | Main problems | Low levels of political pluralism and democracy; less effective rule of law; low income; poor country; extreme poverty; politically and economically dependent on Russia; bad infrastructure; corruption; political troubles | −12 |
| | Main advantages | Strategic position and natural resources | +1 |
| 28. Moldova | Main problems | Political and geographical fragmentation; 'forgotten country'; minority problems; political troubles; secessionist conflict (independent republic of Transnistria); inequality and poverty; huge transformation recession; bad infrastructure; crime; corruption; politically and economically dependent on Russia | −14 |
| | Main advantages | Support and closeness to Romania (EU member); potential for tourism | +2 |

*Source*: Author's elaboration

outlook that it gives, on the basis of a wider institutional and comparative perspective, beyond any attempt to rank the countries.

This general comparative outlook aims to make policy makers aware of the complexity and differences of the transformation process and of the need to implement different policies in different countries.

Moreover, on the basis of this outlook, it can appear clearer that initial conditions were different in all FCEs and therefore transformation policies cannot be similar, as the WC presumed. One cannot foresee similar finishing points for these countries. The transition is a process of institutional change which has to deal with the problems left behind by the previous regime in order to get particular institutions (not necessarily market institutions) serving as tools to reach better living standards (Nagy, 1994). It has to aim instead at particular living standard and welfare objectives accompanied by political institutions such as freedom, democracy and political rights which would give people effective social rights, income opportunities and political participation rights.

## 1.7 Searching for an appropriate transformation therapy

Shock therapy, the package of radical and suddenly implemented reforms, would not have had to be introduced (where it has been introduced) *tout court*, just because such a strategy was chosen, politically and ideologically, to transform the economies from planned economies to market economies. It would have had to analyse the costs and the benefits of the single economic decisions considering trade-offs for each decision. Interdependency between markets and in particular reforms should be considered, as Staehr showed (2005). Political economy arguments were sometimes misleadingly used in order to explain or justify many aspects of the transition process (Svejnar, 1989; Weitzman, 1993; Boycko *et al.*, 1995). For instance, mass privatisation, which included the giveaway of state assets to citizens, was in some countries used to obtain political consensus for reformers; the early retirement of workers was used as a social compensation in order to justify SOE restructuring and to overcome political constraints; liberalisation was implemented in order to make markets more competitive and the state more efficient; and, at the same time, rent-seekers, who took advantages of these decisions, were able to politically and financially support the rulers (Schmidt, 1998; Shleifer and Treisman, 1999; Gerry *et al.*, 2010a).

The following tables analyse the effects of the choices of macroeconomic policies. With some basic theoretical political economy principles, we are able to show, for each policy, the effects in cases of gradualism or shock therapy. In particular, we drew the analysis appearing in the following tables from a relevant critical literature of transition economics, which use tools and arguments of political economy, such as Clague and Rausser (1992); Hare and Revesz (1992); Roland and Verdier

(1994); Rodrik (1994); Blanchard (1997); Kolodko and Nuti (1997); Wei (1997); and Nuti (1999).

In the tables below, the sign '+' indicates a positive effect and the sign '–' a negative effect. Sometimes we will indicate the effect with a '?', which means that the evidence and the economic theory are contrasting on the issue. The last column, 'Result', indicates the total effect for each policy, following gradualism or shock therapy.

*Table 1.7* Price liberalisation

| **Independent variable** | **Dependent variable** | | | |
|---|---|---|---|---|
| **Subsidy reduction** | **Inflation** | **Competition** | **Public budget** | **Result** |
| FAST | + | + | + | 3 |
| GRADUAL | – | – | – | 0 |

Regarding the variable inflation, the faster the subsidies are eliminated and the faster inflation increases, the faster it could be reduced/eliminated (Clague and Rausser, 1992). On the contrary, the slower the reduction of the subsidies, the slower the increase of inflation. However, it will be brought back to a lower level more slowly.

*Table 1.8* Privatisation

| **Independent variable** | **Dependent variable** | | | |
|---|---|---|---|---|
| **Privatisation of public assets** | **Public budget** | **Efficiency of the firms** | **Bankruptcy risk for new firms** | **Result** |
| FAST | – | – | – (i.e., a higher risk) | 0 |
| GRADUAL | + | + | + (i.e., a lower risk) | 3 |

The evidence of privatisation in transition economies suggests that the first mass privatisation – often at lower prices with respect to the real value of the public assets – carried adverse effects (Roland, 1996). Often, this low-cost privatisation was followed either by immediate sales, at higher costs, from the new owners to other purchasers or by failures and bankruptcy due to a very high inclination to risk, determined by the low price at which the public asset was bought during the mass privatisation. This stimulated inefficient and unproductive investments, which were due to a lack of experience of entrepreneurs, lack of information and of private capital able to guarantee innovation and to increase productivity after privatisation.

*Table 1.9* Privatisation (2) (advantages and disadvantages)

| **Forms of privatisation** | **Advantages/disadvantages** | | | | **Result** |
|---|---|---|---|---|---|
| | **Public revenue** | **Fast** | **Equity** | **Know-how and management** | |
| Spontaneous (appropriation) | NO | YES | NO | NO | +1 |
| Selling to foreigners | YES | NO | NO | YES | +2 |
| Mass privatisation | NO | YES | YES | NO | +2 |
| Selling to insiders and managers | NO | YES | NO | YES | +2 |

Moreover, as the table above shows, privatisation is a very difficult issue, because not only does it concern a trade-off between fast or gradual, but it also involves a decision about the type of privatisation employed, which each have particular advantages, such as those described in the table above. In fact, as Roland (1994; 1996) has pointed out, the type of privatisation is a matter of political preference.

At the beginning of transition, the fast opening to international trade caused the collapse of many national enterprises because of the foreign competition (Calvo and Coricelli, 1993; Rodrik, 1994). Many of the enterprises that went under, although less efficient with respect to foreign competitors, were still in a position to create added value; however, they were swept away. According to Blanchard (1997), the increase in unemployment in transition economies can be explained by the closing down and the failure of many of these enterprises, which were forced to abandon the market. In fact, the substitution of private firms in place of public firms took many years to achieve.

*Table 1.10* International trade: barriers and tariffs

| Independent variable | Dependent variable | | | | |
|---|---|---|---|---|---|
| **Tariff reduction and restriction to import-export and capital movement** | **Competition** | **Unemployment** | **FDI attraction** | **Public revenues** | **Result** |
| FAST | + | – | +? | – | 2? |
| GRADUAL | – | + | – | + | 2 |

*Table 1.11* Exchange rate convertibility

| Independent variable | Dependent variable | | | |
|---|---|---|---|---|
| **Exchange rate convertibility** | **World economy integration** | **Devaluation (big/small)** | **Inflation risk** | **Result** |
| FAST | + | – (big) | – (high) | 1 |
| GRADUAL | – | + (small) | + (low) | 2 |

Regarding the devaluation of the exchange rate, the sudden convertibility of the currency would have required a big devaluation in all FCEs. Moreover, competitive devaluation would increase the pressure on inflation (Nuti, 1999).

*Table 1.12* Interest rate levels

| Independent variable | Dependent variable | | | | |
|---|---|---|---|---|---|
| **Interest rate** | **Inflation** | **FDI attraction** | **Monetary sterilisation from central banks** | **Interest on debt** | **Result** |
| HIGH | + | +? | –? | – | 2? |
| LOW | – | –? | +? | + | 2? |

The effect of interest rate levels on investments and on FDI is not clear. Consequently, the results of the attempts of the central banks to sterilise the large flow of foreign liquidity in the second half of the 1990s, stimulated by higher profit margins, remain unclear. However, the sterilising attempts of the central banks were also expensive in terms of loss of foreign reserves (Kolodko and Nuti, 1997). In the end, what would be the definite effect of a rise in interest rates would be an increase in the interest on the public debt.[6]

In light of the description above, it follows that 'shock therapy' was not the best possible choice. Trade-offs, costs and benefits should have been considered by policy makers for each policy (Hare and Revesz, 1992; Wei, 1997). An ideological approach such as shock therapy *cum* WC would merely bring about more social costs. Moreover, the efficiency of these policies would be very controversial and, very often, the benefits of following a gradual policy instead would be higher than the costs, while for shock therapy the reverse would be true.

## 1.8 Institutional change, the learning process and the heritage of planning

A very important issue, which was largely underestimated during transition, or at least in the first decade of it, was the institutional dimension. The debate was much more focused on shock therapy versus gradualism. Obviously, a gradual therapy would have taken the institutional dimension into consideration more if it had been implemented. However, the institutional dimension should include formal rules and informal rules, the mechanisms which allow economic agents to accept and perceive economic rules and institutions. The issue would not be only 'to get the right institutions' but also to make the right institutions work, to create a coherent institutional framework where formal and informal institutions go together. New policies and institutions introduced by design in a short period require time to be accepted and followed by agents. This is particularly true when these new policies and institutions are unknown to most of the agents, as was the case in the FCEs during the passage from a planning economy to a market economy. Knowledge, timing, implementation and acceptance are all components of learning by doing, a process which requires time (Loasby, 2001; Antonelli, 2005). In particular, when introducing new rules and institutions that were never implemented in FCEs, the process can be even more difficult, more costly, longer and not necessarily successful. The case of many

FSRs and Russia in particular are good examples of this, which shows that market rules should be adapted to the context and should not be introduced as a standard formula.

In particular, four categories of formal and informal institutions would be very problematic during transition, when formal institutions do not work properly and the state is characterised by a power vacuum. They are as follows.

### 1.8.1 Property rights

Inefficiency of the system can come from: a) unclear entitlements over property rights; b) uncertainty of economic relations and lack of reinforcement of property rights; and c) lack of self-reinforcement of property rights (Fadda, 1999). The state should make property rights clearer and should implement reinforcement mechanisms.

### 1.8.2 Penalty and incentive systems

Uncompetitive and unproductive activities should be discouraged by the state, government and local authorities.

### 1.8.3 Rent-seeking

When the state and the public administration have unlimited, uncontrolled and opaque power, private rent-seekers can enjoy illegal rents.

### 1.8.4 Trust

State policies can improve trust and reliability. Trust improves economic relations and market mechanisms. Transaction costs are reduced, reliability improves and long-term relationships among economic agents can emerge. Without trust, all this is strongly limited. Moreover, if, in place of trust, hostility and envy are present, economic relationships worsen.

Differences are very pronounced among transition economies with regard to the categories listed above. In particular, in the FSRs, these categories are more problematic than in the CEECs. In the FSRs, one can observe a greater uncertainty over property rights; a system of penalties and incentives which encourages illegal activities, negative informal institutions, corruption and lobbying; a dominant position of a few groups of people and the prevalence of rent-seeking; and a lack of trust and high transaction costs.

When the macro-economic packages of stabilisation were put in place in FCEs radically and abruptly, with no attention to the intensity, speed and sequence of those policies, the consequences were very bad. Lack of information, along with opportunism from people in an advantageous position, played an important role in increasing transaction costs. The practising of market rules was unknown, so benefits went only to people and agents who had more information and strategic positions such as the former communist ruling class, oligarchs, oil businessmen and the mafia. Such a phenomenon existed to varying extents in all FCEs and in particular in the FSRs, with enigmatic examples in Russia. Property rights were not only acquired through legal and normal procedures – fights and controversies among clubs, organisations, families and oligarchs took place in order to gain more rights and benefits. The idea of mass privatisation, distributing property rights to everyone in order to achieve an economic democracy, did not work. The power vacuum and the lack of a state and coherent institutional framework were lethal in the misdistribution of property rights. This did not guarantee a fair privatisation process, which allowed a chaotic situation to develop. Anti-trust organisations and agencies would have been necessary in order to guarantee transparency and legality. However, shock therapy did not allow for such a framework because there was 'no time to waste' and 'no time for building' controlling public agencies.

On the contrary, a strategy of aware and caring change of the institutional dimension would have paid attention in the most delicate phase of transition to cognitive and learning issues such as the building of new institutions, information, knowledge and practices of new rules, inertia towards new rules, and understanding and acceptance of them. Many problems relating to knowledge, understanding and the learning process came into being during transition. The following table tries to summarise some of the new rules and policies introduced at the beginning of transition, the main problems and the issues relating to understanding/knowledge/information.

The table below is just an example in favour of the argument that institutions matter. An awareness of that would help to prevent many problems that shock therapy merely neglected.

Last, but not least, the implementation of economic policies needs to be properly adapted to the social context and accompanied by appropriate information. Public agencies should be absolved of this duty in order to prevent the adverse selection of asymmetrical information and

*Table 1.13* New rules and the learning process

| New variables | New rules | New policies | Understanding | Knowledge/ how to manage | Acceptance | Information | Main problems |
|---|---|---|---|---|---|---|---|
| Exchange rate | Floating | Devaluation/ evaluation | No/little | Missing | Yes/no | Missing | Dualism with informal exchange rate and black market |
| VAT | Direct tax | Abruptly introduced | No/little | Missing | Inertia | Missing | Free-riding |
| Subsidies | As incentives | Hard budget constraints | No/little | No | Inertia | Missing | Cheating and corruption/ opportunism/ lobbying |
| Property rights | Private property rights | Restitutions/ continuation principles | Chaos | Confused | Yes | Missing | Fights/ lobbying/ corruption/ rent-seeking/ bankruptcy |
| Interest rates | Flexible | High | Little | Confused | Yes/no | Missing | High debt/ crunch market/ credit rationing |
| Financial institutions | Private institutions for credit | Customer selection | No | No | Yes/no | Missing | Speculation on ignorance/ financial bubble |

opportunism, especially when policies concern collective goods such as privatisation and subsidies.

The process of economic transition from a planned economy to a market economy is a complex process of institutional change which, to some extent, brings with it the inheritance of real socialism and the rules and institutions of the planned economy. It involves a process where path dependency, habits and former social norms of agents play an important role. Political economy and current social consensus can also act as an inertial force. The solution to the problem therefore depends on many factors, such as external constraints, conditionality, social sustainability, the magnitude of the inertia towards new rules, social conflicts, adaptability, the internal condition of the country, economic levels, cohesion and the ability to occur within the country. The table below tries to give an overall picture of these problems, characterising transition not only as a process of reform but also as a complex and interactive process of institutional change within a framework of political economy, where new rules interact with old institutions and new power groups, and have to cope with inertia and the old power groups of the communist regimes, emerging productive sectors and innovation (Clague and Rausser, 1992).

This table is adaptable to all transition economies, since all of them are experiencing, more or less, the same problems, such as coping with their heritage from the past, institutional reforms, social problems, institutional conflicts, macro-stabilisation, social costs and external constraints. However, these issues are a kind of 'common container' that assume different details and aspects in the single country. Within each country, interaction between the specific issue and the national context yields a particular result different from that in other contexts. Moreover, since not only institutions but also culture matters, transition towards capitalism in each country takes effect accordingly. The change adjusts to a capitalist model following the specific institutional and cultural characteristics of the country and its path dependency. A standard model, implemented using a design strategy, by emulating other country models, would be difficult to set up (Matzner, 1992; Murrel, 1992). An institutional plan which ignores the history, institutions and development path of the specific country would be a failure, as Rodrik (1999: 3) states: 'It is not realistic to expect that national development efforts will converge on a single model of "good economic behaviour"; nor is it desirable that they do so. The lesson of history is that ultimately all successful countries develop their own brands of national capitalism.'

*Table 1.14* The political economy of transition: the main issues in brief

| **Heritage of real socialism** | **Reforms** | **Institutional issues of transition** | **Social costs** | **Domestic and international constraints and conditionality** |
|---|---|---|---|---|
| Insufficient private entrepreneurship and private saving | Macro-economic stabilisation | Governance | Unemployment | Structural reforms suggested by the IMF and WC |
| Distortions within the productive structure | Liberalisation and deregulation | Social conflict and lack of cohesion | Poverty | Adjustment towards the *acquis commaunitaire* and towards the Copenhagen criteria (conditionality for CEECs to meet EU membership) |
| State monopoly | Privatisation and firm restructuring | Conflicts and incoherence between formal and informal rules, old rules and new behaviour, inertia and uncertainty | Loosening of purchasing power of workers and retired people | Trade and integration into the world economy, WTO constraint, WTO conditionality for membership |
| Distortions within trade flows due to the former Comecon specialisation and protectionism | Trade and external convertibility of the exchange rate | Increasing of transaction costs | Increasing of income inequality | Changes to the trade pattern and to the productive structure in order to adjust to international demand |

| | | | | |
|---|---|---|---|---|
| Central planning and price administration. Welfare state and public investment in social dimensions | Pension reform, health reform, education reform and the ending of public subsidies to firms and households | Conflicts over the distribution of new property rights | Dualism between poor and rich regions | Debt sustainability and balance of payment constraint |
| Central planning of investments and industrial effort. Too large SOEs and obsolete capital | New rules and law reinforcement, political economy governance, corporate governance | Institutional chaos and organisational problems, power vacuum, new dominant groups and lobbies | Corruption, crime, illegality, informal economy | Domestic constraint due to savings |
| Underdevelopment/ lack of financial systems, private credit and financial agencies. Lack of capital and capitalists | Property rights distribution | Conflicts between winners and losers of transition | Credit crunch and rationing | Domestic political consensus |
| Soft budget constraints and subsidies to firms | Reinforcing of 'hard budget constraints' | Social consensus | Lower employment levels | International competition |

*Table 1.14* (Continued)

| **Heritage of real socialism** | **Reforms** | **Institutional issues of transition** | **Social costs** | **Domestic and international constraints and conditionality** |
|---|---|---|---|---|
| Inflation (hidden and repressed) | Large SOEs to privatise and to restructure | Governance and rules for FDI | Erosion of purchasing power | World Bank and IMF discipline |
| Different initial conditions and different productive specialisation | Innovation and technology incentives, R&D planning | Inertia and resistance to change | Low wages for unskilled workers | Global knowledge economy pressure |
| Public deficit and debt | Restructuring of the public budget | Inertia, trade union opposition and veto players | Cuts in social expenditure causing cutbacks in welfare (education and health system) | Managing an equilibrium between a domestic social consensus and international organisation discipline |

*Source*: Author's elaboration

There was an attempt in transition economies to design standard institutional plans to be implemented in society. This attempt considered society as a research laboratory. To some extent, institutions can be similar when one deals with market economies: banks, trade laws, financial institutions, job market agencies, Chambers of Commerce, industrial organisations, competition rules, etc. However, market economies are not the same. Rules and institutions emerged in capitalist economies after the Industrial Revolution in England and then in other countries in Western Europe and North America. This was a result of a long process, a historical product of interaction between rules, behaviour and institutions which disciplined the power of markets and created mechanisms for them to work better in the specific context. They limited the destructive effects on the market deriving from asymmetrical information. They concurred to internalise externalities, channelled 'market prices' and guided the direction of changes in them, thus making them not pure market prices but institutionally-guided prices (De Vincenti, 2002: 7).

## 1.9 Final comments

In this chapter I have argued that in transition economies, the end of planning cannot mean the abrupt and mere substitution of markets to planners, because markets do not exist by a miracle and are not created by and do not work through an invisible hand just because the planners disappear. In contrast, the process of transformation must be guided by the state, along with rules and institutions that coherently discipline the economic system in the difficult phase of substitution, in order to prevent a systemic vacuum. Institutions matter as well as political economy. Interaction with persistent behavioural models norms and rules does not allow for a convergence towards a determined model. On the contrary, this will contribute to pushing each transition economy towards a specific model of market economy.

# Appendix A1

## An economic interpretation of the collapse of the Soviet system: technological dilemmas and incentives

If I am going to combine Berend's (2009) view on the fall of communism, explained in the Introduction to this book, with Olson's (1992) perspective on economic systems, I can draw very interesting conclusions. Olson argues that Soviet economies were able to grow faster during the 1950s and 1960s because the society was pushed by an 'encompassing interest' (Olson, 1992). Olson defines the concept of encompassing interest in the following way: if an individual (or an organisation), acting rationally, contributes to the growth of the economy and obtains a consistent part of any increase of the output of the economy, then he or she has an encompassing interest in the society. In other words, individual interests that are adequately motivated and priced, within a framework of virtuous incentives, correspond to collective interests. In the Soviet economy, Stalin had an encompassing interest; he identified himself with the state. The Politburo too was initially pushed by an encompassing interest which coincided with that of the Soviet state. Simultaneously, Soviet officers were continuously motivated and their interests were intimately linked with the success of their firms, offices, towns, municipalities, party sections, etc.

Time went on, and improvement and concentration of power in the ruling class, in a vertical way, without transparency, information or extensive control by the people, left officers, bureaucrats, state managers and directors able to behave more and more in a selfish way, getting more from collusion than from contributing to social output. Therefore, these people started to pursue personal interests, gaining more from the national income than what they contributed to produce. This perverse mechanism left the society with less output to divide. Economic relations and transactions became more inclined to follow this perverse mechanism since it made it possible to get more out of the national income, without control and transparent institutions. In the end, during the 1970s and throughout the 1980s, Soviet societies pervaded these perverse mechanisms, produced less output for all, became less efficient, less productive and lost the encompassing interest which allowed them to grow as fast as Western Europe during the 1950s and 1960s. Income gaps between the East and West increased and economic collapse approached (cf. Table 1 in the Introduction to this book). Even with a strong and stable political apparatus, Soviet planners faced a serious economic disaster which condemned them to disintegration in 1991. The collapse of the Soviet Union was anticipated by the fall of communism in the satellite states of Central and Eastern Europe, which had a similar experience, with strong encompassing interests in the 1950s and 1960s, and overwhelming perverse mechanisms and incentives in the 1970s and 1980s.

The interpolation of Olson's (1992) interpretation with Berend's (2009) explanation of the fall of communism in the Soviet republics and in Central and Eastern Europe brings me to the following reflection: in both approaches, one can identify the crucial role of institutions. These institutions were missing and did not allow, in the first case (Olson's perspective), for a substitution of a national encompassing interest (identified initially and explicitly with the aim of the East economically overcoming and triumphing over the West) with more natural and genuine people-linked interests. These people-linked interests would be: freedom, civil and political liberties, information, transparency, public participation and free economic activities. Such interests could be obtained by diversifying production from defence and heavy industry towards civil technology, light manufacturing and the advanced tertiary sector, which would have improved both the living conditions of people and technology. In the second case (Berend's interpretation), the lack of appropriate institutions and incentives able to stimulate technology and innovation improvement at a firm level was lethal. In addition to these factors, one should add the lack of managerial firms which could have been crucial for a change and for a spin-off development more oriented towards global competitiveness and efficiency.

The table below shows the main problems identified by the two authors and the solutions here proposed. Both approaches, I believe, have a common matrix: the lack of appropriate institutions. In fact, it can be shown that both problems can be represented by a simple game theory with easy solutions.

*Table A1.1* Olson's and Berend's interpretations

| THE ROLE OF INSTITUTIONS IN OLSON'S PERSPECTIVE AND BEREND'S INTERPRETATION OF THE DECLINE OF THE SOVIET SYSTEM | |
|---|---|
| Olson – loosening of encompassing interests | Berend – missed opportunities in technology and innovation |
| Lack of institutions able to substitute the loss of the encompassing national interests | Lack of institutions able to create an environment for firm incentives to produce better technology and innovation |
| **SOLUTION** | **SOLUTION** |
| PEOPLE-LINKED INTERESTS AND PERSONAL INCENTIVES | MONITORING, MANAGER CONTROL AND FIRM INCENTIVES |

Consider the following game structure:

one chief (General Secretary/Politburo)
two state-owned firms with two state managers
two strategies for state managers:
a) report and reveal to the chief about the innovation;
b) hide the innovation.

In a), state managers will face no consequences (no positive incentives are in place). In b), state managers will obtain personal profits. However, if one agent hides the new innovation and the other reveals it, then the first will be severely penalised (imprisonment or even execution – negative incentives). From this structure, the following matrix is obtained.

*Table A1.2* Technological and innovation dilemmas in a command economy

| | **Hide** | **Reveal** |
|---|---|---|
| Hide | (P + 1, P + 2) | (Jail-1, P2) |
| Reveal | (P1, Jail-2) | (01, 02) |

If both managers play 'hide', they can enjoy positive and personal returns (P + 1, P + 2). If an agent plays 'hide' and the other 'reveals', the first will be jailed by the chief and the second will be appreciated and priced, and will keep his or her role of state manager, with the following pay-off (Jail-1, P2). Both will get zero in the event of a simultaneous report (01, 02).

In a static and non-repetitive game, with punishments strongly implemented, obviously the 'reveal' strategy strongly dominates 'hide' and identifies a Nash equilibrium. However, as in the Soviet economies, the game was repetitive and cooperation strategies were more possible. In fact, realistically, bureaucrats, state managers and directors were more prone to cooperate in illegal matters in order to obtain personal returns that were higher than standard social benefits for being state managers. It is likely that the strategy which will dominate in repetitive games is a cooperative one. Therefore, a strategy inclined to maintain the status quo and the prevalence of old technology over new methods is likely to have been what state Soviet managers were following, with perverse and negative effects on the economy as a whole in the long run. This behaviour would be consistent with Berend's (2009) and Olson's (1992) views explained above.

# 2
# The Great Transformation: Recession, Recovery and EU Conditionality

## 2.1 Introduction

This chapter deals with recession and recovery in transition economies during the past 20 years of transformation. International constraints will also be examined. The aim is purely descriptive and informative. As far as the new Member States of the EU are concerned, this chapter will analyse the conditionality and compliance of the candidates. Recession was severe both in the CEECs and the FSRs during the transformation. However, I argue, during the period of transformation and economic recovery, the CEECs were, to some extent, favoured by EU conditionality and membership, while the FSRs were not involved in this process. At the same time, the old EU Member States (the EU-15) benefited greatly from trade with and FDI directed towards the CEECs. In fact, in the CEECs, labour costs are cheap and recourses as well as raw materials are abundant. Nevertheless, although it was a very important issue that influenced transition in the CEECs, EU membership was not the crucial factor in the relatively better performance of many CEECs with respect to the FSRs. Some new Member States, such as Romania, Bulgaria and to some extent Lithuania and Latvia, did not perform better than most of the FSRs. As such, crucial factors for development have to be found elsewhere, as I will show in Part III of this book.

## 2.2 Economic slump and uneven resurgence

As stated by Kornai (2006), the transformation of the CEECs has been unique. On the one hand, it took place peacefully and was an astonishingly fast process towards a Western mode of development. On the other hand, it was characterised by deep economic troubles. It was a process which involved successes and failures that varied considerably among transition countries (Holscher and Gabrisch, 2006).

Transition economies differ significantly in terms of economic performance, although the economic policies advised by international organisations and implemented by national authorities are quite similar. These countries differed with regard to centralised planning, initial conditions and institutional frameworks. The economic structures (productive specialisation, labour division, technologies, output, etc.) were diverse, as were the rules, aims and planning, in spite of common membership of the Communist Bloc (Falcetti *et al.*, 2000).

Economists' views on transformation policies have been quite controversial and diverse (Sachs, 1991; Kolodko and Nuti, 1997; Åslund, 2007). During the 1990s, the debate among economists on the type of transformation and on the mistakes of policy-makers was very intense. Briefly, some economists criticised the timing of implementation, others criticised the intensity of policies and others the need and the appropriateness of such policies. This set of policies delivered important economic shocks, provoking a huge fluctuation in exchange rates which generated effects that were greater than expected.

In many countries (Poland, the Czech Republic and most of the former USSR), the transformation formula was implemented using a shock therapy strategy, as we saw in the last chapter. In others (for example, Hungary and Slovenia), a more gradual approach was adopted. Nevertheless, the aim in both cases was to introduce a market economy and to reduce or eliminate the role of the state in the economy. It is important to stress that countries that adopted a gradual programme of macroeconomic stabilisation, such as Hungary and Slovenia, achieved similar results to those of Poland and the Czech Republic, which implemented a shock therapy programme. By contrast, Russia and Bulgaria, which also implemented a shock therapy programme, achieved very negative results. Moreover, it has to be said that if it is true that Poland's results were the best among transition economies, it is also true that 'Poland did not completely implement shock therapy. Although prices in Poland were liberalised, most of its large SOEs have yet to be privatised' (Lin, 2005: 241).[1]

This seems to confirm that macro-economic policies are context-dependent. They depend on the country or region in which they are implemented. Their success or failure depends on several factors, including initial conditions, local institutions, agents' behaviour and reaction to implemented policies, social context and culture, acceptance by agents, legality and trust, appropriateness of policies, etc.

Most economists today seem to converge towards the idea that, at the beginning of transition, very little attention was paid to all these institutional factors and to the institutional framework of countries in general (Stiglitz, 1998; McArthur and Sachs, 2001; Kolodko, 2004; Rodrik, 2004).

The following table shows which kind of macro-economic strategy, in general, transition economies adopted during the 1990s.

*Table 2.1* Transition and macro-policies

| Countries | Type of macro-economic stabilisation |
|---|---|
| East Germany | Immediately united with West Germany (a particular kind of 'shock therapy'). |
| Czech Republic, Estonia, Latvia, Poland, Slovakia | Speedy reforms, starting with macro-stabilisation. The implementation of privatisation, liberalisation and trade openness policies ('shock therapy' programme). |
| Hungary and Slovenia | 'Gradual' macro-stabilisation, strong institutional framework, gradual privatisation. |
| Albania and Bulgaria | Reforms started very late but then implemented through 'shock therapy'; corruption. |
| Romania and Russia | Reforms started but then stopped, uncoordinated, badly managed; corruption. |
| Belarus and Ukraine | No or insufficient reforms, hyper-inflation, unstable economies and politics; corruption. |
| Armenia, Azerbaijan, the former Yugoslavia (except Slovenia), Georgia | Military conflicts, civil wars, instability of politics and economies, no reforms, except for Croatia, which later started a gradual and successful transition. |
| Other Asian republics of the CIS | Political instability, no reforms, longer and deeper economic recession; corruption. |

*Source*: Lavigne, 1999

It is widely acknowledged that despite some measurement problems that could have occurred during the transformation from a planned to a market economy, such as the existence of an informal economy, statistical problems and the coherence of the accounting system (see Nuti, 1999; Åslund, 2001), the great transformation was concurrent with a huge recession (Kornai, 1994; Svejnar, 2002).

As depicted in the graphs below, in the CEECs at the beginning of the 1990s, cumulative recession resulted in a slump of between 20 and 40 per cent of GDP, whereas in the FSRs it was even worse and GDP fell in some cases by 60 per cent (Transition Report, 2001). At the same time, economic recovery was faster and more consistent in the CEECs (except for Bulgaria and Romania) than in the CIS. The reasons for the different levels of performance probably lie in the diverse initial conditions, different policies and institutions and the mistakes of policy-makers (Gomulka, 1995; Falcetti *et al.*, 2000; Nuti, 2001; De Vincenti, 2002).

After ten years of transition, taking 1989 as a starting point,[2] only a few states reached or exceeded the 1989 level of GDP (Hungary, Poland, Slovakia and Slovenia). After 15 years, the Albania, the Czech Republic and Estonia joined this club. Among the CIS, the situation was severe, and all the FSRs in 2004 were still below their 1989 GDP level, apart from Belarus, Turkmenistan and Uzbekistan. The reason for such these exceptions is to be found in the fact that these three countries were basically still planned economies and never started a true transition process; therefore, they did not undergo a transformation recession experienced by all the other transition economies. After almost 20 years of transition, the situation in most former communist countries does not seem to have stabilised. Moreover, the current economic crisis shows how vulnerable transition economies are with respect to external shocks, with few exceptions. I will not explore the current economic crisis in detail. However, it has to be said that the twentieth anniversary of the fall of the Berlin Wall brought about in almost all transition economies a similar slump to that of 1989–90. Reasons for the current recession are very different. As the figure below shows, the Baltic states, which are open and small economies (classified as competitive capitalist economies in Part II of this book), have been the hardest hit by the current recession, with a slump in GDP of around 12–15 per cent. The extreme export-led model and the uncontrolled openness to FDI seem to be the major causes for this huge slump (Myant and Drahokoupil, 2010). Turkmenistan and Uzbekistan, which on the contrary I will classify as state capitalist economies, have high rates of GDP growth. Other countries such as Poland (+1.3 per cent), Albania (+1.2 per cent), Azerbaijan (+3 per cent), Tajikistan and Kyrgyzstan (+0.5 per cent) managed the recession relatively better.[3] The average rate of recession in transition economies is −5.2 per cent. In 1990, the first year of transition and integration into the world economy for almost all transition economies, the rate of recession was about −4.6 per cent (Tridico, 2007a).

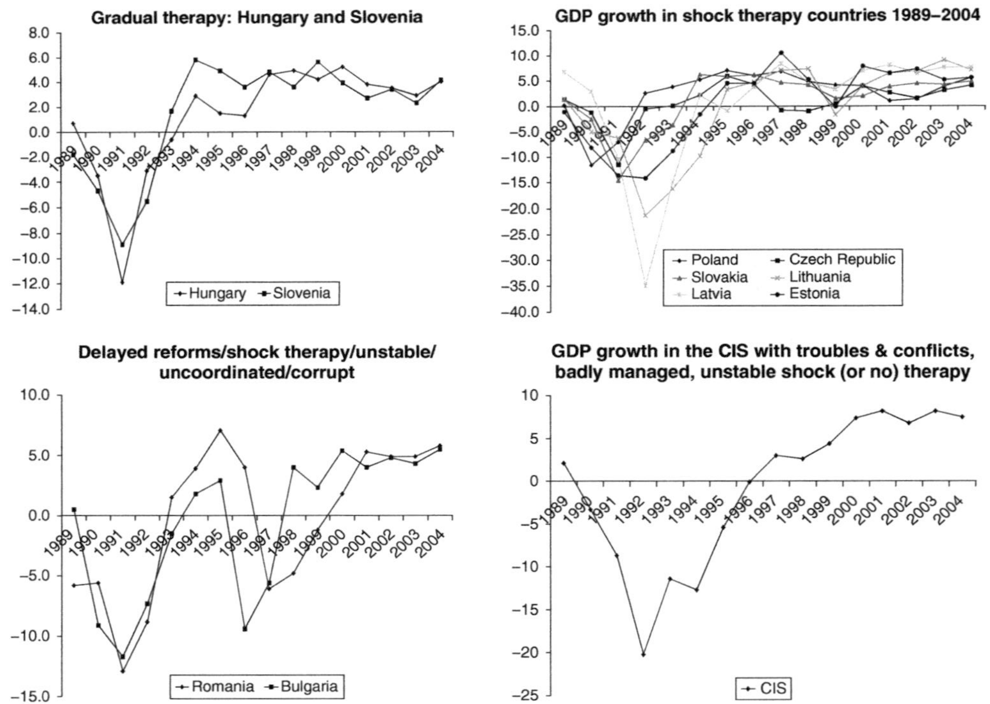


*Figure 2.1* Recession and recovery of GDP in the CEECs and the CIS 1989–2004
*Source*: Transition Reports

Rodrik (2008) claims that integration into the global economy can be both positive and negative depending on the institutions and governance that the country is able to put forward when opening up to the world economy. Weak domestic policies and institutions would increase levels of political vulnerability, with negative consequences on the economic volatility of a country. Thus, when opening up to the world economy, a country would need appropriate institutions of conflict management, international governance, trade strategies and policies, specialisation and state support. This would make it easier to cope with external shocks and crises (Rodrik, 2008).

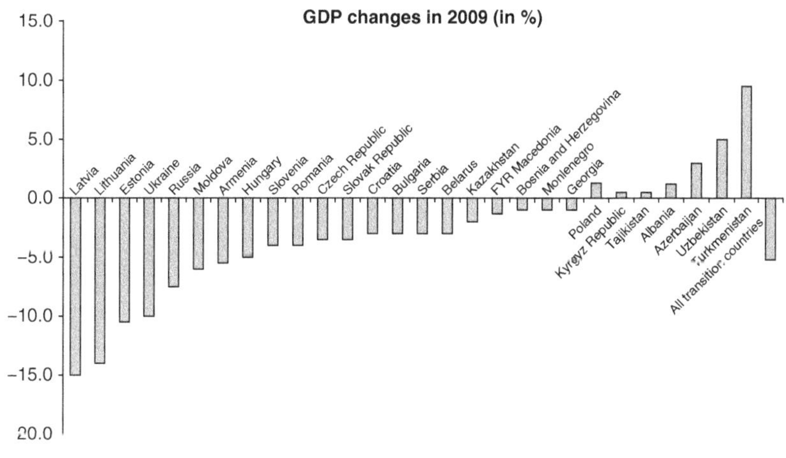


*Figure 2.2* GDP growth in 2009
*Source*: EBRD, 2009

The average GDP level in 2008 of 117 (with 1989 = 100) was not much higher than the level in 1989 considering all the transition economies together. However, the current economic crisis hit all transition economies dramatically, and at the end of 2009, their GDP levels were lower than in 2008. At the same time, because of this second recession, the average level is lower than 117. Many countries, such as Russia, Ukraine, Georgia, Kyrgyzstan, Moldova and Tajikistan among the CIS, and Serbia, Bosnia and Herzegovina, Lithuania and Latvia among the CEECs, also had a GDP level in 2008 that was still below that of 1989 (with Croatia, Montenegro, Romania and Bulgaria just around 100).

*Table 2.2* Levels of real GDP in 2004 and 2008 (1989 = 100)

| CEEC and Balkans | 2004 level | 2008 level | GDP per capita 2008 ($) | CIS | 2004 level | 2008 level | GDP per capita 2008 ($) |
|---|---|---|---|---|---|---|---|
| Slovenia | 120 | 136.5 | 27,168.4 | Russia | 77 | 97.0 | 12,074.5 |
| Czech Republic | 108 | 126.7 | 25,395 | Belarus | 100 | 134.5 | 6,285.5 |
| Estonia | 102 | 113.7 | 16,508.4 | Ukraine | 51 | 60.7 | 3,937.0 |
| Poland | 135 | 156.5 | 13,838.9 | Kazakhstan | 94 | 124.5 | 8,736.4 |
| Hungary | 115 | 119.6 | 15,326.1 | Armenia | 89 | 131.3 | 3,711.2 |
| Lithuania | 84 | 99.8 | 14,017.8 | Turkmenistan | 105 | 160.3 | 2,915.6 |
| Slovakia | 114 | 142.4 | 18,248.9 | Azerbaijan | 71 | 163.0 | 5,507.4 |
| Croatia | 91 | 104.8 | 15,552.4 | Georgia | 41 | 73.5 | 2,845.0 |
| Latvia | 83 | 98.0 | 14,909.1 | Uzbekistan | 107 | 144.8 | 1,007.4 |
| Albania | 129 | 154.5 | 4,066.1 | Kyrgyzstan | 75 | 94.2 | 952.5 |
| Bosnia and Herzegovina | 57 | 78.9 | 4,833.5 | Moldova | 41 | 57.5 | 1,766.0 |
| Serbia | 60 | 81.1 | 6,761.0 | Tajikistan | 62 | 91.9 | 794.8 |

| Montenegro | 72 | 101.1 | 6,509.0 | CIS | 76 | 111 | 4211 |
|---|---|---|---|---|---|---|---|
| Romania | 92 | 113.2 | 9,186.5 | All transition economies | 94.7 | 117 | 12,013.9 |
| Macedonia | 78 | 95.7 | 4,761.3 | | | | |
| Bulgaria | 84 | 105.7 | 6,561.1 | | | | |
| CEEC 5+ | 116 | 131 | 19,647.3 | | | | |
| CEEC 5− and Balkans | 86 | 107 | 9,582 | | | | |
| All CEEC + Balkans | 96 | 119 | 14,614.9 | | | | |

*Note*: *CEEC 5+* are the five most advanced CEECs: the Czech Republic, Estonia, Hungary, Poland and Slovenia. *CEEC 5−* are the five least advanced CEECs: Bulgaria, Lithuania, Latvia, Romania and Slovakia. *Balkans* are the rest of the Balkan countries including Albania, Croatia, Macedonia, Montenegro and Serbia. *CIS* are the FSRs that are today part of the CIS.
*Source*: Transition Report, 2009

## 2.3 The labour market and the explosion of unemployment

Most of the former communist countries were characterised by full employment of labour and very often by situations of excess of aggregate demand over supply. This was a consequence of a bad price management policy by planners, who kept prices artificially lower (Nuti, 1986). In former communist countries, planners and managers pursued objectives in physical terms and not in value. All the state companies were adapted to the plan with fixed quantitative objectives centrally decided thanks to 'soft budget constraints'. Their production had to respect the demands of the plan and not the effective demands of the economy (Kornai, 1986). This caused huge distortions and inefficiencies in production. The constraints were not suggested by the prices whose variations (increases or decreases) could be good signals for the amount of goods to produce, but were determined centrally, and very often on the basis of the preferences of individual managers and planners. The directors of the state companies, having fixed objectives in physical terms, paid attention not to the efficiency of production but to the amount produced. The objectives could have been, for example, a determined amount of nails and not the quality and the diversity of every single nail, while for a transportation company, the objective could have been the number of kilometres to cover and not the amount or the quality of the goods transported.[4]

Production was not regulated by prices. Managers had personal preferences and objectives. The planners' rational choices did not substitute market efficiency (Portes, 1993). Managers were pursuing physical objectives such as job creation and higher levels of production, spurred on by the prices and rewards offered by the regime. A direct consequence of this situation was the excess of labour demand and of aggregate demand. Full employment was not an economic issue but a political preference, regulated by adverse choices by managers and corrupt and incompetent planners (Nuti, 2009). It was not an economic problem: it was a bureaucratic/administrative issue. The objective for the managers of the state companies was not the productivity of labour, the quality of the goods produced, the efficiency of the company or the organisation of the firm. The number of jobs and the level of production that the company was able to yield were of paramount importance. Obviously, in such a situation, real wages, decided centrally, remained at very low levels.

The transformation towards the market economy was accompanied by the emergence of hyper-inflation, which until then had been kept artificially low. During communism, inflation was controlled through the repressed form of shortage of goods and queues at retail shops. Now liberalisation brought about an explosion of unemployment. In terms of GDP, Eastern Europe did not manage to catch up with Western Europe, but in terms of unemployment rates it managed to do so very quickly. Job destruction without job creation contributed to the increase of the unemployment rate to double-digit figures in the first years of transition. Unemployment exploded in 1990 and increased steadily thereafter in many countries. This was coupled with decreasing wages during the early stages of transition and increasing wages during the later stages, in a similar fashion across almost all transition economies.

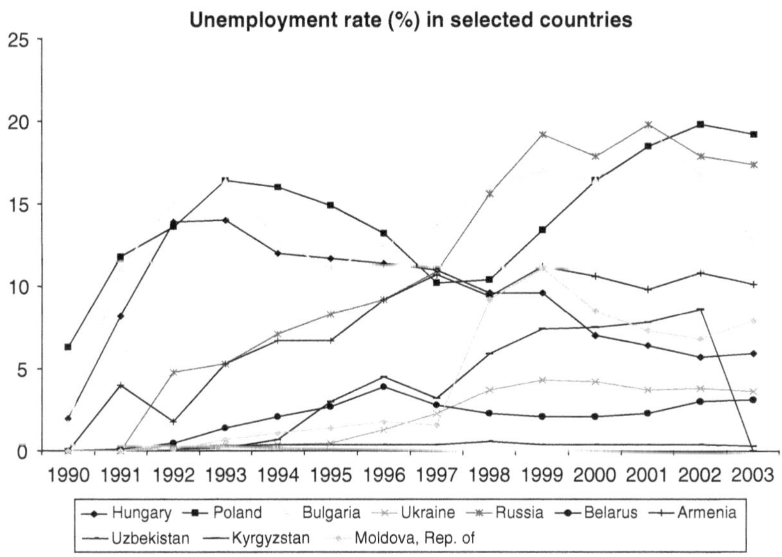


*Figure 2.3* Unemployment rates during the 1990s
*Source*: Transition Report, 2004

After 20 years of transition, average wages in transition economies are one-third of the average wages in Western Europe. In fact, contrary to other prices, wages during transition were kept lower in order to boost competitiveness. The OECD (2000) estimated that on average, 60 per cent of the earning workers in transition economies are below the poverty line. Even if the recovery of GDP to some extent occurred in several former communist countries, after the recession of the early 1990s, the labour market remained a problematic issue. Unemployment is still high in many transition economies. This is because, as Blanchard (1997) argued, the fall in production and the closing down of many SOEs were not immediately counteracted by private firms and capital. The graph below demonstrates such an issue.

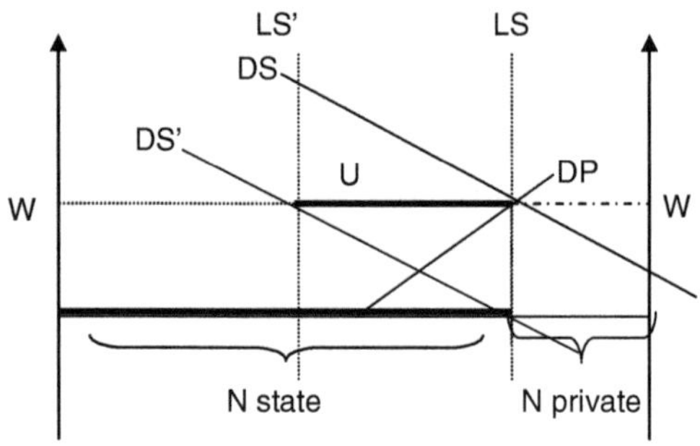


*Figure 2.4* Employment dynamics in former communist countries
*Source*: adapted from Blanchard, 1997

On the horizontal axis from left to right are the employment of SOEs (N state) and private employment (N private). On the vertical axis is the same level of real wages (W). The line DS represents the labour demands of the state companies, decreasing with respect to wages, from left to right, while the private demand for labour (DP) decreases with respect to wages from right to left (LS = labour supply). After 1989, the labour demands of the SOEs (DS) contracted drastically (to DS′). In the first few years it was not replaced by sufficient private expansion in terms of labour demands in order to be able to offset the withdrawal of the SOEs and to converge towards the new labour supply (LS′). The result was the explosion of mass unemployment (U).

In fact, during the first years of transition, new firms emerged and many were privatised. However, most of them lacked capital, experience and knowledge. They were small in size and were not able to absorb the huge fall in production and employment caused by the withdrawal of the state from the economy. Bigger investments and firms only arrived later, with the flow of Western FDI. In a more dynamic vision, we can add that, as the state withdrew, private expansion took place slowly along with many difficulties. Therefore, unemployment remained at high levels during the 1990s.

According to Nuti (1999), dynamics of unemployment in the FCEs, described by Blanchard (1997), can be interpreted in two ways. The first of these follows a classic approach: the greater the levels of unemployment, the greater the pressure on wage reduction and therefore the greater the profit rate, with beneficial effects on capital accumulation, economic growth and further employment. The second interpretation follows the neoclassical approach: the greater the levels of unemployment, the greater the resistance to privatisation and to the restructuring of state companies, because of the additional risks of unemployment implicit in the processes of restructuring. Both these interpretations explain the existence of high unemployment levels.

Moreover, an insufficient level of saving and a deficit in the current account requires an inflow of FDI. Such an inflow did not happen at the beginning of transition. Foreign firms did not have faith in investing in FCEs. FDI only started to arrive in the second half of the 1990s in transition economies and in particular in the CEECs which had the prospect of joining the EU and therefore could attract FDI from it (Bedi and Cieslik, 2002). In fact, after the Copenhagen Council in 1993, which offered a concrete prospect to the CEECs to join the EU, conditionality and harmonisation towards the *acquis commaunitaire* made an increase in FDI possible. The impact of FDI is twofold. On the one hand, it may have an impact on the economy, equalising the current account, increasing production and employment. On the other hand, it influences norms and institutions in the country to which it is provided. Foreign firms do not face the issues of inertia and institutional problems of adapting firms and organisations to market rules, because they did not carry with them a communist legacy. Such an inflow of FDI was probably led to an increase in employment levels and a reduction in unemployment levels at the end of the 1990s.

The same story can be described when one looks at the employment rate. In transition economies, the employment rate of the adult population (aged 15 and over) declined consistently from around 70 per cent at the end of the 1980s to an average of 51 per cent in 2008. This huge decline is attributed mainly to the transformation recession of the early 1990s. The following transition was not able to return the economies to pre-transition levels of employment, even though in some countries like Poland, the Czech Republic, Slovenia and other advanced CEECs, economic activity level reached and surpassed the pre-1989 level of activity.

Some countries, in particular some of the CIS, managed to better protect employment and to maintain higher levels of employment with less job destruction during the early 1990s. These countries today have an average employment level of 54 per cent, which is far above the figure of 48 per cent for the less advanced CEECs and even higher than the levels

*Table 2.3* Employment levels of countries as a percentage of population (aged 15 and over)

| **Countries** | **1991** | **1992** | **1993** | **1994** | **1995** | **1996** | **1997** | **1998** | **1999** | **2000** | **2001** | **2002** | **2003** | **2004** | **2005** | **2006** | **2007** | **2008** |
|---|---|---|---|---|---|---|---|---|---|---|---|---|---|---|---|---|---|---|
| Albania | 49 | 48 | 47 | 47 | 48 | 48 | 47 | 48 | 48 | 47 | 47 | 46 | 46 | 46 | 46 | 46 | 46 | 46 |
| Armenia | 38 | 37 | 36 | 36 | 36 | 38 | 37 | 38 | 37 | 37 | 38 | 39 | 39 | 38 | 39 | 38 | 39 | 38 |
| Azerbaijan | 57 | 56 | 56 | 56 | 55 | 56 | 56 | 57 | 57 | 57 | 57 | 57 | 58 | 59 | 59 | 59 | 61 | 60 |
| Belarus | 58 | 57 | 56 | 55 | 54 | 54 | 54 | 53 | 52 | 52 | 52 | 52 | 52 | 53 | 52 | 52 | 52 | 52 |
| Bosnia and Herzegovina | 42 | 42 | 41 | 40 | 41 | 47 | 44 | 44 | 42 | 41 | 41 | 41 | 41 | 41 | 41 | 40 | 42 | 42 |
| Bulgaria | 45 | 48 | 43 | 43 | 44 | 44 | 43 | 43 | 41 | 38 | 40 | 41 | 42 | 43 | 44 | 46 | 46 | 46 |
| Croatia | 50 | 50 | 50 | 49 | 49 | 48 | 48 | 47 | 46 | 44 | 44 | 44 | 44 | 45 | 45 | 45 | 46 | 46 |
| Czech Republic | 58 | 58 | 57 | 57 | 57 | 57 | 56 | 56 | 54 | 54 | 54 | 54 | 53 | 53 | 53 | 53 | 54 | 54 |
| Estonia | 61 | 60 | 58 | 57 | 55 | 54 | 53 | 53 | 52 | 51 | 51 | 52 | 52 | 51 | 53 | 54 | 55 | 55 |
| Georgia | 57 | 57 | 55 | 55 | 56 | 57 | 57 | 56 | 56 | 56 | 58 | 56 | 57 | 55 | 55 | 55 | 55 | 54 |
| Hungary | 48 | 48 | 45 | 44 | 43 | 43 | 42 | 43 | 44 | 45 | 45 | 45 | 45 | 45 | 45 | 45 | 45 | 45 |
| Kazakhstan | 63 | 60 | 61 | 63 | 61 | 60 | 60 | 60 | 60 | 60 | 62 | 63 | 63 | 63 | 62 | 62 | 64 | 64 |
| Kyrgyz Republic | 58 | 58 | 58 | 58 | 58 | 59 | 59 | 58 | 59 | 58 | 58 | 56 | 57 | 58 | 58 | 58 | 58 | 58 |
| Latvia | 58 | 57 | 55 | 53 | 54 | 46 | 49 | 49 | 48 | 47 | 48 | 50 | 51 | 51 | 52 | 55 | 55 | 55 |

| | | | | | | | | | | | | | | | | | | |
|---|---|---|---|---|---|---|---|---|---|---|---|---|---|---|---|---|---|---|
| Lithuania | 54 | 55 | 54 | 51 | 51 | 51 | 51 | 52 | 52 | 49 | 48 | 49 | 50 | 49 | 50 | 51 | 51 | 50 |
| Macedonia, FYR | 37 | 37 | 36 | 36 | 36 | 35 | 34 | 35 | 35 | 35 | 37 | 36 | 33 | 32 | 33 | 34 | 34 | 35 |
| Moldova | 58 | 58 | 57 | 56 | 55 | 55 | 54 | 53 | 51 | 51 | 50 | 49 | 47 | 45 | 45 | 46 | 45 | 45 |
| Poland | 53 | 52 | 51 | 50 | 50 | 50 | 50 | 50 | 48 | 46 | 45 | 43 | 43 | 43 | 44 | 45 | 47 | 48 |
| Romania | 56 | 58 | 60 | 59 | 61 | 60 | 60 | 59 | 59 | 58 | 58 | 52 | 52 | 50 | 49 | 50 | 48 | 48 |
| Russian Federation | 57 | 60 | 59 | 57 | 55 | 54 | 52 | 51 | 51 | 53 | 54 | 55 | 55 | 55 | 56 | 56 | 57 | 57 |
| Serbia and Montenegro | | | | | | | | | | | | | | | | | 42 | 44 |
| Slovak Republic | 55 | 54 | 53 | 51 | 51 | 52 | 51 | 51 | 49 | 48 | 48 | 48 | 49 | 48 | 49 | 50 | 52 | 53 |
| Slovenia | 55 | 51 | 47 | 52 | 53 | 53 | 53 | 54 | 53 | 53 | 53 | 53 | 51 | 54 | 54 | 55 | 54 | 54 |
| Tajikistan | 54 | 52 | 50 | 47 | 45 | 43 | 43 | 44 | 44 | 45 | 47 | 48 | 49 | 50 | 51 | 51 | 54 | 55 |
| Turkmenistan | 56 | 56 | 56 | 56 | 56 | 56 | 56 | 58 | 59 | 59 | 59 | 59 | 59 | 59 | 58 | 58 | 58 | 58 |
| Ukraine | 57 | 56 | 57 | 57 | 57 | 57 | 57 | 56 | 49 | 49 | 50 | 51 | 51 | 51 | 53 | 53 | 53 | 54 |
| Uzbekistan | 54 | 53 | 52 | 52 | 52 | 52 | 53 | 54 | 54 | 54 | 55 | 55 | 55 | 56 | 56 | 56 | 57 | 58 |

*Source*: World Bank, online database

in the advanced CEECs (51.5 per cent). Such a dynamic is an indicator of the path of transformation among transition economies as regards the labour market. In the CIS, economic restructuring was less marked and employment levels stayed at higher levels. In the CEECs, economic restructuring caused more intense job destruction. However, while the most advanced CEECs were able to initiate a stronger process of job construction, the less advanced CEECs still lagged behind in this process and are in a worse position in comparison to all transition economies. The figure below illustrates this dynamic.

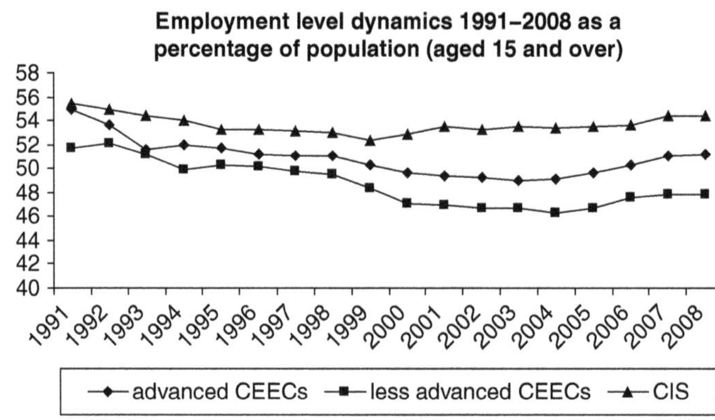


*Figure 2.5* Employment levels
*Source*: World Bank, online database

There are various reasons for such low employment rates besides the collapse in output and the difficulties of recovery. First of all, there is the huge informal sector which hides the real consistency of employment. Secondly, there is the process of job creation and job destruction which has not really brought about satisfactory results so far. Also, there is still an significant rate of employment in agriculture which is not visible in the official statistics. Such employment concerns people who are living in the countryside and growing foodstuffs. However, they are neither officially looking for a job nor employed as proper farmers, and therefore cannot be considered unemployed or employees. This phenomenon is a strong legacy from the past when people, not having access to collectivised agricultural foods and affected by shortages, were growing their own food. Interesting research about these people can be found in the recent work by Richard Rose (2009). He claims that most households who grew food in FCEs were not farmers. In Russia, the proportion growing food who were not employed in agriculture was of five (people growing food) to one (the farmer) (Rose, 2009: 56), in Czechoslovakia four to one and in Bulgaria three to one.

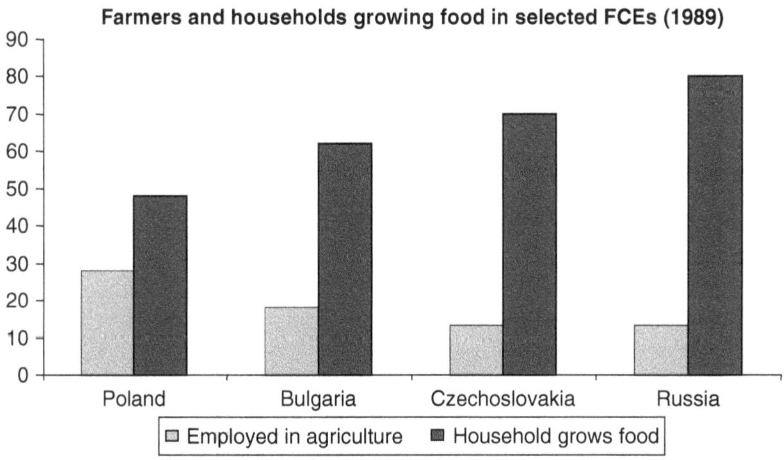


*Figure 2.6* Households growing food in FCEs
*Source*: Rose, 2009

During transition, the situation did not improve much, in particular in FSRs, as the figure below shows (Gerry and Li, 2010; Marelli and Signorelli, 2010).[5] Employment in the agricultural sector is still very important at around 36 per cent in 2008, having increased as a proportion of the employment sectors from 33 per cent in 1989.

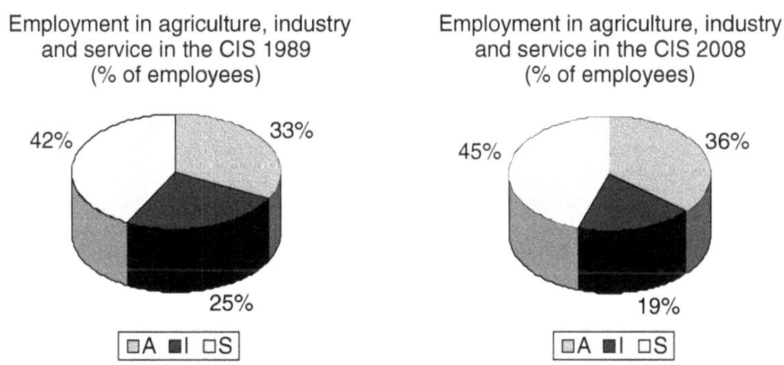


*Figure 2.7* Structural employment in FCEs 1989–2008
*Source*: World Bank, online database

The situation only looks a bit better in the CEECs, where the levels of employment in the agricultural sector are today around 14 per cent, which is less than in 1989, when they were around 22 per cent (see the appendix to this chapter for a detailed table with data on employment structure by country).

Today, the unemployment rate in transition economies, on average, is around 11 per cent, with some peaks for Bosnia and Herzegovina, Montenegro and Serbia equal to 42 per cent, 35 per cent and 31 per cent, respectively. Obviously, the reasons for these rates are attributed to the past conflict in the former Yugoslavia. However, when these three special cases are excluded, the unemployment rate remains high at around an average of 8 per cent. The figure below shows data for all transition economies. The current crisis will likely have more dramatic effects on unemployment in 2011.

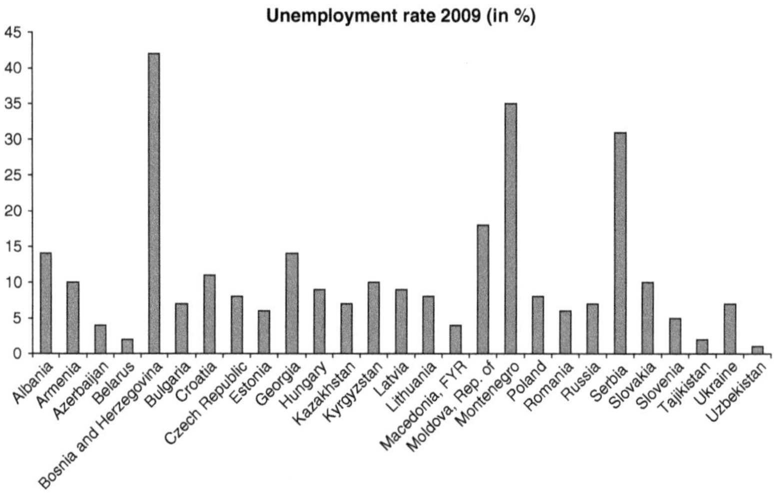


*Figure 2.8* Unemployment rates in 2009 among transition economies
*Note*: Turkmenistan unemployment rate not available for the last few years
*Source*: EBRD, 2009

## 2.4 The impact of EU enlargement on the transition of the CEECs

In this section I will focus more on the CEECs, since the transition there was to some extent special because it benefited from the promise of EU membership, which then became a reality for all candidates from

Central and Eastern Europe. Croatia and Macedonia are candidate countries. Croatia, which is in a more advanced phase of development, started negotiations with the EU in 2006, while accession negotiations with Macedonia have not yet started. EU membership for the other former Yugoslavian republics (Montenegro, Serbia, Bosnia and Herzegovina and Kosovo) and Albania remains difficult and will remain uncertain for the time being, although all of them are officially classified as potential candidates. FSRs are not involved in the EU enlargement process, apart perhaps from Ukraine, whose candidacy is strongly supported by Poland and to some extent Georgia and Armenia, whose future relations with the EU largely depend on the future accession of Turkey (another EU candidate country), which however is not considered in this analysis.

The enlargement process of the EU to include ten former communist countries, i.e., Poland, the Czech Republic, Slovenia, Estonia, Hungary, Lithuania, Latvia, Slovakia (which joined the EU in May 2004), Bulgaria and Romania (which joined the EU in January 2007), represented a very important condition during transition and a goal which all of them aimed to reach as soon as possible. The negotiation process and the adoption of the *acquis commaunitaire* played an important role in the transformation of institutions and rules in the CEECs and was one of the main conditionalities during transition. In fact, many scholars saw transition towards a market economy and integration into the EU as two sides of the same coin (Prausello, 2003; Carlucci and Cavone, 2004). In fact, one of the most important steps in the process was the European Council of Copenhage,n which established three crtieria for the FCEs of Central and Eastern Europe to become part of the EU, which were a political criterion, an economic criterion and an institutional criterion:

1. The presence of stable political institutions to guarantee democracy, the primacy of the rule of law, human rights and minority protection.
2. The existence of a vital market economy able to cope with competition pressure and market forces within the EU.
3. The institutional capability for the new Member States to respect communitarian obligations and to adopt European law, i.e., the so-called *acquis communautaire*.

These three criteria were a strong conditionality during transition for the CEECs. It would be reasonable to argue that, to some extent, most of the CEECs performed better during transition because of the EU conditionality. At the same time, however, it could be argued that most of the CEECs had better initial conditions than the FSRs and fewer corruption and institutional problems. This allowed them to attract FDI and therefore to grow faster.

In the remaining part of this section, I will focus mostly on three countries, i.e., the Czech Republic, Poland and Hungary. Several reasons justify this choice. First of all, it is because of their representation of the region: they are the biggest economies among the CEECs. Secondly, they had the best economic performance and, to some extent, they adopted different strategies. Thirdly, they were the first countries to reach their 1989 levels of GDP and attracted most of the FDI in the region. They are three out of the five best-performing transition economies mentioned earlier (along with the two small economies of Estonia and Slovenia).

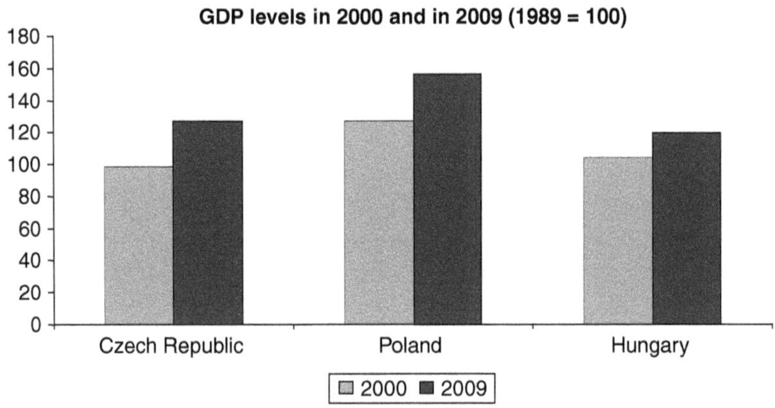


*Figure 2.9* GDP levels in the Czech Republic, Poland and Hungary
*Source*: Transition Reports, 2001 and 2010

The Czech Republic, Poland and Hungary represent 63 per cent of the entire GDP of the ten new EU Member States. They are among the most advanced transition economies in terms of reforms and progress towards a market economy (Transition Report, 2001), and are therefore among the most attractive countries for foreign investors. Finally, Hungary and Poland were the first, in 1991, to sign an Association Agreement with the EU, which is the first step towards membership. The Czech Republic signed the Agreement in 1993.

Economic growth was positive first in Poland, in 1992, after three years of recession, in the Czech Republic in 1993 and then in Hungary in 1994.

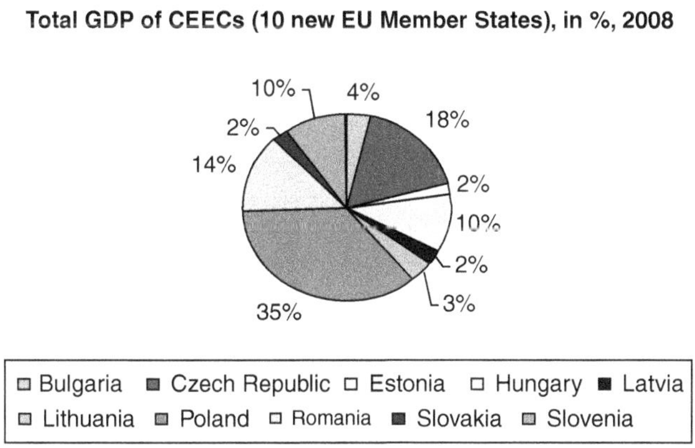


*Figure 2.10* The biggest countries (in terms of GDP share) among the CEECs
*Source*: Transition Report, 2009

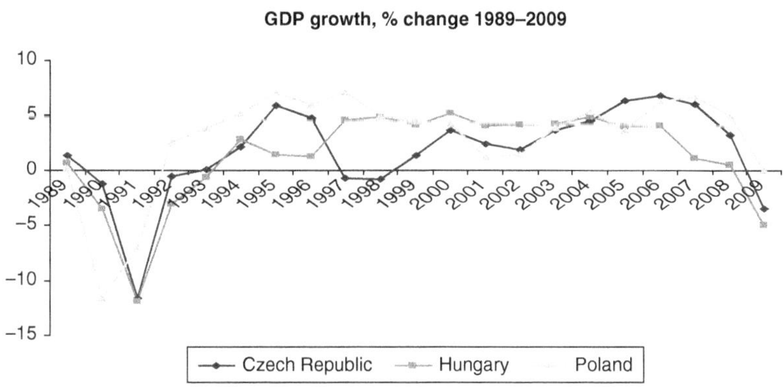


*Figure 2.11* GDP growth in the Czech Republic, Hungary and Poland
*Source*: Transition Reports, 2001 and 2010

The EU enlargement in Eastern Europe has some immediate consequences for the EU and for CEECs, as the table below shows. For the EU, first of all, the population (and the size of markets) has increased; secondly, per capita GDP, which on average changed consistently, has decreased; then, most importantly, there has been a change in the distribution of structural funds, with a shift from the poor regions of old European Member States towards the poor regions of new Member States (basically all the new members).

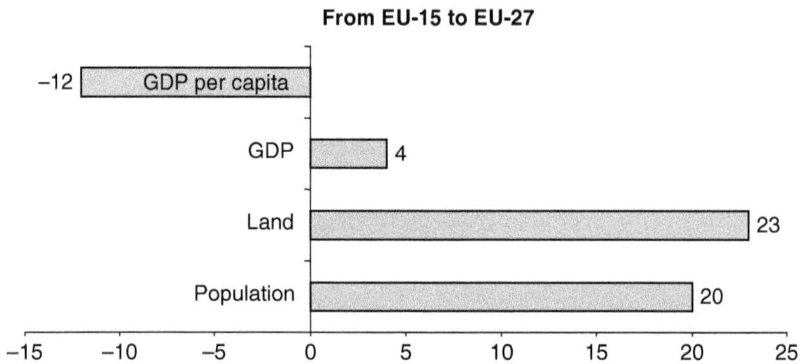


*Figure 2.12* Most evident implications of EU enlargement to incorporate CEECs 2004–7 (values in %)
*Source*: EU Commission

A very sensitive issue for the relation between new and old EU Member States is the Common Agricultural Policy (CAP). The agricultural sector is very important for all CEECs, because it still plays an important role in terms of employment and GDP contribution. Therefore, the CAP subsidies are very consistent for new Member States. The MacSharry reforms in 1992 were further modified in June 2003 in order to reduce the agricultural budget and to no longer link subsidies to production levels but to land dimensions in the form of unique direct payments to agricultural firms which respected certain criteria, such as cross-compliance (i.e., sustainable environment conditionality), productivity improvements and green innovation (De Filippis, 2002).

As regards cohesion policies, the old objective 1) of the EU Cohesion Policy Programme states that regions having an average GDP per capita of below 75 per cent of the EU income would be entitled to EU structural funds. Therefore, these funds are now mainly dedicated, for the 2007–13 EU Programme, to new Member States. Until 2004 (and 2007 for Bulgaria and Romania) new Member States received pre-accession funds (see the table below). This was not a 'Marshall Plan', as many politicians claimed. It was an important funding plan which helped new Member States regarding EU conditionality in several sectors, such as transport, agriculture, technology and the environment (Mayhew, 1998). On the other hand, the EU, and in particular EU firms, enjoyed significant advantages in terms of delocalisation of production towards the CEECs, new investments with high profits, lower labour costs and economies of scale towards new markets and consumers, along with an increase of exports.

*Table 2.4* Pre-accession EU funds to CEECs (millions of euros)

| CEEC | PHARE | SAPARD | IPSA | Total |
|---|---|---|---|---|
| Bulgaria | 100 | 52.1 | 105.8 | 257.9 |
| Czech Republic | 79 | 22 | 71 | 172 |
| Estonia | 26 | 12 | 29 | 67 |
| Hungary | 97 | 38.2 | 90 | 225.2 |
| Latvia | 30 | 21.8 | 47.6 | 99.4 |
| Lithuania | 44 | 29.8 | 53 | 126.8 |
| Poland | 398 | 168.7 | 354 | 920.7 |
| Romania | 242 | 150.6 | 243.3 | 635.9 |
| Slovakia | 49 | 18.3 | 47.6 | 114.9 |
| Slovenia | 25 | 6.3 | 15.8 | 47.1 |
| Total | 1,090 | 519.8 | 1,057.1 | 26,669.9 |

*Notes*:
**PHARE**: Poland and Hungary: Assistance for Restructuring their Economics
**SAPARD**: Special Accession Programme for Agriculture and Rural Development
**IPSA**: Instrument for Structural Policies for Pre-Accession
*Source*: EU Commission

However, all this was no longer sufficient *per se* to boost economic development. Empirical evidence among new Member States is controversial and there is no clear relationship between membership to the EU and growth. Bulgaria and Romania are typical examples of countries showing a lack of this relationship, as are Slovakia, Lithuania and Latvia, which shows that the relationship between EU Association Agreements and economic development is not consistent. Still, the average GDP per capita among the CEECs is a fraction of EU-15 income, and EU conditionality needs to be accompanied by a process of development and of institutional change in order to enable informal rules, which may otherwise inhibit economic development, to change.

Transition is a complex and gradual process which includes the creation of institutions, the allocation of property rights, the certainty of economic relations and the interaction of these factors with many other social, economic and political variables such as education, health, improvements in technology, political rights and participation, capability and social opportunities. Moreover, during transition, the evolution

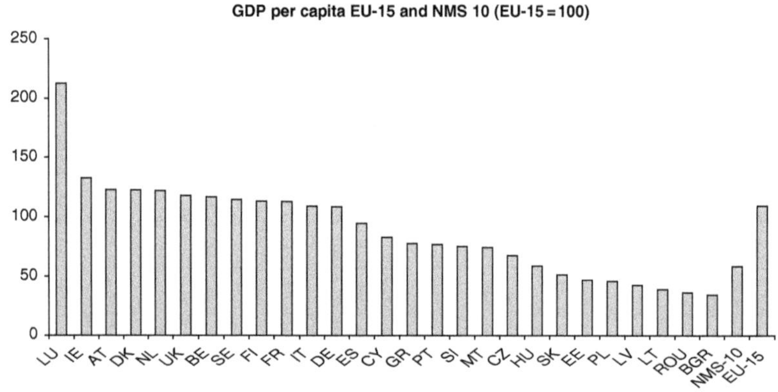


*Figure 2.13* Levels of GDP per capita in the new EU (2007)
*Note*: NMS: new Member States
*Source*: Eurostat

of these institutions must be coherent and the economy must be organised and governed with an appropriate governance, without an ideological approach and with proper political decisions and collective actions which would benefit the people and their needs, because in the end, the satisfaction of needs means development. All these factors, and in particular an institutional dimension, will be explored in a critical and positive way in Part II.

As regards differences in terms of GDP between new and old Member States, one can say that they are still very large, and a catching up within the enlarged EU-27, six years after the first important eastern enlargement of the EU, is very difficult to imagine, at least for the majority of the new Member States.

Apart from the case of Luxembourg's GDP per capita of 75,800 euros at 2009 prices, which has remained steadily very high in Europe, the tendency is to find high variability in GDP figures across Europe. For example, Bulgaria, the poorest of the 27 EU countries, has a GDP per capita hovering around 4,400 euros (US$6,600) and Romania is not too far ahead with 5,500 euros at 2009 prices. Macedonia, an EU candidate, could potentially be the poorest member nation with an income of 3,100 euros at 2009 prices (Eurostat, 2009). This contrasts with the current average income per capita in the EU-27, which is 24,300 euros, with that of the EU-15 averaging 28,200 euros at 2009 prices. The new 10 Member States from Central and Eastern Europe which joined the EU between 2004 and 2007 plus Croatia, Macedonia and Turkey, the last three EU candidate countries, have an average GDP per capita equal to 9,125 euros (2009 prices). And yet there are substantial differences across the board. For instance, if one were to compare Slovenia, the richest among the new Member States, to Portugal, the poorest country of the EU-15, Slovenia ranks higher in terms of GDP per capita. In fact, it is almost as rich as Greece, the second-poorest country of the EU-15.

The figure below tries to express these differences in a more accurate way, using US$ in Purchasing Power Parity (PPP). In this way, income in new Member States is actually higher than at current prices, since the purchasing power of those countries is higher, given the lower national price levels.

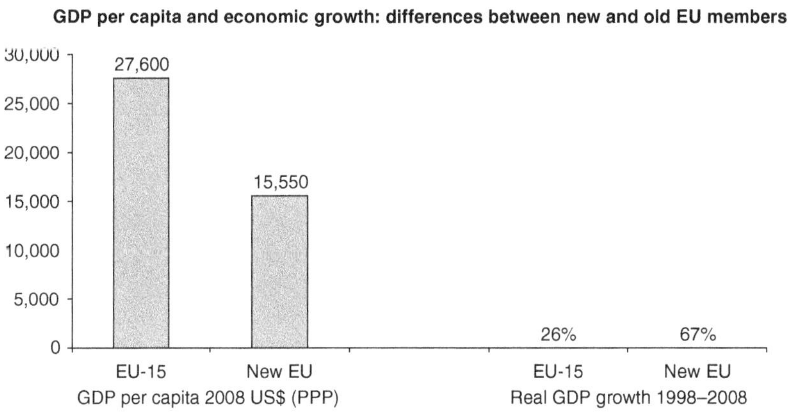


*Figure 2.14* A comparison between the old and new Member States of the EU
*Source*: Eurostat, 2009

Obviously, cumulative economic growth in the last ten years among new Member States was higher than among old Member States. However, this is no longer sufficient to reduce the disparities between them (in the appendix to this chapter, a more detailed empirical analysis of income differentials and reduction in the disparities among the EU-27 is presented).

## 2.5 FDI and international organisation constraints

The promise of membership to the EU acted as a guarantee for foreign entrepreneurs wishing to move their capital and to set up their business in candidate countries, first in the Czech Republic, Hungary and Poland,

and later in all of the CEECs. Hungary, which was initially considered a safer country, was the first to start attracting FDI. However, in the second half of the 1990s, when Poland also became a more stable country, it, together with the Czech Republic, attracted the biggest share of FDI. The graph below describes the evolution of FDI in the three countries which attracted the most FDI.

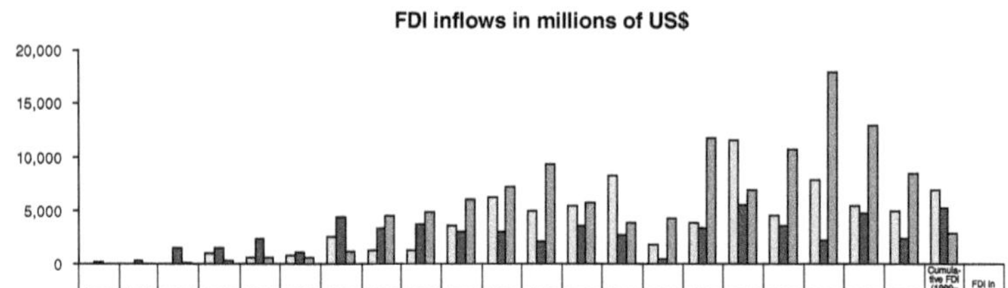


| | 1989 | 1990 | 1991 | 1992 | 1993 | 1994 | 1995 | 1996 | 1997 | 1998 | 1999 | 2000 | 2001 | 2002 | 2003 | 2004 | 2005 | 2006 | 2007 | 2008 | 2009 | Cumulative FDI (1989–2009) per capita in US$ | FDI in 2009 (in % of GDP) |
|---|---|---|---|---|---|---|---|---|---|---|---|---|---|---|---|---|---|---|---|---|---|---|---|
| Czech Republic | | | | 983 | 563 | 749 | 2,526 | 1,280 | 1,259 | 3,575 | 6,220 | 4,942 | 5,474 | 8,282 | 1,814 | 3,941 | 1,163 | 4,598 | 7,930 | 5,500 | 5,000 | 6,954 | 4.6 |
| Hungary | 187 | 311 | 1,459 | 1,471 | 2,328 | 1,097 | 4,410 | 3,335 | 3,715 | 3,070 | 3,060 | 2,151 | 3,573 | 2,722 | 479 | 3,405 | 5,586 | 3,640 | 2,197 | 4,763 | 2,400 | 5,314 | 3.1 |
| Poland | | | 117 | 284 | 580 | 542 | 1,134 | 4,445 | 4,863 | 6,049 | 7,239 | 9,327 | 5,804 | 3,901 | 4,284 | 1,176 | 6,951 | 10,720 | 17,970 | 12,950 | 8,500 | 2,967 | 2.5 |

Czech Republic ■ Hungary ■ Poland

*Figure 2.15* FDI in the Czech Republic, Hungary and Poland during the 1990s and 2000s
*Source*: Transition Report, 2001

Poland is first in terms of cumulative FDI, while the Czech Republic has the supremacy in terms of FDI per capita, followed by Hungary. The same can be said with respect to FDI as a percentage of GDP. With regard to the origins of FDI, 39 per cent of cumulative EU capital flows come from Germany, which was a strong supporter of the eastern enlargement of the EU, 15 per cent from the Netherlands and 12 per cent from France. The Italian share was 4 per cent. In terms of the number of investment projects, Italy is in second place, with 19 per cent of the total share, while Germany remains in first place with 27 per cent of projects.[6] The French capital flows are mostly concentrated in Poland and Romania, while German and Dutch FDI go mainly to the Czech Repubic, Hungary and Poland. Scandinavian FDI is mainly concentrated in the three Baltic countries, while the Italian capital flows are concentrated in the Balkans and Romania. Table A4 in the final appendix at the end of this book illustrates in great detail the FDI in all transition economies during the 1990s and 2000s.

FDI has two objectives: 1) to conquer new markets; and 2) to use them as productive bases for further exports. In fact, many multinationals invested heavily in the CEECs during the 1990s in order to create a competitive advantage based on lower labour costs, a skilled labour force and marketing positioning. In less than 10 years, the CEECs became a place for old EU firms to delocalise and internalise production (Manzocchi and Beatrice, 2001a; Montalbano, 2002).

International specialisation changed consistently thanks to these new flows of FDI in former communist countries. An interaction between job destruction and job creation in the EU and in the CEECs took place, and its effects are still taking place. The CEECs are countries very close to the core of the old Europe, with a skilled labour force and a mature industrial structure, although this was obsolete at the beginning of the 1990s. A relatively lower country risk and EU membership made these countries very attractive for European investors, who enjoy labour costs there equal to half or one-third of the EU-15 average (Markowski and Jackson, 1993). Multinational firms in the CEECs are interested in exploiting profits coming from different sources, such as market size, cheap labour and natural resources. In the first case, the objective is to conquer new domestic and profitable markets. In the second case, FDI is mostly concentrated in the industrial sector, exploiting lower skilled labour costs. In the third case, the advantages come from investing in heavy industry that can exploit natural resources and raw materials. In all three cases, the production is often turned towards the exporting sector.

Moreover, the policies of CEECs to attract FDI were very incisive since they were able to strategically create special zones where FDI could enjoy advantageous fiscal tax conditions (PAIZ, 2001).[7] However, despite these special zones, much FDI goes to central zones and capital cities/areas, where it can also benefit from better infrastructure and higher human capital levels (Litwack and Qian, 1998).

FDI contributes to institutional and structural change. New FDI brings about new forms of management, knowledge, organisation, strategies and marketing, know-how and agencies.[8] It also brings new rules to business and has a huge impact on economic organisation in general. On the basis of the huge literature on the subject (Dunning, 1977; Ohlin *et al.*, 1977; Krugman, 1998; Rodrik, 1995; Irvin and Kroszner, 1999; Bevan and Estrin, 2000; De Santis and Vicarelli, 2001; Iapadre, 2001; Manzocchi and Beatrice, 2001b; Lissowska, 2001; Montalbano, 2002; Helpman, 2006), we can summarise the impact of FDI in the following ways:

1. It contributes to the surplus in the balance of payments.
2. It increases exports, because usually FDI is more competitive for produce in the exporting sector.
3. It increases productivity and competitiveness.

4. It may have spill-over effects and can influence the starting up of new domestic investments and market segments.
5. It affects new human capital formation.
6. It contributes to change the balance of power and the system of lobbying business club organisation.
7. It contributes towards changing the behaviour of agents, economic rules and institutions.

Together with the attraction of FDI in CEECs, the Czech Republic, Hungary and Poland in particular increased their trade flows with the EU. These two factors, FDI and trade, are reported as key factors in the further development of these three countries in some articles (Manzocchi and Beatrice, 2001a). Clearly, evidence is controversial on this topic and there are economists who argue that FDI contributed to an increase in the commercial deficit in some transition economies because foreign investors imported capital goods, technology and other services from their own country in massive amounts (Weresa, 1999). However, FDI definitely contributed to the integration of the new EU Member States into the world economy, and these countries were also affected by other international organisations and international conditionalities

*Table 2.5* International agreements of the CEECs during the 1990s

| | GATT/WTO | IMF (Art. VIII) | European Association | EU full membership |
|---|---|---|---|---|
| Bulgaria | Dec. 96 | Sept. 98 | Mar. 93 | Jan. 2007 |
| Czech Rep. | Jan. 95 | Oct. 95 | Oct. 93 | May 2004 |
| Hungary | Jan. 95 | Jan. 96 | Dec. 91 | May 2004 |
| Poland | Jul. 95 | Jun. 95 | Dec. 91 | May 2004 |
| Romania | Jan. 95 | Mar. 98 | Feb. 93 | Jan. 2007 |
| Slovakia | Jan. 95 | Oct. 95 | Oct. 93 | May 2004 |
| Slovenia | Jul. 95 | Sept. 95 | Jun. 96 | May 2004 |
| Estonia | Nov. 99 | Aug. 94 | Jun. 95 | May 2004 |
| Latvia | Feb. 99 | Jun. 94 | Jun. 95 | May 2004 |
| Lithuania | May 01 | May 94 | Jun. 95 | May 2004 |

*Source*: Transition Report (2001) and European Commission

such as the WTO and the IMF. In fact, during the 1990s, the new EU Member States also experienced a transition towards membership of those organisations, as Table 2.5 shows. Moreover, during the 2000s, the new EU Member States also became members of NATO.

The European enlargement, according to the Regular Report on Enlargement of 2002, should have initially followed the differentiation between CEEC-Helsinki and CEEC-Luxembourg. According to this differentiation, enlargement of the EU to incorporate certain CEECs should be accomplished in two phases. The first phase should include five countries, as established by the European Council in Luxembourg in 1997.[9] The second phase should include the remaining five countries, which were less advanced in terms of the reform process, as decided by the European Council in Helsinki in 1999[10] (European Commission, Regular Report on Enlargement 2002). However, in the end, the Copenhagen Council in December 2002 decided to extend the first wave of enlargement to CEEC-Luxembourg plus Slovakia, Latvia and Lithuania in 2004 and to postpone the accession of Romania and Bulgaria until 2007.

## 2.6 The transformation of the trade pattern

The transition of the FCEs is sometimes erroneously perceived as a transformation towards the 'standards' of the EU, meaning by this not only the reduction of the gap in GDP per capita but also convergence in the institutional and social dimensions. On the contrary, in my view, each country has its own path of development which includes the transformation and acquisition of institutions and social standards that are different in each context. It also includes a process of institutional change which in turn contains several features, such as the change in economic agents' behaviour and the understanding of particular policies, and the radical changes in the productive structure, the rules of production, the partner trades in the international economy, the form of competition, the wage nexus and the form of money constraints. None of this is achieved in a short space of time, nor can it be observed through the growth of GDP.[11] The reduction of differences in income, although an important issue, seems too reductive with respect to the most general and complex problem of economic development in FCEs.

The surface level of economic development is represented by GDP growth. The analysis of economic development means the explanation of rules, policies and variables which allow for a change in the productive structure of the country, the improvement of living conditions of people and the increase in all forms of capital (human, social and physical). These changes would have to be accompanied by a coherent institutional change that is able to manage the social conflicts and to attenuate the external and international shocks (Rodrik, 1999). The institutional dimension should create the appropriate economic environment to allow individuals to accumulate skills and firms to accumulate capital in order to increase output (Jones and Hall, 1998), so that adverse selection and bad incentives (corruption, crime, free-riding, rent-seeking, etc.) are avoided, transaction costs and opportunism are reduced and greater advantages are created for all.

In the CEECs, transition also means the transformation of trade patterns, which changed radically in the past 20 years. These patterns used to be oriented towards FCEs only, while now they are very much integrated into the EU. In fact, in the place of the former Soviet Union and Comecon, one can find today, in the import-export figures, the EU. The best example of this change is Poland, which is the biggest of the Central and Eastern European economies. In 1989, the FSRs accounted for 33 per cent of Polish imports and for 28 per cent of its exports, while ten years later, in 1999, this role was taken over by Germany, which counted for 38 per cent of Polish exports and for 27 per cent of its imports.[12] In 1999, only 5 per cent of Polish imports came from Russia and only 2.6 per cent of Polish exports were directed towards it (Economist Intelligent Unit, 2000). Such a pattern, as illustrated below, is very similar to that in other CEECs. In a way, the relationship between Germany, Poland and Russia is a paradigmatic example of the European context with respect to the current European political situation and economic influence. For years, Poland was alternatively under the domain or the influence of Germany and Russia (Davies, 2001). Nowadays it is 'the turn' of Germany, which is the biggest and most important EU economy.

*Table 2.6* Main trading partners of the CEECs (percentage of total) in 2005

| **Exports to** | | **Imports from** | |
|---|---|---|---|
| GERMANY | 36.1% | GERMANY | 25.2% |
| ITALY | 6.5% | ITALY | 9.4% |
| NETHERLANDS | 5.3% | FRANCE | 6.8% |
| FRANCE | 4.8% | RUSSIA | 5.9% |
| UK | 4% | UK | 4.6% |

*Source*: Economist Intelligence Unit, 2005

Until 1989 it was 'the turn' of Russia, and usually in Europe, the country which controls Poland has the greatest influence in Central and Eastern Europe (Davies, 2001).

The structural change that occurred in the economy of the CEECs enabled the changes in the trade patterns, and today these economies are fully part of the EU single market. However, they had to change production, restructure their economies and transform their productive infrastructure. During the 1990s, they were subject to high social costs in term of unemployment. Most CEECs had an international specialisation that was functional to Comecon needs and to FSR requirements. Heavy industry was the most important industry in most CEECs. Therefore, the change towards the more diversified EU pattern was very costly, because it had to adjust to EU demands and technical norms.

The new model encompasses the possibility of exporting high technology products and services with higher added value. Moreover, EU membership requires continuous investments in innovation and organisation in order to maintain a highly competitive position that is able to compete with old EU firms. For some countries such as Poland and Romania, this also means the restructuring of the agricultural sector characterised by high levels of employment (around 25–30 per cent) and by lower levels of productivity. In Poland and Romania the percentage of GDP contributed by the agricultural sector is equal to 5 per cent, which is similar to the figures of Hungary and the Czech Republic, where however the percentage of people employed in the agricultural sector is much smaller (around 6 per cent). For all new Member States it meant restructuring big former SOEs and attracting foreign capital that could foster innovate and productivity.

Today the EU plays the main role in the import-export flow of the CEECs (see Figure 2.16). The flow of trade between the EU and the CEECs has increased enormously. By the end of the 1990s, it already represented 70 per cent of CEEC capital flows. The balance is slightly in favour of the EU. All the CEECs have been opened to international trade and have converged towards EU average tariff levels. Small countries like the Czech Republic, Slovakia and Estonia are very open economics, with models that are more and more oriented towards a export-led model, while Poland, Romania and Bulgaria remain rather more closed. However, all of them abolished all the restrictions between them and the EU on 1 January 2003 and have adopted a Common Foreign Tariff (CFT) towards third countries at 3 per cent.

The change in the model of trade is fundamental because it also involves norms and the behaviour of agents who were not familiar

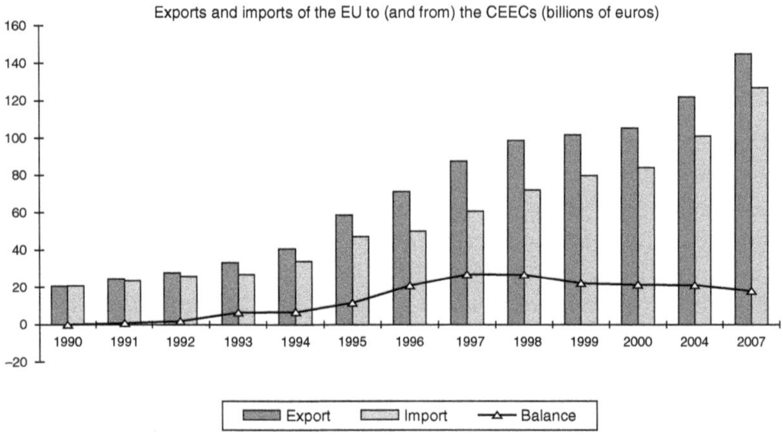


*Figure 2.16* EU-CEEC trade 1990–2007
*Source*: Eurostat

with new import-export rules, international demand, technical requirements, marketing, strategies of sale, etc (MacBean, 2000). The impact of the integration into the EU and the world economy is therefore huge from both an economic and an institutional point of view. The balance of trade, as the figure above shows, is in favour of the old EU-15, which exports more to the CEECs than it imports from them. This is to underline the better competitiveness of the old EU Member States compared to the CEECs. The opening up of trade brings with it pressure and worldwide competition, which modify domestic issues and power relations within national economic powers and policy preferences, putting social cohesion at greater risk. Therefore, social institutions which would be able to attenuate social conflicts and to manage new power forces are necessary in order to keep social peace and to lower social costs (Rodrik, 1999).

## 2.7 Final comments

The transformation of transition economies has been profound and recession has been severe, both in the CEECs and in the FSRs. However, most CEECs began to undergo a more consistent process of economic development that did not happen in most FSRs. The reasons for this are several. One of them, which was analysed in this chapter, is EU conditionality and membership, which had a positive effect on most CEECs.

In fact, the impact of the EU on the CEECs has been very important during transition, in particular in terms of FDI and trade, which were promoted by the prospect of EU membership. It is likely that more FDI and trade with the EU-15, along with EU aid, contributed to a faster GDP recovery in the CEECs than in the FSRs, which were not affected by EU membership. In terms of foreign relations, the eastern enlargement modified the EU's approach towards the FSRs too. In particular, thanks to the lobbying of some countries like Poland, the EU is increasingly interested in what happens in Ukraine, Belarus and the Caucasus republics, which were always considered not to be a part of European affairs. On the contrary, today the prospect for these countries, in particular for Ukraine and Belarus, of being part of the EU in the future is no longer unthinkable.

However, EU membership was not the crucial factor in creating better development in the CEECs. Several cases of bad performance still remain among CEECs such as Romania, Bulgaria and to some extent Lithuania and Latvia. As such, other factors seem crucial for development, as I will show in Part III. These factors have to be found in the emergence of social capital and in the institutional framework of the society which shapes political institutions and further development.

# Appendix A2

*Table A2.1* Employment levels by sector in percentages, 1989–2008

| Sector | Countries | First year data available in parenthesis if not 1989 | Last year data available in parenthesis if not 2008 | Countries | First year data available in parenthesis if not 1989 | Last year data available in parenthesis if not 2008 |
|---|---|---|---|---|---|---|
| A | Albania | (1994) 67 | (2006) 58 | Armenia | (2001) 5 | (2006) 46 |
| I | Albania | 11 | 14 | Armenia | 23 | 16 |
| S | Albania | 22 | 28 | Armenia | 68 | 38 |
| A | Bulgaria | 19 | 8 | Azerbaijan | 32 | 39 |
| I | Bulgaria | 42 | 36 | Azerbaijan | 29 | 13 |
| S | Bulgaria | 36 | 57 | Azerbaijan | 35 | 48 |
| A | Croatia | (1996) 20 | 13 | Georgia | (1998) 49 | 53 |
| I | Croatia | 29 | 31 | Georgia | 10 | 10 |
| S | Croatia | 51 | 56 | Georgia | 41 | 36 |
| A | Czech Rep. | (1993) 8 | 3 | Kazakhstan | (2000) 27 | (2004) 34 |
| I | Czech Rep. | 43 | 41 | Kazakhstan | 20 | 17 |
| S | Czech Rep. | 49 | 56 | Kazakhstan | 53 | 49 |
| A | Estonia | 21 | 4 | Kyrgyz Rep. | 33 | (2006) 36 |
| I | Estonia | 37 | 36 | Kyrgyz Rep. | 25 | 19 |
| S | Estonia | 42 | 60 | Kyrgyz Rep. | 35 | 44 |

| | | | | | | |
|---|---|---|---|---|---|---|
| A | Hungary | 19 | 5 | Moldova | 35 | 33 |
| I | Hungary | 35 | 32 | Moldova | 29 | 19 |
| S | Hungary | 41 | 63 | Moldova | 33 | 48 |
| A | Latvia | (1996) 17 | 8 | Russia | (1990) 14 | 9 |
| I | Latvia | 27 | 29 | Russia | 40 | 29 |
| S | Latvia | 55 | 64 | Russia | 46 | 62 |
| A | Lithuania | (1995) 21 | 8 | Tajikistan | (1991) 45 | (2004) 56 |
| I | Lithuania | 29 | 30 | Tajikistan | 23 | 18 |
| S | Lithuania | 51 | 61 | Tajikistan | 26 | 26 |
| A | Macedonia | (2001) 24 | 18 | Ukraine | 19 | 17 |
| I | Macedonia | 33 | 31 | Ukraine | 9 | 24 |
| S | Macedonia | 43 | 50 | Ukraine | 15 | 59 |
| A | Poland | 25 | 15 | Uzbekistan | (1995) 41 | (1999) 39 |
| I | Poland | 38 | 31 | Uzbekistan | 19 | 19 |
| S | Poland | 36 | 55 | Uzbekistan | 35 | 35 |
| A | Romania | 28 | 29 | Avg. CIS | 33 | 36 |
| I | Romania | 45 | 31 | Avg. CIS | 25 | 19 |
| S | Romania | 27 | 40 | Avg. CIS | 42 | 45 |
| A | Serbia & Mont. | (2005) 24 | 25 | Avg. CEEC | 22 | 14 |
| I | Serbia & Mont. | 27 | 26 | Avg. CEEC | 34 | 31 |
| S | Serbia & Mont. | 49 | 49 | Avg. CEEC | 44 | 55 |
| A | Slovakia | (1994) 10 | 4 | | | |
| I | Slovakia | 40 | 40 | | | |
| S | Slovakia | 50 | 57 | | | |
| A | Slovenia | (1993) 11 | 10 | | | |
| I | Slovenia | 44 | 34 | | | |
| S | Slovenia | 45 | 55 | | | |

*Note*: A: Agriculture, I: Industry, S: Service
*Source*: World Bank, online database

## Convergence and divergence processes among the old and the new EU Member States

After the recession of the early 1990s, the new Member States grew more than the EU-15 over the last 10–11 years. Average growth in the CEECs (the ten new Member States) and in Croatia and Macedonia (new EU candidates) between 1997 and 2008 was around 4.6 per cent annually. This is higher than the average EU-15 growth for the same period, which was below 3 per cent and would be even smaller if one excludes Ireland, which experienced an extraordinary rate of growth in the last two decades. Therefore, on average, GDP per capita in the new Member States increased more than in the EU-15 and it increased from 45.5 per cent in 1997 to almost 61 per cent in 2008, as the table below shows.

*Table A2.2* Average GDP per capita (in PPP) in EU and candidate countries (in %)

| **Group of countries** | **1997** | **2008** |
|---|---|---|
| EU (27 countries) | 100 | 100 |
| EU (15 countries) | 115.5 | 110.8 |
| Standard deviation of income in the EU-27 | 25.5 | 20.9 |
| GDP per capita in the ten new Member States plus Croatia and Macedonia | 45.5 | 60.9 |

*Source*: Eurostat, 2009

The standard deviation of average income declined and to some extent one can notice a so-called sigma convergence (the reduction in income dispersion among countries). The figure below shows data for the ten new Member States and the two former Yugoslav republics that are current EU candidates (Croatia and Macedonia).

However, this does not underline a catching-up process between the old and new EU Member States, for several reasons. One of these is that we are considering the period of fast growth in the CEECs after the second half of the 1990s and we are excluding the recession period at the beginning of the 1990s which was very consistent throughout all transition economies. As the table below shows, paying attention to the fact that in 1989 the geographical shape of several countries was

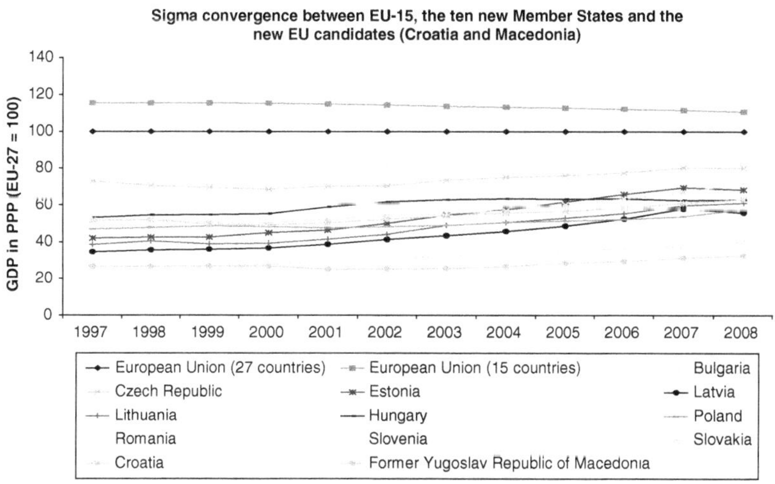


*Figure A2.1* Income differentials within the new EU
*Source*: author's elaboration based on Eurostat, 2009

different, average GDP in 1989 among the CEECs with respect to the EU-15 was higher than it was in 1997 (45.5 per cent). Therefore, the standard deviation, which declined in the last decade, remained at the same level during the previous decade.

*Table A2.3* GDP per capita (PPP) among FCEs in percentages of the EU-15 GDP

| Countries | 1989 |
|---|---|
| Bulgaria | 35 |
| Czechoslovakia | 65 |
| Hungary | 57 |
| Poland | 38 |
| Romania | 39 |
| Yugoslavia | 45 |
| Average (of above) | 47 |
| Soviet Union | 49 |

*Source*: Berend, 2006

Secondly, we are considering a club of countries considered as the most advanced in terms of transition and closer to the EU. In fact, since 2004, most of them have been part of the EU. No sigma convergence is noticeable if we consider all transition economies together (including the FSRs). Finally, one could argue that, apart from the case of some fast-growing countries in the EU-15 (such as Ireland, Spain, Finland and Greece), the old EU Member States experienced a process of slow growth over the past two decades. Hence, the decline in the standard deviation between old and new EU Member States is to be attributed more to EU stagnation than to the new Member States catching up. In fact, the figure below shows more clearly that a process of convergence was not occurring. On average, the CEECs increased their GDP per capita, but income differentials among them remained the same. The standard deviation in 1997 among the CEECs only was around 17.3, while in 2008 it was around 16.5. Countries like the Czech Republic and Slovenia, with better initial conditions in 1989, are still much richer today than other CEECs because they grew consistently over the last two decades. Countries like Romania and Bulgaria, which were much poorer, are still poorer today and did not experience any catching up. Similar stories apply to Macedonia, Latvia and Lithuania. Poorer countries did not grow faster. Any form of correlation between a lower level of GDP and faster growth can be excluded.

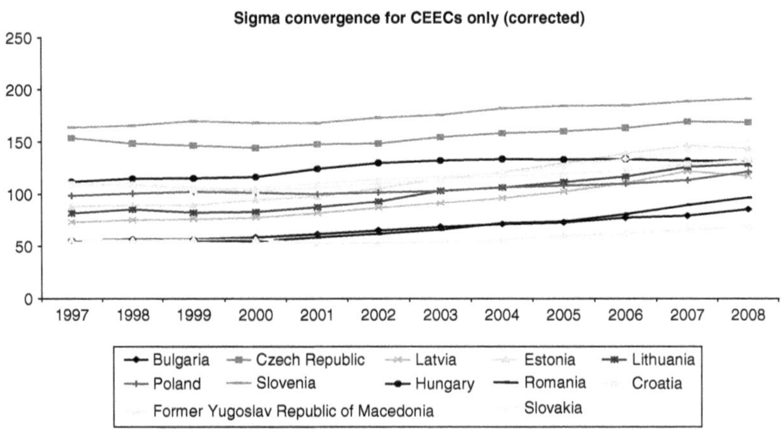


*Figure A2.2* Income differentials within the new Member States and candidates
*Source*: author's elaboration based on Eurostat, 2009

Such a statement, that poor countries did not grow faster, would be confirmed by a simple regression model which considers the initial GDP per capita of countries (*GDP*(1989)) as an independent variable and the rate of growth ($g$) as a dependent variable over the last two decades. A term of error '$\varepsilon$' and a constant '$a$' are considered in the model, as is shown by the equation below:

$$g = a - \beta \cdot GDP(1989) + \varepsilon$$

In general, according to neoclassical models of growth, an absolute 'beta'-convergence (i.e., a convergence in the rate of growth) would occur among countries. Poor countries are supposed to grow faster than richer countries. If the results are statistically significant and the beta coefficient of the model is negative, then an absolute convergence would occur (Sala-i-Martin, 1996): countries which have an initially higher GDP level would grow more slowly than countries with an initially lower level of GDP.

The model above would need to be tested for causality. However, empirical studies across the world and countries on this issue show very controversial findings and unclear results (Pomeranz, 2000; Boggio and Serravalli, 2003), and this also applies when transition economies are included in the analysis (Andreff, 1998; Manzocchi and Beatrice, 2001a; Montalbano, 2002; Sarajevs, 2003; Falcetti *et al.*, 2006). It is not the objective of this book to test for causality or to analyse the convergence in any depth, which was however excluded by many studies. It is sufficient here to state that correlation between var. GDP89 and growth 1989–2009 is very weak.

| | GDP89 | Growth 1989-09 |
|---|---|---|
| GDP89 | 1.0000 | |
| Growth 1989-2009 | -0.0088 | 1.0000 |

The scatter figure below confirms that an inverse decreasing relation cannot be characterised.

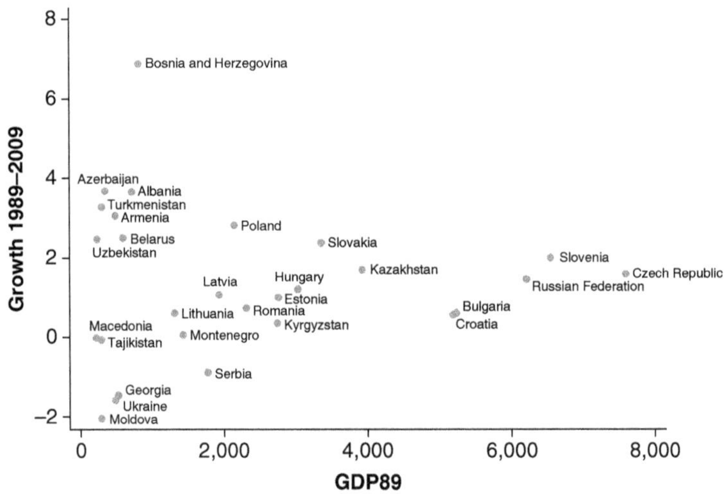


*Figure A2.3* Scatter GDP 1989 and average growth 1989–2009
*Note*: data for Bosnia and Herzegovina refers to 1996–2008
*Source*: author's elaboration based on EBRD data

Besides, if one looks at the average rate of growth in the table below, it would be immediately clear that poorer countries did not grow faster. Indeed, it could be said that this does not generally happen among countries, apart from very few exceptions, being limited to certain periods of time and to a limited number of countries (Boggio and Serravalli, 2003).

*Table A2.4* GDP per capita (in US$) 1989 and 2008

| | GDP per capita in 2008 | GDP growth average 1989–2009 | GDP per capita 1989 (the earliest available year in parenthesis if not 1989) |
|---|---|---|---|
| Albania | 4,066 | 3.65 | 721 |
| Armenia | 3,711 | 3.06 | 488 |
| Azerbaijan | 5,507 | 3.67 | 346 |
| Belarus | 6,286 | 2.50 | 593 |
| Bosnia and Herzegovina | 4,834 | 6.88 (1996–2008) | 818 (1996) |

| | | | |
|---|---|---|---|
| Bulgaria | 6,561 | 0.60 | 5,238 |
| Croatia | 15,552 | 0.55 | 5,193 (1990) |
| Czech Republic | 25,395 | 1.58 | 7,590 |
| Estonia | 16,508 | 1.00 | 2,760 (1992) |
| Georgia | 2,845 | −1.46 | 524 |
| Hungary | 15,326 | 1.19 | 3,027 |
| Kazakhstan | 8,736 | 1.70 | 3,924 |
| Kyrgyzstan | 952 | 0.35 | 2,745 |
| Latvia | 14,909 | 1.06 | 1,930 (1993) |
| Lithuania | 14,018 | 0.59 | 1,310 (1992) |
| Macedonia, FYR | 4,761 | −0.08 | 293 |
| Moldova | 1,766 | −2.05 | 293 |
| Montenegro | 6,509 | 0.05 | 1,431 (2000) |
| Poland | 13,839 | 2.81 | 2,147 |
| Romania | 9,186 | 0.72 | 2,319 |
| Russian Federation | 12,075 | 1.46 | 6,202 |
| Serbia | 6,761 | −0.90 | 1,773 (1996) |
| Slovakia | 18,249 | 2.37 | 3,351 |
| Slovenia | 27,168 | 2.00 | 6,540 |
| Tajikistan | 795 | −0.02 | 216 |
| Turkmenistan | 2,916 | 3.28 | 298 |
| Ukraine | 3,937 | −1.59 | 480 (1992) |
| Uzbekistan | 1,007 | 2.47 | 233 |

*Source*: GDP per capita 2008 and GDP growth are from EBRD (2009). GDP per capita 1989 is from EBRD (2009) and from the World Bank Development Report (1992)

# Part II

# Institutional Change and Varieties of Capitalism in Transition Economies

# 3
# Institutional Change: Old and New Institutionalism

## 3.1 Introduction

This chapter puts forward a brief review of old and new institutionalism. This is functional to the next chapter, where I will use these concepts to build my model of institutional change in transition economies. Moreover, this chapter also analyses the main definitions and classifications of institutions. Broadly speaking, institutions may be defined as a set of rules, social norms and prescribed patterns of correlated behaviour which affect social interaction and therefore structure economic organisation (Foster, 1981; Knight, 1992; Nugent and Lin, 1995; Hodgson, 2006).

## 3.2 Institutions and institutional change

Many economists, aware that institutions, rules and social norms matter, have tried to explain their origins. However, this is a very complex and difficult field that still remains unexplained. Walton Hamilton (1932: 84) stated that '[a]n institution has no origin apart from its development'. In other words, it is difficult or impossible to find the specific origins of an institution. Over the centuries, one can find evidence of institutional origins throughout history. Generic origins can be perceived in the old biblical and pastoral communities as well as in the more consolidated Aztec, Maya and Inca societies. According to Bush (1988), institutions find their own origin within each specific society, following this scheme: *Society → System of Institutions → Institution*. Nevertheless, Malinowsky stated (1960: 117): 'there is no way we could know the historical origin of a society'.

Economies are organised around institutions, and all markets depend and function strictly according to their specific institutions. Figure 3.1

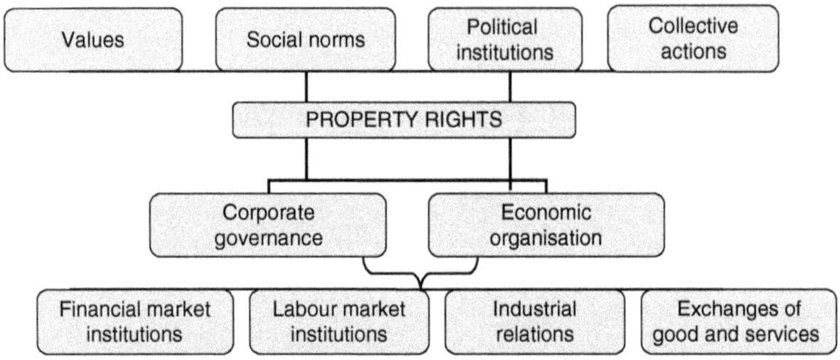


*Figure 3.1* Institutions, property rights and economic organisation

provides a framework representing the way in which advanced and industrialised economies are in general organised around institutions.

To some extent, a reconstruction of the history of advanced and industrialised economies can help in discovering the origins of institutions. In general, one could agree with Powell and Di Maggio (1991: 3) that: 'Institutions arise and persist when [they] confer benefits greater than transaction costs (that is, the cost of negotiation, execution, and enforcement) incurred in creating and sustaining them.' Matzner (1993) argues that there are many different reasons which affect the foundation of institutions in industrial and modern societies:

- First of all, there is the existence of uncertainty. Institutions reduce uncertainty, render economic relationships stable and create common rules and languages in which single agents can operate in order to protect themselves from accusations of illegality and from the aggressive actions of other agents. Institutions create mechanisms through which individuals act to make loans, to invest, to sell and to buy, within a stable framework, governed on the one hand by formal institutions such as law and on the other by informal behaviour such as reputation and trust.
- Institutions enable the deciphering and circulation of a large amount of information among agents.
- Fast transactions in the current age of the microchip and digital information increase price volatility. Within this context, institutions, rules and standard behaviour can be useful in reducing agent speculation.
- Last but not least, institutions are crucial in the creation of an environment where education, innovation and knowledge – all useful

elements for economic development – are available to people and can be accessed by them.

The attention of institutional economists has increasingly moved towards institutional change and evolution rather than concentrating on its origins, because, in the end, *change makes development possible* (Ostrom, 2007) The dynamics of institutional change occur over time; they are contextualised in the concept of the evolution of economies (Hodgson, 1998) and are affected by the interaction of agents' behaviour and by technological progress.

Institutional theories that try to explain institutional change as being based on competition and the market with its selection mechanisms are direct descendants of Adam Smith's thesis of the invisible hand. The market would select the most efficient (in the Paretian sense) economic forms of organisation through maximisation and the adaptation of agent behaviour (Knight, 1992). By contrast, theories in which the interactive behaviour of agents, the context, the relationship with the external world and the reactions to it are perceived in an evolutionary rather than a mechanical way as playing the main role in institutional change make reference to the old tradition of institutionalists, such as Veblen, Mitchell and Commons (Polany, 2001).

North (1990) explains how differences in economic performance could be strongly influenced by the way in which economic institutions evolve in a given historical period and in a given social context. Institutional evolution depends on specific factors, such as newly introduced law and also the prevailing history of a given country, its values, traditions and path dependency (Ostrom, 2005; Beck and Laeven, 2006).

Therefore, the evolutionary distance between economic institutions can be very different from country to country, since it is affected not only by formal rules, law and constitutions, which can be similar among countries, but also by informal rules. Given that, and taking into consideration the assumption of the old institutional economy, which asserts that institutions clearly affect economic performance, two fundamental issues remain to be explored:

1. How institutions evolve, considering in turn:
   - origins and causes of institutional change; and
   - phases of institutional change.
2. How institutions affect economic performance – this can be observed through:

- theoretical models; and
- empirical evidence.

In the following part of this chapter, I will focus on these two aspects, presenting some models of institutional change and reviewing some literature which shows the causal relationship between institutions and development.

## 3.3 Models of institutional change

By studying institutional change, a useful comparison can be made between the extent to which the end of colonialism has affected economic development differently in Asian and African countries and the extent to which the end of planned economic systems in the CEECs has resulted in different outcomes in terms of economic performance among the countries concerned (Pryor, 2006). Despite the similar constitutions and new formal rules adopted by the different countries, the socio-economic development of these countries has differed drastically. Therefore, we can legitimately suppose that not only do formal institutions affect social and economic development but that informal institutions have an impact as well. North (1990) explains economic performance on the basis of institutional evolution. Moreover, institutional evolution depends on specific factors, such as a country's history, values and traditions, which in turn give its context specific features. Therefore, the evolutionary path of institutions can vary widely across different countries as long as it is not determined solely on the basis of formal rules and constitutions. Hence, the essential question is how institutions evolve and what determines institutional change.

Hodgson (1995), in the same vein as the old institutional school, finds many similar features between the evolutionary processes of institutions and natural biological evolution. As in the Darwinian process, institutions evolve by adapting behaviour to new circumstances because human habits – procreators of institutions – are constrained by a form of natural selection. Following this approach, changes in institutions are strictly endogenous. Socio-economic evolution is considered to be the transformation of a system through endogenously generated changes.

I believe that there are four ways through which institutions can evolve. The paths of change can be described as follows:

1. Technology → formal and informal change → new behaviours and habits.

2. By design → formal change → new behaviours and habits → informal change.
3. Change in values → new behaviours and habits → informal change → formal change.
4. Revolution → formal change → informal change.

The passage from formal to informal change, and vice versa, is not immediate. In fact, an interaction always takes place. In the beginning, inertia hinders the evolution of institutions because new institutions need to be absorbed and accepted by people's behaviour, which, in turn, is affected by former rules and habits:

1. As regards the first path in the list above, Veblen's idea of cumulative change explains the dynamic of progressive institutional change. Basically, it starts with technological innovation, which alters habits and behaviours in a community; this in turn causes innovation in the sciences.[1] Following the logic of Veblen's claim, institutional change moves from technological change and then follows a cumulative process.
2. In a sense, Veblen's idea of cumulative change is also the basis for any formal change, which is the second path outlined above. That is why Veblen argues that technological innovation alters habits, both directly and indirectly, through change in the formal framework. Moreover, as Neale rightly states, '[a]n institution does not stand alone. It fits into a system of institutions, so changing institutions means that the rules of other institutions must adapt and so change' (Neale, 1988: 245).
3. A change in values, the third path listed above, is another spin-off of institutional change (Fadda, 2002). By following this approach, an imaginary chain of the process of the creation and transformation of institutions can be built up:

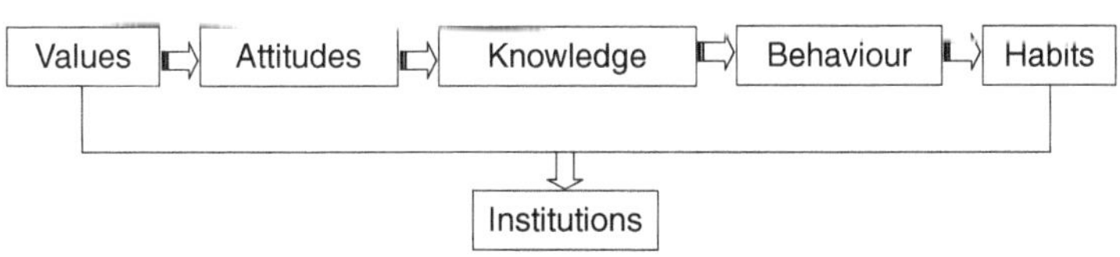


The change in values is a sufficient condition to create a change in institutions, but as Fadda (2002: 21) argues, such a change is not a necessary condition because one could have a change in institutions but values could remain unchanged. In fact, an institutional change can occur, by law or by design, even if the values of people in a given area are the same.

4. Finally, institutional change can arise as a result of revolution, changes in power relations among social clusters, radical transformations in organisations, dramatic changes in the political and economic system of a state, etc. One of these events will change the formal constitution and the formal framework of a society, but not the behaviour of people (at least not immediately). In fact, informal rules will follow previous norms and patterns of behaviour with a significant risk of inconsistency with the new formal framework while it is in the process of being built. Old informal constraints will still be present and persistent. In the beginning, there is inertia and the transformation will be affected by path dependency, which in turn will affect the evolution of institutions (Beck and Laeven, 2006).

The case of post-communist transition economies is very relevant when analysing institutional change and when testing some of these institutional economic theories.

## 3.4 Old institutional economics

In the old institutional economics (OIE) model, rational choices are substituted with habits produced by social norms and accepted behaviours. In this case, preferences, beliefs and choices are all products of an evolutionary adaptation to new circumstances determined by habits. A change in values and beliefs causes a slow evolution of individual habits and subsequently in the choices made. According to old institutional economists, the connection between institutions and habits is clear and immediate. 'Institutions are a set of thought common to the generality of men' (Veblen, 1919: 239). '[An] institution is a way of thought or action of some prevalence and permanence, which is embedded in the habits of a group or the customs of a people' (Hamilton, 1932: 84). On the other hand, Wesley Mitchell (1950: 373) states that institutions are merely convenient terms, widely prevalent and highly standardised social habits.

In accordance with old institutionalism, the imitation and emulation of behaviours lead to the spread of habits and to the emergence or reinforcement of institutions (Summers, 1992). Institutions standardise behaviours and this helps to transmit habits to new members of the group. In this way, institutions embed *collective action*. All individual actions (which, in Commons' words, are defined as *transactions*) are embedded in a framework of collective action. These collective actions are regulated and controlled by laws, social customs, organisations and individual behaviour in terms of bargaining, negotiating and transacting. Therefore, collective action determines all individual economic relations:

> [I]ndirectly, by establishing the working rules which govern the bargaining relations between people, which establish the permissible limits of coercion and duress which individuals and organisations may bring to bear on each other.
>
> Directly, by sanctioning certain rationing devices for allocating such scarcity-values as have not been distributed by bargaining. All governmental tax and expenditures programs are included in this category, as well as the decisions of going concerns like corporations and labour unions.
>
> Indirectly, by establishing the working rules on which the production process [can] go forward through the managerial direction by some of the work of others. (Chamberlain, 1963: 75)

In conclusion, from Commons' point of view, economic relations among agents and economic distribution of goods depend on the way in which the actions of collectives affect transactions (or individual actions).

A majority of the old institutional school would be ready to subscribe to the statement that most of what people do is governed by the institutions of their society. This 'institutional proposition' means, in a wide sense, that culture defines the permissible and the forbidden, right and wrong, the admirable and its opposite, as well as giving content to these definitions with rules for behaviour and thus providing opportunities as well as limits (Neale, 1988).

There is a substantive amount of literature that refers to old institutionalism. First of all, there is Hodgson (1998), who tried to give a broad definition of 'institutions'. This involved five characteristics:

1. All institutions involve the interaction of agents with crucial information feedback.
2. All institutions have a number of characteristic common conceptions and routines.
3. All institutions sustain, and are sustained by, shared conceptions and expectations.

4. Although they are neither immutable nor immortal, institutions have relatively durable, self-reinforcing and persistent qualities.
5. Institutions incorporate values and processes of normative evaluation. In particular, institutions reinforce their own moral legitimation: that which endures is often – rightly or wrongly – seen as morally just.

According to Paul Bush (1988: 49), '[s]ociety may be thought of as a set of institutional system[s]. An institutional system may be thought of a set of institutions. Institutions may be defined as a set of socially prescribed patterns of correlated behaviours'. We can continue this line of thought by asserting that behaviour is correlated to values. At the bottom of this structure, there are certain values, and institutional change takes the form of an alteration in the value structure of institutions. Still, Neale (1988: 227) defines institutions in accordance with the old institutionalism definition: '[a]n institution is of the nature of a usage which has become axiomatic and indispensable by habituation and general acceptance'. However, Foster (1981: 907) adopts a more simple – but in my view more useful – term, defining institutions as '[p]rescribed patterns of correlated behaviours'.

All these definitions have a great impact on the building of new economic theoretical models and of institutional change. The 'institutional proposition' deeply troubles the neoclassical approach of rational choice and the maximising of the individual. It changes the terms of decision making so that economic agents can make choices. Social norms and habits channel and regularise economic agent behaviours. They limit the range of rational choices and they constrain economic actions and transactions.

### 3.4.1 Institutional change within the paradigm of OIE

The position of OIE is very different from the neoclassical approach. OIE takes into consideration power relations and collective actions, social groups, lobbies and dialectic relationship among social forces in order to explain the process of institutional change. Transaction costs, crucial for new institutional economics (NIE), play a marginal role in the context of OIE's institutional change.

The change in relative prices, which from an NIE perspective is very important in the process of institutional change, is considered in OIE to be a consequence of the change of institutions. Moreover, the minimising of transaction costs is a concept which does not belong to OIE.

In fact, according to the old institutionalists, old and inefficient economic institutions can persist even when economically inefficient if they guarantee the pursuit of their original objectives, and when the power groups, the guarantors of these institutions, still consider them appropriate for the protection of their interests and as necessary in achieving their objectives. This theoretical approach is therefore sociological with respect to the fact that economic institutional change is subject to an evolution that in itself contains a dialectic process between groups and social forces, each one of which is interested in either changing or preserving a certain set of institutions. The final result will depend on the force of each group and on the decisions of the dominant groups in a given period and historical context.

The tradition of the old institutional school finds many similar characteristics in the process of institutional change to the evolutionary process in the natural world, as described by Darwin's biological evolutionary theory. The evolution of institutions undergoes a similar process to the natural system in Darwinian evolution[2] (Veblen, 1898) and it is perceived as implicit in all economic systems that institutions change, evolve, survive and disappear in a selective biological way. Institutions, driven by human behaviour, evolve and adapt to new socio-historical circumstances, because human habits – the procreators of institutions – are determined by natural selection in a process of adaptation and survival (Hodgson, 1995). Institutions that are able to change survive. Following this approach, institutional change is endogenous. Economic evolution is therefore considered to be transformation of an economic system through endogenously generated changes.

The same is true of firms. They follow 'routines' in their behavioural models, which have the same function as genes in biology (Nelson and Winter, 1996; Dosi, 1988). Genes are persistent characteristics of the organism, so routines are persistent characteristics of firms. Genes are inherited from one organism to another, so the routines of a firm pass from an old enterprise or plant to a new one. Genes survive the selective processes, though some emerge better and stronger than others, in the sense that they survive in new circumstances, adapt easily, improve their characteristics and perform better. The routines of a firm show a similar story: they can survive in the selective processes of the population (of an industry) and improve their performances, reinforcing their characteristics, adapting to new circumstances and performing better (Wilson, 1975; Penrose, 1952).

Following Bush's approach of the sequencing creating institutions described above, social behaviour creates institutions (Bush, 1988).

At the basis of behaviour and habits, one can find values (Friedland and Alford, 1987). In fact, according to OIE, at the basis of the institutional framework, one can find values that are strictly correlated with behaviours. Consequentially, institutional change and the evolution of institutions within the OIE paradigm is a change in the values of a society, in the power relations, groups and forces of that society, and in the values on the basis of which those forces, powers and groups act, shaping collective actions and final institutions.

One of the most important contributions to the theory of collective action comes from Olson (1965). Olson maintains that in a structure of games and interactions, the non-cooperative solutions represent the dominant strategy. His main contribution lies in the fact that he characterised collective action as an instrument through which human behaviour is obliged to avoid free-riding phenomena: social groups, norms, membership of particular groups, reputation, laws, punishments and incentives can be very incisive in forcing an agent to adopt a corrected behaviour that is socially fair and is not opportunistic, thus reducing free-riding.

Obviously, collective actions have a cost, in the sense that the organisation of a group, the legislative process, the expenses of an organisation, the activity of lobbying and so forth are all expenses of collective actions that are supported by the community (Olson, 1965). But, in the long run, through good governance, organisations, groups, laws and policy makers will reduce these costs. As such, institutional change, in this theoretical framework, is a product determined by those organisations, groups and actions which make institutions more, or less, convenient through the reduction of costs and the advantages and disadvantages that they create for the community.

This approach has found promising grounds for development in game theory, where social groups and lobbies are players, their strategies are guided by values and their choices are determined by their objectives (Schotter, 1981). In the games, change is the result of interaction between the players, and the dominant strategies belong to the stronger groups.

## 3.5 New institutional economics[3]

Since the emergence of consensus on the importance of institutions (North, 1990), neoclassical economists have tried to adjust their theoretical paradigm to the institutional dimension, re-evaluating its importance as part of economic analysis. Institutions were considered to be an economic variable affecting the behaviour of economic agents. As such, 'institutions matter' and the main concern was to 'get the right institutions' (Williamson, 1981). It was in this context that NIE[4] emerged, aiming to revise neoclassical economics and its policies.

NIE attempts to insert into the neoclassical paradigm the role of institutions as constraints on economic choices (Libecap, 1998). NIE uses methodological individualism in order to justify aggregate behaviour and representative agents. On the contrary, OIE rejects this basic 'neoclassical' assumption.

In the NIE understanding, institutions, in a broad sense, can be both formal and informal. Informal institutions are defined as norms, rules and habits, which constrain economic agents to some extent. However, informal institutions are not substitutes for rational choices, as in the old institutionalism approach; instead, they create habits for rational choices (Hodgson, 1998). By contrast, formal institutions are generally defined as the sphere of law, with constitutions, regulations and organisations. There is a direct connection between formal rules and the political-economy structure in governance, property rights and a judiciary system. Thus, the reinforcing of formal institutions is guaranteed by the legal system.

According to Williamson, transaction cost economics provides a better explanation of the human reality and social interactions characterised by bounded rationality problems, information asymmetries and opportunism (1985: 125). Nevertheless the form of economics is oriented towards maximisation. In fact, NIE does not focus on collective dimension explanations, power relations and space dynamics. The only problem is to find out and characterise all the relevant costs. Hence, maximisation is always possible if transaction costs succeed in capturing institutions and the consequent frictions (Williamson, 1985: 127).

North, who takes a position between old and new institutionalism, defines institutions as 'the rules of the game in a society or, more formally, [institutions] are the humanly devised constraints that shape human interaction' (1990: 3). Here, institutions are a means of reducing uncertainty in economic relations and of remedying market failures. North's institutional approach is closer to the OIE theory when he states that institutions do not necessarily have to be efficient, while power relations and lobbies are very important: '[i]nstitutions are not necessarily or even usually created to be socially efficient; rather they, or at least the formal rules, are created to serve the interests of those with the bargaining power to devise new rules' (1990: 16). In fact, North's approach is sometimes considered to be a *bridge* between OIE and NIE theory (cf. Groenewegen *et al.*, 1995).

However, imperfect information, agents' bonded rationality and different sorts of asymmetries cause rises in transaction costs. In this 'imperfect economic world', institutions reduce uncertainty and provide more stability to economic relations. North states that the total cost of production consists of the input costs of labour, land and capital (transformation costs) and of transaction costs, together with costs derived from exchanging, protecting and enforcing propriety rights and acquiring information: 'Once we recognize that the costs of production are the sum of transformation and transaction costs, we require a new analytical framework of microeconomic theory' (North, 1990: 28). Nevertheless, he accepts the theory of transaction costs and its impact on institutional change.

The main difference between NIE (1) and OIE (2) can be summarised as follows:

1. Institutions → Preferences → Maximisation → Choices
2. Institutions → Choices

Hence, in the old institutionalism paradigm, economic behaviour is not *price-guided* but institution-supported (Matzner, 1993). An institution-supported behaviour finds its own essence in the reality of the economic system, where decisions are socially determined by values, rules, habits, reputation, etc., and are politically guided by power forces, organisations, lobbies and even families. Changes in values and beliefs cause a slow evolution of individual habits and subsequently the choices of individuals. In this way, institutions stimulate *collective action*. For Commons (1934), all individual actions (i.e., *transactions*) are embedded in a framework of collective action. These collective actions are regulated and controlled by laws, social customs, organisations and individual behaviour in terms of bargaining, negotiating and transacting.[5] As such, Commons acknowledges that economic relations and the distribution of goods depend on the way in which collective actions affect transactions.

### 3.5.1 Institutional change within the paradigm of NIE

The theory of institutional change in the NIE approach is based on a fundamental assumption:[6] that institutions reduce the economic costs of transacting and hence the agents would use the institutions in order to reduce transaction costs (North, 1990). The behaviour of agents will follow the direction of the relative change in prices. At the new prices and with the new methods, the old institutions will no longer be able to reduce transaction costs (North, 1990), so the institutions will change. From this, it is clear that for NIE the concept of an efficient institution refers to institutions able to reduce transaction costs, acting within a framework of rational behaviour oriented to the maximisation of profits, as in neoclassical theory. Firms will react to the change in relative prices by modifying their production methods, combinations of inputs and selling strategies, and will thereby also modify the institutions on the basis of which they act.

However, many neo-institutional economists (such as Demesetz, 1967; North, 1981; and Alston, Libecap and Schneider, 1995) underline and acknowledge the fact that historically one of the most important motivations for institutional change, beyond price maximisation, was change in the relative endowment of productive factors which enabled the emergence of fundamental institutions such as property rights.[7] These economists acknowledge the possibility of changes which are idiosyncratically linked to the past, within a framework of path dependency (Aoki, 2001).

Another path of institutional evolution is explained by Nugent and Lin (1995), who state that institutions do not always evolve efficiently. Nugent and Lin criticise the 'functionalist' approach to institutional change, which assumes that competition in a free market would assure the emergence of efficient institutions and therefore the elimination of inefficient ones. On the contrary, they argue that a non-efficient path of evolution of institutions is absolutely possible: institutional rigidity and natural inertia in the adaptation of agent behaviours could prevent or hinder, even for long periods of time, institutional adaptation to environmental changes that have already occurred, in this way causing slow institutional evolution that is out of step with recent formal and technological changes (Nugent and Lin, 1995: 2314).

Finally, it is important to mention those theories that rely on 'spontaneous order' as the origin of institutional change. The spontaneous emergence of conventions and rules in the community produces the evolution of institutional change (Sugden, 1998). A convention can begin to change when more and more people believe that other people will follow the change. This simple explanation implies that norms do not necessarily evolve towards solutions that are Pareto-efficient (Sugden, 1989: 94). Some practical conventions can generate from 'expectations' that are crucial for giving stability to certain rules and institutions becoming 'normative expectations'. On the basis of these 'normative expectations', some economic institutions will emerge and will then just be codified by laws rather than created by laws. The change in normative expectations creates a successive change in the economic institutions (Sugden, 1989: 73–4).

## 3.6 Institutions and economic development

The link between institutions and economic growth is one of the most debated themes within both institutional and economic growth literature (Ostrom, 2007). Institutional economics criticises both endogenous and exogenous growth theories for being unable to explain the growth process in developing countries in particular, or the divergent and convergent forces occurring between them and developed economies. Some developing countries are able to achieve a very high rate of growth, much higher than any other developing or developed economies, while others never started a true process of growth (Olson, 1996a; Olson *et al.*, 1998).

Some of the modern institutional theories mostly attribute the differences in rates of growth to the quality of institutions, governance abilities, the specific advantages of a particular territory, social capital, trust and other 'non-material factors' (Scott, 1987; Knack and Keefer, 1995; Becattini, 2000; Bellandi, 2003). Trust is a resource that does not involve a cost. It is based on a fundamental but personal assumption, perception and experience. Trust and other norms, such as loyalty, a positive attitude towards cooperation between economic agents, consolidated relationships between agents, certainty of property rights, social opportunities and rights, a respect for contracts, management of social conflicts and social cohesion, shape the 'social infrastructure' of a country; it is this infrastructure that is essential for the start of a development process in a developing country (Raiser *et al.*, 2001; Kornai *et al.*, 2004; Sabatini, 2008). All the social values and norms that impose respect, the common observance of some rules and principles, the conviction of the honesty and reliability of the other agent, and respect for the rules and agreed contracts increase exchanges, stimulating cooperation processes and the sharing of technologies, knowledge and information. Uncertainties in economic relationships and information asymmetries diminish and the transaction costs decrease, to the great advantage of productivity and economic growth.

Other economists focus their attention on the governance abilities of a country. In particular, Olson *et al.* (1998) elaborate a model on the basis of which they explain how good governance and institutional quality, captured by some institutional indices,[8] increase economic growth and determine the main differences in output between countries. The same idea was developed by Acemouglu *et al.* (2001), who however think that economic development has its origins back in the past that find their basis in the historical institutions of every country.[9] Jones and Hall (1998) showed that the differences in output between countries are mainly explained by differences in the 'social infrastructure', that is, the differences caused by economic institutions. The differences in social infrastructures are the most important factors in explaining the different magnitudes of 'residual growth', which in turn is the main factor in income differences. Finally, Rodrik (1999) explains the improved economic performance of countries after the Second World War in terms of the presence of more appropriate social institutions able to mitigate social conflicts and external shocks.

These contributions, beyond their attachment to OIE or NIE, have the same theoretical paradigm in common when explaining economic development. Such a paradigm can be expressed by the following flow diagram:

| Social and institutional infrastructure → (Input) → Productivity and output per capita |
|---|

This paradigm has been largely ignored or under-estimated during transition of FCEs.

## 3.7 Transaction costs and collective action in the model of institutional change

Nugent and Lin (1995) defines institutions as a set of behavioural rules established to govern social interaction. Knight (1992) adds that institutions structure social interaction. According to these definitions, two notions of institutional economics, i.e., transaction costs and collective action, are important, and both play a crucial role in my model. However, transaction costs do not emerge solely by reason of imperfect information, bounded rationality and asymmetries, as in the NIE paradigm. In its classical form, NIE suggests that transaction costs are constituted by:

1. service costs, such as legal costs, accounting costs and intermediary financial costs;
2. costs of collecting information, exchanging and of protecting and enforcing propriety rights.

Most importantly, in the framework of institutional change in the CEECs and FSRs, the classical definition of transaction costs is no longer sufficient because property rights are not yet well distributed and consolidated. Moreover, the uncertainty and instability of economic relations and conflicting groups cause an extra cost during the acquisition of new property rights. As such, I wish to add two other categories of costs to transaction costs. I call these additional categories of transaction costs *bargaining transaction costs* and *costs of acquiring property rights* (extra transaction costs). These two costs are the costs, *sensu strictu*, incurred in bargaining for a contract and negotiating a sale or purchase of every single good, resource or service in a situation in which property rights are not yet distributed, which is therefore a situation very different from the one described by NIE where (normal) transaction costs can emerge (Coase, 1937; Williamson, 1985). In the NIE approach, negotiation costs of selling and buying are included, as are exchanging costs of goods as represented by retail services, costs of negotiating contracts and costs relating to property rights protection. Bargaining transaction costs derive from transactions made by economic agents who are directly in contact with one another, who do not share the same information, who do not know each other's preferences and who have different aims and strategies, as well as different sets of values. This category of costs can be very wide because it could involve legal, semi-legal and illegal costs. In fact, bargaining transaction costs can concern every market transaction. In such a situation, it is evident that costs will be affected by the power of clusters, the social position of agents and political decisions. Moreover, costs of acquiring property rights, a particular type of institutional transformation cost, is an extra cost that is *ex ante* with respect to transaction costs. On the basis of this extra cost, larger transaction costs will be incurred. Therefore, both categories of costs – bargaining transaction costs and costs of acquiring property rights – could strongly challenge neoclassical market prices as being derived from transformation costs only. By contrast, in this new approach, the neoclassical definition of competition would change and prices would be defined by institutions and not by the market.

Hence, in my model, which is put forward in the next chapter, costs will emerge from the inconsistency between formal and informal rules in economic transactions as well as from actions of power groups which act in an opposing direction in order to achieve their own interests. This could include lobbying activities, organised crime and corruption, new and old organisations, and adverse attitudes of people unwilling to change in order to conform to the new rules. The existence of values that differ from those promoted by these new formal rules push people to behave in different ways. The formal framework prescribes different rules that are often in contrast with the behaviour of those who act in accordance with previous values. This inconsistency causes uncertainty in economic relations, inefficiency in the economic process and a squandering of time and resources. The direct consequences are much more serious than those stemming from 'normal' transaction costs. In fact, they are not usual transaction costs, as defined by NIE, where they are caused by economic exchanges, protecting and enforcing property rights, and the acquisition of information. Instead, they are extra costs affecting both economic relations and transaction costs.

In the case of transition economies, the costs of acquiring property rights can be very widespread in society because property rights in these countries, although regulated by law, are still evolving. Formally (by design) there is certainty in terms of the distribution of property rights, but informally the certainty of property rights is not yet consolidated and extra costs will emerge.

In addition, as Commons explained, collective actions mould people's behaviour in all types of transactions. His concept of institutions is intrinsically connected to the definition of collective action: '[w]e may define an institution as Collective Action in control, liberation and expansion of individual action' (Commons, 1934: 69). Collective action, according to Commons, ranges all the way from social customs to the many organised 'going concerns'. In other words, he refers to collective action as 'going concerns', meaning the *activities* of organisations such as trade unions, families, corporations, banks, governmental agencies, etc. These are organised groups, containing conflicts of interest among themselves and opposing other organised groups. A conflict of interests arises from a scarcity of resources. In addition, Commons refers to collective action as patterns of conduct, social customs and laws approved or sanctioned by society. One can say that lobbies and social groups are very important agents of collective actions. For instance, when an individual sells or buys a good or service from another individual, he or she acts within the sphere of collective action represented by social rules, contract laws, habits, propriety rights, membership of an organisation, membership of a powerful family, etc. Therefore, collective action determines all economic relations of individuals, but it can easily be the case that while formal institutions suggest a particular behaviour and a strategy to reach such aims, informal institutions suggest an opposite behaviour. Hence, lobbies, new laws, old social customs and new and old organisations interact with one another disharmoniously, affecting people's behaviour, causing inconsistency among economic agents and therefore causing uncertainty and instability in economic relations.

In this framework, economic behaviour is far from being price-guided or, at least, the prices are far from being determined by competitive markets. Instead, economic behaviour is 'institution-guided', that is, individual actions are controlled by collective actions and they are not necessarily economically efficient. Individual actions will follow and will be defined by institutions, lobbies, social norms, habits, values and organisations, which have nothing to do with the concept of price-guided attempts by rational agents to maximise utility (Matzner, 1993). Therefore, in my opinion, collective actions affect individual actions and transaction costs emerge, among other sources, from the inconsistent interaction of agents, causing high costs, as explained above.

## 3.8 Final comments

On the basis of this brief overview of the literature, one can state that institutions are not only important for economic development but are also endogenous to economic development (Maddison, 1995). Moreover, economic development should be considered as a process which starts with institutional change, together with a change in informal rules and power groups which would otherwise inhibit development and act as obstacles to innovation and knowledge (Kuznets, 1965). This is very relevant for FCEs, since development is about change and transition involves institutional, structural and systemic change. During the change (or the transition), the main issue would be to get the right institutions to adapt those which do not fit well, to keep the old institutions which could still work and to overcome the inefficient ones. Once this is done, the implementation and reinforcement of institutions need to be put forward. As such, an institutional theoretical analysis is necessary in order to understand these mechanisms.

Moreover, during institutional change, idiosyncratic phenomena are very likely to occur, especially during periods of great and fast technological change which artificially speeds up social changes (Murrel, 1992) or during dramatic changes and revolution. Fast technological change and dramatic institutional change counteract the slow and natural adaptation of behavioural rules, values and habits (Lissowska, 2001). The idiosyncrasy seems to characterise institutional change in communist countries in particular, which are affected on the one hand by abruptly induced but intended changes as a result of the great transformation of 1989 and on the other hand by the limited transformation of values and habits informally persistent in the relevant society (Tridico, 2004). This can result in conflict between social groups, agents and sets of institutions during the transition from a planned ecomony to a market economy, as will be shown in the next chapter.

# 4
# A Model of Institutional Change in Transition Economies

## 4.1 Introduction

In this chapter I will introduce a model of institutional change in transition economies, in which the behaviour of agents is affected not only by formal institutions such as new laws and organisations but also by social norms, those old values and habits which influence the shape of new institutions. The analysis is inserted within a political economy framework, where political preferences, social constraints and consensus as well as international conditionality matter. I will argue that institutional costs, which go beyond mere transaction costs, are emerging from the lack of consistency between formal and informal rules, and negatively affect economic performance (an extra cost of transaction). Among FCEs, an important example of this is given in what I call the 'dichotomy thesis'. Adaptation and changes in the social behaviour of people are difficult and take time, as many surveys today show (New Russia Barometer, 2005; Levada Centre nationwide survey 2008).

## 4.2 Interaction and inconsistency between formal and informal institutions: the dichotomy thesis

In this section I will try to give a real representation of what has been stated theoretically in the previous chapter and I will show how an extra cost will emerge if formal and informal institutions are not consistent.

The transition from a planned economy to a market economy is not only an economic transformation but also involves the culture of capitalism, other values, different institutions, property rights, costs and time (Olson, 1996b). In fact, I would claim that at the heart of transition is institutional transformation. Capitalism is not only a different

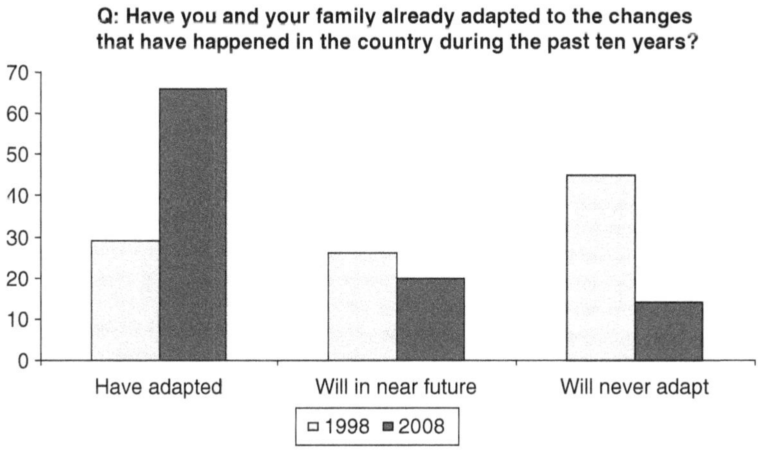


*Figure 4.1* Russia's adaptation to transformation
*Source*: Levada nationwide surveys, October 1998; March 2008

system of allocating resources, it brings with it a 'new style of life' as well. During the transition, there is interaction between formal institutions, determined by the new system, and informal institutions of the old ethos, which are essentially determined by behaviour that is contingent on the past.

It could be argued that in FCEs the new formal rules are in conflict with the prevailing informal rules determined in the past. The discrepancy between formal and informal rules causes an increase in transaction costs. By contrast, if the formal change is in accordance with the informal rules, the transaction costs are lower and production will rise. The problem is that informal rules are not a policy variable. When there is no agreement between formal and informal rules, policy makers cannot directly change informal rules; however, they can directly influence the formal rules.

Hence, if any evolution towards new game rules takes place, it will be affected by the old behavioural norms and by previous rules and prevailing habits. In fact, the groups unwilling to change will try to protect their own interests by *rent-seeking*[1] and *lobbying*. Thus, contrasting norms will cohabit and the transaction costs will be much higher than in one harmonious society, with consequent negative effects on economic performance.

We could have a society in which economic agents act in opposite directions because they use different and opposing goals and strategies to achieve their aims. Two different sets of norms can be identified. One is supported by evolutionary groups, willing to change, who think that they could have more chances in the new system, while the other is supported by people who think that they could obtain more advantages under the old rules. This is what I call the *dichotomy thesis*. I use this hypothesis to explain why high costs – which affect economic growth – emerge if institutions are not consistent. The interaction and inconsistency between these two forces could be dangerous because this could curb economic growth. In fact, this interaction could be much more costly in terms of transaction costs, lobbying activities, bribes, lost time and the power relations of groups. Moreover, this chaotic situation could create space for *illegal intermediation groups* such as corrupt bureaucrats, the mafia and people who exploit a dominant position for personal interests. The dichotomy thesis works very easily: briefly, it claims that old habits, previous behavioural patterns, the old ethos and the existence of old lobbies and all the informal institutions curb the dissemination of new formal institutions and their reinforcement; as Fernandez and Rodrik (1991) have argued, uncertainty will emerge and the reform process can be inhibited. That is why the presence of uncertainty favours great opposition to the change, even though those same reforms would benefit the majority.

As such, the transformation becomes slow and conflicting. The costs increase and this reduces economic performance.

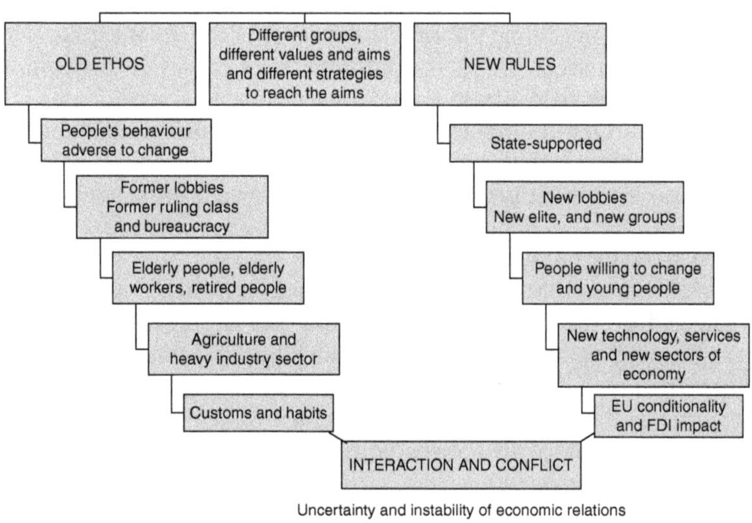


*Figure 4.2* The dichotomy thesis
*Source*: author's elaboration

The new institutions are built on the interactive dichotomy between old rules and new formal rules, supported by two different groups. The inconsistency between these will affect economic growth by hindering the stability and certainty of economic relations. Consequently, such a situation will favour the emergence of illegal or semi-legal groups, which will affect all the transactions in the economy, causing significant extra costs.

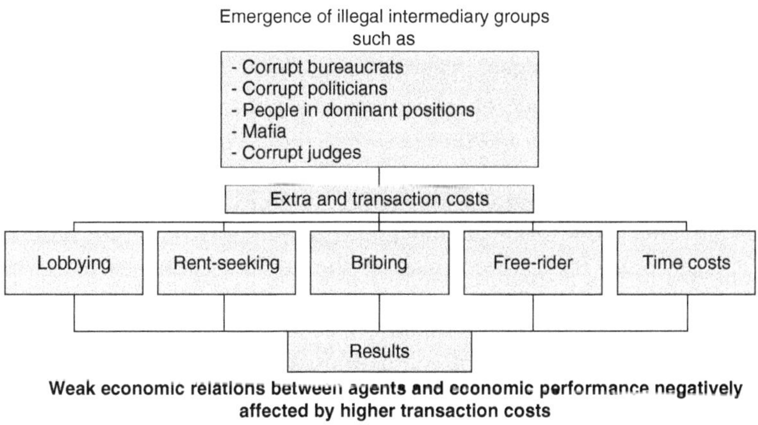


*Figure 4.3* The emergence of oligarchs and of illegal and semi-legal groups
*Source*: author's elaboration

In this situation, transaction costs such as information costs, exchange costs and the costs of enforcing and protecting property rights will be much higher than in a normal situation. In particular, *bargaining transaction costs* will be very high. Moreover, the *acquisition costs of new property rights* within a vicious circle of corruption and lobbying will generate an extra cost, which in general is part of the institutional transformation. Hence, inefficiency and negative economic performance will be caused by these extra costs, which, in turn, will curb the rate of growth of the economy.

My dichotomy thesis is built on the basis of ten episodes and observable stylised facts common among CEECs and FSRs, such as the following:

1. The resistance of farmers and heavy industry workers (and connected lobbies) to formal change and the restructuring of

agriculture and heavy industry (brought about, basically, by a need for harmonisation with the CAP prescriptions and with the EU internal market rules as far as CEECs are concerned, and with FDI and integration into the world economy for all transition economies). The change is also opposed by retired people and bureaucrats who were part of the former ruling classes and who are unwilling to accept the new rules of a market economy.[2]

2. A significant increase in regional divergence (denoted basically by considerable differences in terms of GDP per capita and unemployment) between poor and rich regions and between big cities and villages or small towns. This divergence increased during the 1990s and the dichotomy is between winners and losers in the transition process (Gorzelak, 1998).
3. A cumbersome bureaucracy, which is not yet well adapted to the new formal institutions of a market economy. Bureaucrats and civil servants come from an old planned economy structure and, in most cases, they are not used to the new concerns of the market economy.
4. The uncertainty and instability of prices whose costs, in many cases, do not depend on competition and input costs but on special bargaining, relationships, bribing costs, social customs, habits, etc. (Johnson *et al.*, 1999).
5. The significant presence of a *grey or black market*, as opposed to a legal market, and often tolerated by governments at the beginning of transition (Schneider and Enste, 2000).
6. The emergence of oligarchs, oil and resource-seeking groups, and new and old ruling classes who are able to rob the country, to sell the spoils abroad and to take advantage of institutional chaos.
7. Tax evasion and illegal practices (bribing and corruption) in economic transactions by some groups and agents:
    - to avoid a lengthy bureaucratic process;
    - to achieve their own aims more easily; and
    - to run more efficiently in the new economic contest, avoiding rules and processes that are not yet well known.
8. An informal sphere of institutions negatively affecting economic relations. One can observe a number of informal economic relations other than corruption among economic agents in search of information, seeking and providing credit, stipulating contracts, making business, becoming involved in political campaigns or entering politics.

9. A lack of trust between foreign and local investors.
10. Minimal use of banking and financial services.

Given the concept of extra costs mentioned above, I claim that the transition process is much more costly than mainstream economic theory suggests. In fact, FSRs and CEECs not only incur the 'normal costs' of this process, i.e., social costs (unemployment and poverty), financial costs (budget deficit, increase in debt and trade balance deficit), industrial costs (enterprise restructuring and changes in industrial and trade patterns), inflation and a cost of disinflation, devaluation of exchange rates, etc.,[3] they also incur other costs or a loss of benefits for society because of divergent aims, different values and conflicting interests among different clusters. In short, these costs, or the loss of benefits, are the consequences of the following issues:

- Bribing, corruption and tax evasion.
- Bureaucratic and administrative inefficiency.
- Political resources involved in the protection of particular interest groups and privileges.
- Property rights, distribution costs, and conflicts and uncertainty concerning property rights, resulting in an increase in the cost of their distribution and consolidation.
- Higher transaction costs.
- Lack of trust, resulting in an increase in transaction costs and a decrease in economic exchange.
- Different values, aims and interests of social groups and lobbies, which divert and bias resources towards illegal activities.
- Lower social capital and weaker economic relations.

Therefore, although a macro-economic stabilisation could take place, as it has taken place in CEECs and FSRs during the early years of transition, at a micro-economic level, the inconsistency between formal and informal rules and the dichotomy between the two forces which support those two sets of rules will negatively affect economic performance.

An interesting perspective through which to observe the change and the inertia occurring during the transformation is the analysis of the New Russia Barometer XIV (Rose, 2009). This is a survey that includes questions about what people consider 'a normal society'. There is almost unanimity in Russia (96–99 per cent) in considering a society with the following characteristics to be normal: 1) opportunities to improve living conditions; 2) lower inflation; 3) no fear for crime; 4) employment opportunities for all; 5) welfare services to help the needy; 6) a lack of government interference; and 7) fair treatment of everyone by public officials.

*Table 4.1* When will society become normal?

| **Q. How long do you think it will be before Russia becomes a normal society? (answers in per cent)** | | | | | | | |
|---|---|---|---|---|---|---|---|
| | **2001** | **2003** | **2004** | **2005** | **2007** | **2008** | **Change** |
| Already normal | 9 | 15 | 10 | 10 | 17 | 29 | +20 |
| 1–5 years | 5 | 10 | 12 | 8 | 11 | 11 | +6 |
| 6–10 years | 27 | 34 | 33 | 31 | 22 | 20 | –7 |
| Never | 9 | 11 | 11 | 8 | 9 | 6 | –3 |
| Difficult to know | 50 | 31 | 34 | 43 | 41 | 34 | –16 |

*Source*: Centre for the Study of Public Policy, New Russia Barometer, 2005

The obstacles to normality are different, and people interviewed mostly believe them to be: corruption, unemployment and low wages, government behaviour, the transition towards a market economy, the legacy of the past and various others, as the figure below shows.

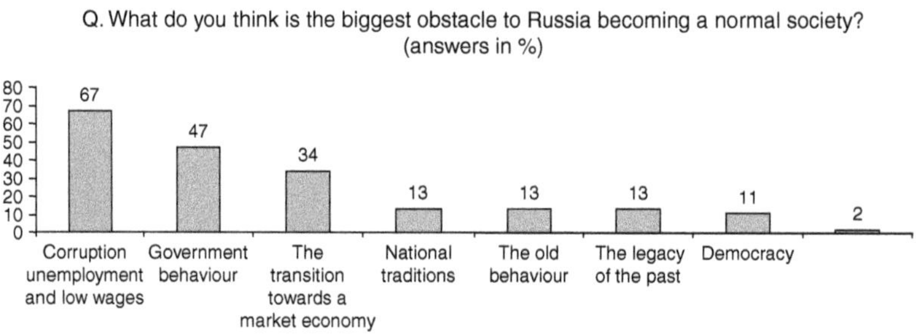


*Figure 4.4* The journey to normality
*Source*: Centre for the Study of Public Policy, New Russia Barometer, 2005

As one can see, corruption is a very important obstacle to normality, and this also includes a lack of a legal framework able to prevent these distorted informal behaviours. Corruption also underlines a very little sense of social capital endowment (Putnam, 1993; 2005). Corrupt countries are countries where *civicness* (à la Putnam) and civil society is very much under-developed. Public resources are therefore wasted and extra costs of transaction emerge. The figure below shows the percentage of firms in transition economies wasting recourses because of informal payments to public official (bribes) in order to get 'things done'.

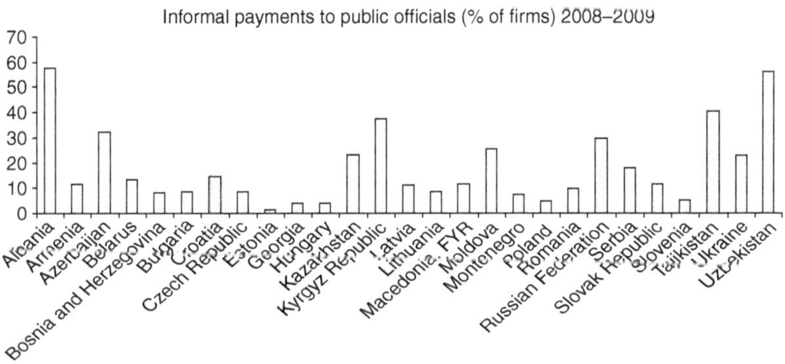


*Figure 4.5* Bribes in transition economies
*Source*: World Bank, online database

## 4.3 The dynamics of institutional change in transition economies

The case of transition economies is a very interesting one for evolutionary institutional theory and is particularly useful in verifying the validity and consistency of the different theoretical approaches as applied to the transformation which took place in Central and Eastern Europe during the 1990s. First, however, we need to clarify exactly what is meant by the *institutional* definition of transition economies.

CEECs and FSRs are referred to as 'transition' economies, implying a sort of *economic journey* from starting point A to point of arrival B. The transition (or transformation) from a planned economy towards a market economy is often conceived as a period of time during which ideally the introduction of specific reforms leads to a perfect economic model (Sachs, 1991). The concepts of both transition towards a market economy and accession to the EU for some of the transition economies are dealt with in the same way; they are perceived as *two sides of the same coin*.

Today, this definition of transition and the neoclassical consensus over the transformation of FCEs has largely dissipated. It seems that it is neither economically acceptable nor methodologically correct to apply this concept of transition to CEECs and FSRs (Nuti, 1999). Empirical evidence shows that there can be no starting or arrival points in an economic system. Therefore, there cannot be a 'perfect transition' towards a 'perfect model' of the economy. Economics is a social science, a superstructure of a socio-political organisation that is both determined by, and in constant interaction with, human behaviour. For this reason, economic evolution is subject to modifications and changes in path evolutions, and does not follow predetermined paths.

On the contrary, it seems much more realistic to assume, following the OIE proposition, that economic behaviour is guided and defined by institutions (both formal and informal) (Neale, 1988: 230). We could therefore describe transition not as a linear transformation from point A to point B but as a generally uneven process represented by a diagram that represents transition as a circle which starts with the distribution of property rights. An institutional cost for the acquisition of property rights will emerge. During the acquisition of property rights, interaction between formal and informal institutions will occur and inertia towards new behavioural models will hamper institutional evolution. Consequently, the conflicting process between groups supporting these two sets of institutions will cause uncertainty in economic relations, curb economic performance and raise the cost of transactions.

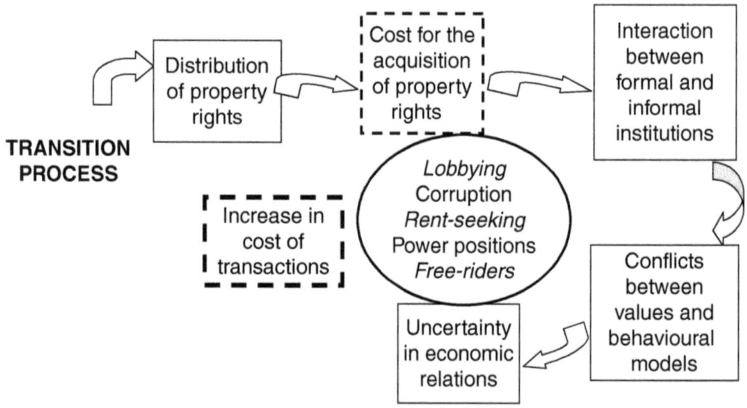


*Figure 4.6* The transition process
*Source*: author's elaboration

Within this circle, lobbies (power groups that try to maintain or conquer dominant positions and obtain greater rent), the practice of corruption and the presence of free-riders will negatively affect this conflicting process, causing inefficiency in transactions and curbing economic performance.

There is a wide consensus today regarding the fact that institutions are extremely important for the economic *performance* and growth processes in a country. Furthermore, these institutions are the product of human behaviour and habits, consolidated in a series of values which are, in their turn, the expression of leading groups and social classes. These values often do not allow for the production and reproduction of neoclassical mechanisms (the 'right' reaction to change in prices, profit maximisation, etc.). Moreover, these values evolve, but their evolution is not immediate. It is the result of a long historical and social process. By considering all these aspects, it should be possible to analyse the 'transition' of CEECs and FSRs from a planned economy system towards their own model of a market economy and, ultimately, towards EU accession. From this point of view, 'transition' is not an *economic journey* from point A to point B, but rather an institutional evolutionary process which brings about:

- the reinforcement of institutions;
- consistency between formal and informal institutions; and
- certainty and stability in economic relations.

Moreover, following this evolutionary approach, the introduction of market rules and capitalist institutions should be consistent with the cultural heritage of a given country and with the evolution of a people's set of values. It follows that transition cannot be a radical and fast process; rather, it should be a gradual process of adaptation, as many evolutionary scholars would claim (Clague and Rausser, 1992; Hare and Revesz, 1992; Roland and Verdier, 1994). As regards EU accession, for example, a strong injection of reforms similar to those adopted in the other Member States could produce negative results in those countries whose institutions, behaviours and values are too different from those introduced by the reforms. There could be a dangerous discrepancy between normative organisational institutions (formal institutions) and institutions conceived as behavioural rules, social norms and acquired habits (informal institutions). The process of EU enlargement to incorporate the CEECs has to consider all these aspects in order to achieve full political and social cohesion inside a united and enlarged Europe.

During the past 20 years, the role of institutions, and in particular the role of institutions at the beginning of the transition process, has been largely under-estimated or ignored. As we have observed previously, at the beginning of the transition process the prevalent idea among economists and international economic organisations was an 'anti-institutional' approach to resolve the economic problems of transition economics. The WC in some of its ten points 'suggested' abandoning many institutions of economic policy and the results were very bad in terms of social costs and institutional stability, with chaos and disorganisation ensuing.

In line with the institutional proposition described in the previous chapter, I argue that if the formal economic institutions are neglected, informal institutions and processes of spontaneous forces prevail (Pejovich, 1999; Fadda, 2002). This informal institutionalisation may also be *parastatal* or illegal. Examples include the mafia, organised crime, a corrupt bureaucracy, an informal economic network among agents, lobbies, etc. These forces fill the systemic vacuum. This kind of informal institution will generate an informal economy, an unofficial economy that will not be taken into account in either the official economic or official data. Moreover, economic relations will be weakened and transaction costs will increase, which will negatively affect economic growth. Thus, two parallel economies could emerge, each of which will be supported by two opposing groups in dangerous competition.

## 4.4 Transition economies: a *sui generis* evolutionary model

In an evolutionary approach, the transition process entails new kinds of social behaviour and new types of interaction among economic agents. New behaviour and interaction with old persistent behavioural models will create new institutions (Matzner, 1993). In turn, these new institutions will perpetuate new social behaviour. This concept of transition is very different from the one which considers a transition as a set of reforms such as laws, constitutions, organisations and governmental agencies that would transform planned economies into market economies and it supports a gradualist approach (Kregel and Matzner, 1992; Roland, 1994).

The institutions are not exogenously defined and unchangeable. They have a social nature, so they evolve slowly but continuously. Once this is established, the crucial questions are what is the origin of their evolution and how do they evolve? For NIE, the cause of institutional transformations is the change in relative prices and enterprise reactions to them (North, 1990), as opposed to *old institutionalism*, in which the changes in price follow institutional transformations (Bush, 1988).

Formal rules are also the product of social evolution. If change in the formal framework of society is slow and in accordance with the natural evolution of society's values and habits, then the risk of inconsistency is quite low. But if the formal rules are abruptly imposed by an exogenously designed political process, then that risk is much higher.

Many economists agree that institutional transformation lies at the heart of post-communist transition. However, different conceptions of institutions create different interpretations of that term. After the dissolution of the Communist Bloc in 1989, Central and Eastern Europe and a little later the FSRs began a transformation towards a market economy. The change was very significant: both the economic and the institutional frameworks were significantly changed. In the CEECs and FSRs there are guarantees relating to private property, new banks, new economic and administrative organisations, and other formal institutions exogenously imposed in a short time and by political decisions. Yet the behavioural rules have not completely changed. Informal economic institutions are far from completed. Economic agents often continue to think in terms of a previous economic logic. I argue that this inconsistency between formal and informal institutions affects economic performance. It prevents the linear and advanced development of CEECs because it causes uncertainty and instability in economic relations.

Given the concept of institutions, which includes both formal and informal institutions, it is no longer sufficient to change formal institutions in order to achieve another system. What is more important is to 'change the mentality' of economic agents. I argue that old institutions may continue to function in the new system even if they are inefficient because current institutions are contingent on the past. There exists a self-reinforcing process that allows for the path dependency of institutions. Moreover, interaction between new formal rules and old social customs will affect the evolutionary path of institutions. In fact, in European transition economies, certain institutions survive, even if they appear inefficient, while others disappear. That is why each society has its own history, its own path of development, its own habits and its own behavioural rules, in other words its own values.

In addition to the path-dependency theory, other factors have to be taken into consideration in order to explain an institutional change in the CEECs. First of all, there is the *interaction between formal and informal rules and the inertia caused by this relationship*. The interaction between the new formal framework of institutions which is about to be built and the dominant behaviour of people in a certain period in turn triggers new rules and new behaviour. Hence, not only the legacy of the past but also this interaction will affect the building of new institutions. I argue that the point to take into consideration is how people react to this formal change. The resulting new institutions are undefined and uncertain, *sui generis* models which will depend on different elements such as the legacy of the past, the interactions between formal and informal rules, and the former behaviour of people constrained by the new formal framework. In sum, informal institutions affect formal institutions in two ways:

- first, by putting pressure on the institutional framework to cause and to influence change of the formal framework;
- secondly, by the interaction between the dominant behaviour (informal rules) and the new framework that has already been built (but which is not necessarily consistent with this).

As such, a particular type of institutional evolution has taken place in transition economies. I would say that it is characterised by several factors such as: path dependency, a new formal institutional framework exogenously imposed by political decisions, changes in the structure of market demand, interaction with the outside world, any informal institutions still present, conflicts and interaction between discordant rules, generational conflicts because of different values and the capacity of the state to implement and enforce new rules. In the words of Lissowska (2001: 1), '[d]iachronic relations are prevailing and synchronic discordance is highly probable'.

## 4.5 The stages of the processes in transition economies

The transition from a planned economy to a market economy goes through three phases. The first is a *chaotic phase*. This is characterised by what Blanchard calls a *power vacuum*. In this phase, power groups and policy makers decide to change the system and therefore to implement new radical policies. In this phase it is likely that new groups will emerge, legal or illegal organisations can easily take advantage of the chaos, and criminals and the mafia can exploit the power vacuum 'to start up their business' on a large scale. Moreover, an informal economic network can be set up, an unofficial economy can grow, and black and grey markets (already present in the former communist countries) can expand. In the CEECs such a situation took place between 1989 and 1990, while in the FSRs it took place during the first part of the 1990s. However, it should also be recognised that several Central European countries such as Poland and Hungary had already gone through a type of reform process during the 1990s, and this contributed in shaping, to some extent, the developments which followed.

Then, following an ideal timing of reforms, a second phase, which can be called the *stabilisation phase*, should come next (Wei, 1997; Svejnar, 2002). This phase is characterised by the implementation of a macro-economic stabilisation programme. Radical policies are put in place in order to change the system and to develop the market economy and its institutions. This phase would also help governments to build appropriate institutions which could be crucial for further economic growth (Gerry *et al.*, 2010a). This phase was the subject of much debate in former communist countries when choosing the 'best possible' market economy model between 1990 and 1992. However, most of those involved in the debate agreed that macro-economic stabilisation should mean the liberalisation of prices first of all in order to eliminate distortions caused by the artificially and badly administrated prices of the former planners. Such a distortion in prices did not allow for the efficient allocation of productive resources and goods. As Nuti (1986) explained, such a distortion was one of the origins of repressed and hidden inflation during the 1980s. During socialism, the problem was that prices were badly controlled and therefore were not free to clear the market. Thus, elimination of the gap between demand and supply, a factor that had been strongly present in former communist countries since the second half of the 1970s, was necessary (Simatupang, 1994). This mismatch was the origin of high inflation as well as the well-known phenomenon of queues outside shops. Restrictive monetary and fiscal policies had to be implemented in order to achieve the aim of price liberalisation.

Despite this, many differences existed among economists in terms of which economic approach to take in a complex transformation strategy. Besides the policies of macro-economic stabilisation, there were other more controversial policies involved in the debate over an appropriate stabilisation programme package for the early 1990s. These include:

1. the institutional direction of institutional change;
2. trade patterns, main partners and main specialisations;
3. the convertibility of the exchange rate and foreign investment regulation;
4. the restructuring of state-owned enterprises, privatisation and deregulation;
5. market institutions, property rights and the legal system;
6. commercial law;
7. corporate governance.

Ideally, all these items belong to the sphere of institutional change. The extension and implementation of the policies concerning institutional change are part of a third phase of the transformation process (Boycko *et al.*, 1995). This phase can be called the *cconsolidating phase* (Linz and Stefan, 1996). However, in many countries in transition, several items listed above, and in particular the restructuring of state-owned enterprises, privatisation, deregulation and convertibility of the exchange rate, happened prior to this phase, often in a very chaotic way (Kolodko and Nuti, 1997). In several CEECs, this was initially during the phase of economic growth, starting in 1992–3. In FSRs it took place after 1995, but was quite unstable. In my view, this is the most delicate phase of transformation. Put simply, one can say that recovery in CEECs after a recession in terms of GDP levels depends on the stabilisation programme, but sustainable growth depends on the consolidating phase. Moreover, neither accession to international organisations, such as the OECD or NATO, nor EU accession marks the end of this period.

This third phase follows macro-economic stabilisation and price liberalisation. This phase concerns the adjustment of behaviour to macro-economic changes. The consolidating phase involves social and economic transformation, modification of behaviour and attitudes of economic agents, changes in social norms and changes in the formal framework of society. This phase is characterised by a change in ownership patterns, led by new institutions and a new system of property rights. During this phase, formal and informal institutions interact with each other dichotomously, building new institutions that allow for economic growth. The extent to which the economy will be affected by transaction costs, economic disequilibria, social costs and loss of benefits will depend on this institutional interaction and on the inconsistency between the formal and informal set of institutions during the evolutionary process of transition.

In this phase, the most important factors are *institutions*. The economic agents and the power groups in society will often be in conflict. Different interest groups will emerge and a number of social conflicts will accompany the transformation. The transition in this phase reveals that it involves a dialectical process where conflicting interest groups will try to gain an advantage, thus affecting the evolutionary process of the economy and of society. My main argument is that the inconsistency of formal and informal institutions and the dichotomy of groups supporting their own set of institutions cause a lack of trust between economic agents, uncertainty and instability in economic relations. Therefore, the transaction costs in the economy will rise. The structural cost of transition to a market economy will be very high and the rate of economic growth will be curbed.

In the third phase of the transition process, the position of institutional and evolutionary economists should be examined. According to them, '[T]he Big Bang not only ignores the lessons of history, it fails to provide the social and economic conditions necessary to create a market economy. The basic error lies in the mistaken belief of the spontaneous emergence of capitalism and market economy once property rights are privatised, prices are set free, the currency is stabilised and unregulated competitive markets are introduced. This error of spontaneity creates serious impediments to discussion of the policies that will have to be formulated in a successful transformation strategy' (Kregel and Matzner, 1992: 35). Moreover, in line with evolutionary economics, Murrel (1992: 52) states that even 'old, inefficient institutions may be better than ones that are planned, but which do not yet exist'. This is why – I would say – it takes time for planned institutions to be understood and accepted in terms of people's behaviour, while old institutions, even inefficient ones, can offer a framework in which people can act coherently immediately.

In conclusion, one can say that a minimum reform package exists and should be implemented in order to begin the transition towards a market economy. For many transition economies, this package consisted of the macro-economic stabilisation programme and price liberalisation, both of which aimed at curbing inflation. At the same time, the policies of the *consolidating phase* should be consistent and appropriate in order to avoid social conflicts as much as possible (Fernandez and Rodrik, 1991). These policies could intervene in the distribution of property rights and allow economic agents to accept the new rules of doing business, such as competition and cooperation, new institutions in the labour market, new market strategies, regulation and collaboration with foreign investors. In this process, the role of a stable Weberian state is crucial.

## 4.6 An interpretation of institutional change in transition economies

Like Knight (1992), I consider institutional change to be a slow historical process that takes place and develops through interactions between agents, social groups, organisations and dominant groups. As such, institutional change can be pushed ahead, as observed earlier, by four factors or movers: technology, changes in the value structure (informal change), changes in the formal sphere (constitutions and law) and a sudden great transformation (such as revolution). Using a concept of

Fadda's: 'Institutional change is a slow historic process, and it starts (because institutions are no longer efficient) when the technological or environmental conditions allow for such a change, or the aims of dominant groups support the change or still when power relations among the social groups change' (Fadda, 2001: 51). 'Efficient' here does not mean that they have to minimise transaction costs; institutions can be said to be efficient so long as they are committed to their original aims.

I present a model where all these factors of institutional change are taken into consideration within a framework of political economy, crossing different discipline borders with an interdisciplinary approach. The point is how these factors can produce consistent change to allow for a steady and strong new institutional structure. In particular, formal and informal institutions can produce new institutions which may or may not build a steady and consistent framework of economic rules. I define 'informal institutions' as a set of *social norms*, conventions, moral values, religious beliefs, traditions and other *behavioural norms* that have passed the test of historical time and that determine individual as well as organisational behaviour in the pursuit of their aims. The informal institutions can be called the *old ethos* or the *carriers of history* (Pejovich, 1999: 142). These informal rules are part of the dynamic evolution of a community and its cultural heritage. In addition, these rules are self-reinforcing over the course of time through mechanisms such as imitation, tradition and other forms of teaching. They also serve as sanctions which facilitate the self-reinforcing process such as community membership, reputation, and fear of expulsion and of being the only one not to respect the rules. There is an inbuilt threat in this Hobbesian type of competition[4] that allows the rules to be respected, since otherwise social relationships would become violent.

On the contrary, formal institutions are generally defined as the legal sphere, with constitutions, regulations and organisations. There is a direct connection between formal rules and the political-economic structure, such as governance, property rights and the judiciary system. Thus, the reinforcing of formal institutions is guaranteed by the legal system. According to these formal and informal rules, economic agents will manage their business, act and operate on the markets, and make their decisions. For these reasons, it is very important to have a consistent framework of institutions and no discrepancy between formal and informal institutions. The model of institutional change can be formalised and simplified using the interaction between formal and informal norms as an independent variable, and the emerging new institutions as a dependent variable.

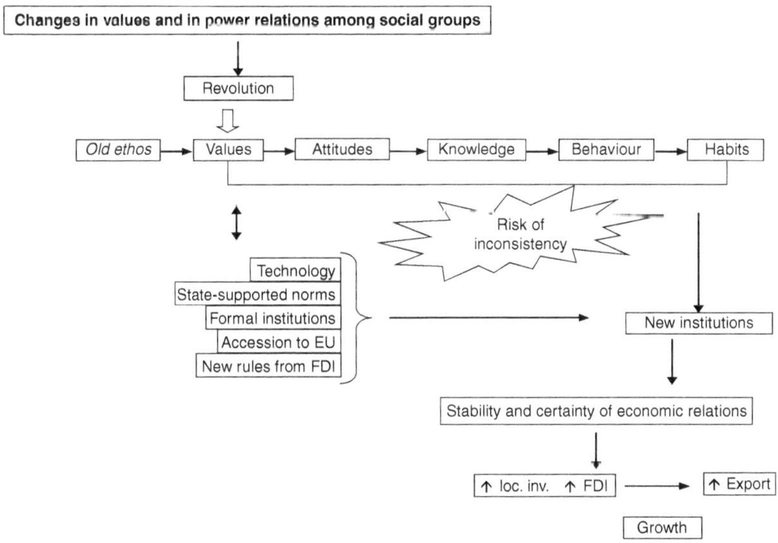


*Figure 4.7* Scheme of institutional change in transition economies
*Note*: loc. inv. = local investments
*Source*: author's elaboration

The idea of the model, and the hypothesis behind it, is that at the beginning of the transformation in the CEECs and FSRs, the risk of inconsistency caused uncertainty in economic relations and fragility in economic performance. When the institutional framework is steady and when the inconsistency between formal and informal institutions is reduced, growth is faster, eliminating the fragility in economic performance. That is why consistency between formal and informal institutions gives stability and certainty in economic relations and reduces transaction costs. This model shows the dynamic path evolution of institutions, in which all the movers of institutional change listed above (values, technology, law and revolution) are present. It is obvious that the shaping of institutions depends on the interaction between formal and informal institutions. Values and technology are fundamental elements of the evolutionary process in this model. As in Veblen's idea of cumulative change (Veblen, 1919: 231–51), I assume that values and technology affect each other mutually; they are not in a subordinate relationship. Veblen's idea of cumulative change explains the dynamics of progressive institutional change. Technological innovation alters values and habits, and in turn new values and habits cause innovation in the sciences. There is a risk of inconsistency because the old ethos of the former communist countries and the informal rules could clash with the new national laws and the new institutions established by a need for harmonisation with EU legislation for the CEECs, and with the FDI inflows for all transition economies. In such a conflicting situation, the transaction costs will be very high.

In transition economies, the EU accession process and the significant increase in FDI inflows have had a strong impact on growth and trade as well as on the institutions of the CEEC and FSR economies. FDI affects economic growth in two ways: first, it brings new rules into the economic process such as technology, labour organisation and market strategy; secondly, if institutions are able to establish stability and certainty in economic relations (this also means the protection of propriety rights), there will be more FDI, which will likely have a positive effect on economic growth. Hence, on the one hand, more and more FDI will be attracted, while on the other hand, the economic agents will be able to find information and institutional support to invest and to export.

However, from an institutional point of view, in each country the economic institutional pattern emerges endogenously, as a consequence of the interaction between external influence and domestic constraints, political preferences and social consensus, in accordance, as much as possible, with the individual culture, history and set of values of the country. Once all these decisions are taken and new institutions are set up, people and economic agents should follow them consistently and persistently if the economy is to perform well. The new rules should be consistent and credible, and a legal system should guarantee institutions such as certainty of ownership, respect for law and commercial contracts, and enforcement and monitoring of property rights.

As Rodrik states (1999: 3): 'Macroeconomic stability and high investment rates have been common [in the countries that have performed well], but beyond that many details have differed. Correspondingly, the rules of the international economy must be flexible enough to allow individual developing countries to develop their own "styles" of capitalism, in the same way that countries such as Japan, Germany and the United States have in the past evolved their own different model.'

## 4.7 Final comments

In the first years of transition, the most important aim of governments was macro-stabilisation (Balcerowicz, 1993): the fight against inflation, the reduction of debt, the liberalisation of prices and the privatisation of public assets. Mainstream economists argue that all these aims were necessary to allow for economic growth. Nevertheless, these results were not sufficient conditions to stimulate long-term and sustainable growth. If we look at the economic performance and at the social indicators in FSRs and CEECs, we notice that in general the data are quite surprising and controversial. On the one hand, particularly in the CEECs, there was a significant recovery in GDP levels, a positive annual change in the labour productivity of industry, relatively high investment rates and enterprise restructuring, a strong capability to attract FDI, a reduction in inflation, low public debt and low deficit figures compared to the EU average. In sum, we could say that during the past 20 years the stabilisation programme, particularly in the most advanced CEECs, has produced almost complete nominal convergence towards the Maastricht criteria, i.e., the macro-economic criteria that would allow CEECs to join the eurozone. On the other hand, one can find among FSRs and CEECs not only high unemployment rates, a growing inequality rate, a considerable index of poverty and a worsening of life expectancy (as I will show in Part III of this book) but also high and extra transaction costs, corruption and lobbying, and inertia towards change.

In other words, despite the fact that CEECs and FSRs have done remarkably well in general with regard to financial stabilisation, these economies are still affected by numerous problems which curb economic performance. In my view, one of the most neglected of these problems, which has been analysed in this chapter, is the inconsistency between the new institutional framework and informal institutions. Not enough attention was paid to the role of informal institutions. As I emphasised above, the institutional framework and, in particular, the consistency between formal and informal institutions are very important for economic development. Informal institutions are also part of the economic process and are not exogenously given. Informal institutions resist change or take more time to change because initially there is inertia. The interactions between the old ethos and informal institutions and new rules were bound to bring problems affecting the consistency of behaviour, with consequent negative effects on economic performance.

# 5
# Varieties of Capitalism and Socio-Economic Models in Transition Economies

## 5.1 Introduction

In this chapter, after having briefly outlined the formal change that occurred in transition economies, mainly through EBRD indices, I will classify them according to their socio-economic models and I will test whether the type of system has an impact on the development path of the country, considering both economic growth and some socio-economic indicators. Following the varieties of capitalism literature (Jessop, 2002; Amable, 2003; Amoroso, 2003; Brenner, 2005; Coates, 2005), countries will be classified according to their main macroeconomic characteristics and institutional variables drawn from the EBRD, such as enterprise and privatisation, market and competition, trade and openness, financial system, wage nexus and social investments. Following this classification, I found five types of socio-economic models among FCEs: the *competitive capitalist model*, the *corporative model*, the *dirigiste model*, the *hybrid model* and the *state capitalist model*.

## 5.2 The transformation towards market institutions: EBRD indicators

The assumption which underlies this book is that the diversity of development experienced by transition economies is in large part due to the diversity of institutions. In order to show the link between institutions and development, EBRD, World Bank and Freedom House indicators are used.[1] As we will see, political institutions like the Freedom Index (from Freedom House) and the Voice and Accountability Index (from the World Bank) associated with socio-economic variables such as education and health expenditure are very important for human development, which in turn affects GDP. By contrast, EBRD indices and institutional variables are relevant and useful in order to classify countries among the different types of socio-economic model characterised.

The EBRD elaborates some indices of institutional reforms for transition economies. These are also useful in investigating the successes and failures of reforms towards a market economy. However, these indices pay little attention to political institutions and informal institutions. By contrast, Word Bank governance indicators also focus on this second set of institutions. The following table and figure show GDP (per capita, levels and growth) and the average EBRD indices for each country (Figure 5.1) and for groups of countries (Table 5.1) among transition economies.

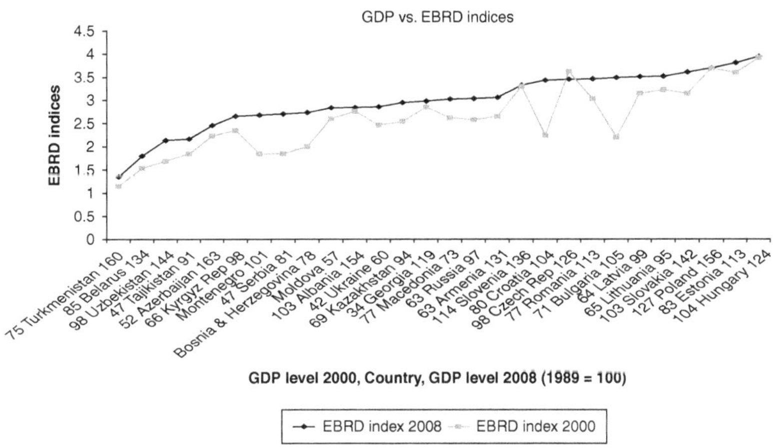


*Figure 5.1* EBRD indices and GDP levels in 2000 and 2008
*Source*: EBRD, Transition Reports

However, progress in terms of GDP does not seem to be directly affected by progress in institutional reforms as characterised by the EBRD (i.e., market institutions). Obviously, the debate about this is very vivid and results are sometimes very controversial (De Melo *et al.*, 1996; Falcetti *et al.*, 2006), in particular when a factor of causality is involved in the analysis. However, in this analysis I take into account the correlation between economic growth and these indices, and the results

*Table 5.1* GDP vs. EBRD institutional indices

| **Group of countries** | **CEEC 5+** | **CEEC 5– and Balkans** | **All CEECs and Balkans** | **CIS** | **All transition economies** |
|---|---|---|---|---|---|
| GDP per capita 2008 (in US$) | 19,647 | 9,582 | 14,614 | 4,211 | 12,013 |
| Average economic growth 1989–2008 (in %) | 1.7 | 1.2 | 1.5 | 1.1 | 1.4 |
| Average of EBRD indices 2009 | 3,649 | 3,182 | 3,416 | 2,522 | 3,192 |

*Source*: EBRD, Transition Report

are not significant or unclear. By contrast, a strange paradox seems to emerge when one considers EBRD progress and GDP levels together. It is possible to identify two extreme groups of countries and a third group which lies inbetween these two:

1. The first group comprises the most advanced countries in terms of EBRD institutional reforms, with the highest levels of GDP, considering 100 as the level of GDP in 1989.
2. The second group is made up of a set of countries which never started a process of reform or are very slow reformers. However, this group has a relatively high GDP level, since these countries never experienced a huge fall in GDP due to systemic transformation at the beginning of 1990s, as other transition economies did.

The figure below tries to approximately represent this paradox. It is interesting to observe that Turkmenistan, which is still considered a quasi-planned economy with a private sector share of GDP equal to 25 per cent, has the lowest EBRD average index (1.35) but the highest level of GDP after Azerbaijan, given the 1989 level as equal to 100. The same applies to Belarus, Uzbekistan and Azerbaijan, which have the lowest EBRD indices but the highest GDP levels. On the other hand, we have Poland, Hungary, Slovenia and the Czech Republic, which have high GDP levels and the highest EBRD indices. Between

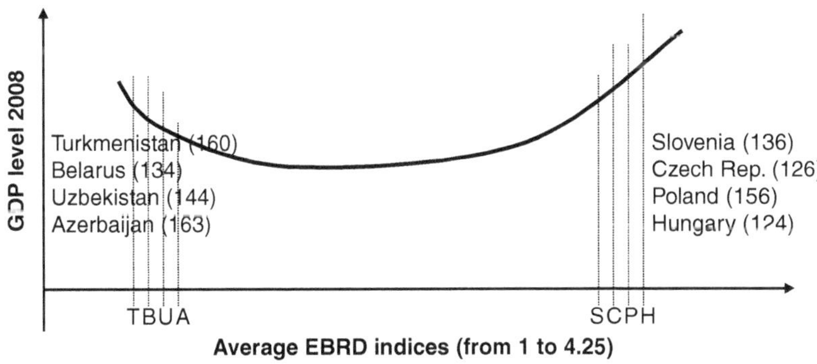


*Figure 5.2* GDP levels versus EBRD indices (note: GDP level 1989 = 100)

Azerbaijan (A) and Slovenia (S) on the x-axis, which represents the level of EBRD indices, are all the countries with low-to-middle levels of reforms (a third group). Simultaneously, these countries are also characterised by low-to-middle GDP levels, in comparison with the 1989 levels, measured on the y-axis. On the basis of this, it can be assumed that economic recovery and GDP growth among transition economies are not strictly connected with market economy reforms, contradicting the EBRD projection (see the correlation matrix in the appendix to this chapter).

*Table 5.2* Correlation of GDP growth to EBRD indices

| | growth89-09 | ebrd_ind09 |
|---|---|---|
| growth89_09 | 1.0000 | |
| ebrd_ind09 | -0.1574 | 1.0000 |

*Source*: author's elaboration based on EBRD data

However, although EBRD indices are not correlated with growth, I assume that institutions matter. But the question is which ones? I maintain, and I will show, that interaction between appropriate institutions – not strictly market-related – improves the level of human development, which in turn leads to higher levels of GDP. In fact, countries can implement specific institutions and policies that identify a specific model of development. As I will show in the next section, socio-economic models differ considerably among transition economies, as does economic performance; several types of models within varieties of types of capitalism can be identified.

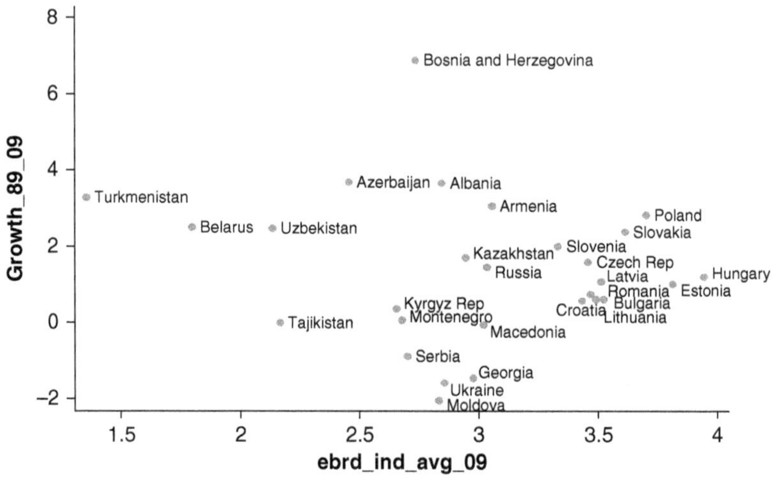


*Figure 5.3* Scatter EBRD index 2009 and GDP growth 1989–2009
*Note*: this scatter is confirming, in a more analytical way, the paradox shown in Figure 5.2, where countries with lower and higher EBRD indices grew faster during the 1989–2009 period. The case of Bosnia and Herzegovina is not relevant, since the data refers to the 1996–2009 period. In any case, it is not possible to characterise here a positive relation between EBRD and growth.
*Source*: author's elaboration based on EBRD data

## 5.3 Varieties of capitalism and growth in transition economies

Generally speaking, countries can be classified according to their type of economic system, which can be characterised by some particular institutional forms and macro-economic factors such as domestic competition, role of the state, international trade and openness, and monetary forms. Following this approach, Amoroso (2003) and Jessop (2002) identified four types of economic systems, such as the Anglo-Saxon model (or competitive capitalism), the corporative model (corporative capitalism), the dirigiste model and the social-democratic model. To these models, Choi Chonj Ju (2004) and many others (e.g., Qian, 2003; Yeager, 2004) added the current model of the socialist markets represented in particular by China and Vietnam.[2] Bruno Amable (2003) found similar stories in his book *The Diversity of Modern Capitalism*, with five different ideal types of capitalism, taking into consideration five institutional forms (product market competition, the wage-labour nexus, the financial sector, social protection and education). He put together the dirigiste and the

*Table 5.3* Socio-economic models and their main characteristics

| **Characteristics** / **Models (leader country)** | **Competition** | **Economic regulation** | **Main economic actors** | **Relationship between public and private actors** | **International economic relation** | **Taxation** |
|---|---|---|---|---|---|---|
| Anglo-Saxon model (USA, UK, Ireland) | Promoting free competition | Deregulation, withdrawal of the state from the economy | Firms, corporations, markets | Residual public sector: market-oriented | Global competition | Low taxes, no or little progressive rate |
| Corporative model (Germany) | Balancing cooperation and competition | Decentralised | Tripartite structures (business clubs, trade unions, government) | Public-private partnerships | Protection of strategic sectors in an open economy | High taxation to finance welfare state |
| Dirigiste model (France) | State control, regulated competition | National accumulation and regulation strategy | Private and public sectors | Public-private partnerships under state guidance | Protectionism | High taxes and collective recourses |
| Social-democratic model (Scandinavian countries) | State-controlled liberalisation and competition | Knowledge and innovation as economic guide for regulation | Public and private firms and ethical corporations | Public-private partnership in order to realise social cohesion | National actors, moderate free competition, open economy | High wages, career perspective, high and progressive tax rate |

*Table 5.3* (Continued)

| Characteristics / Models (leader country) | Competition | Economic regulation | Main economic actors | Relationship between public and private actors | International economic relation | Taxation |
|---|---|---|---|---|---|---|
| Socialist markets model (China, Vietnam) | Balancing between forms of liberalisation and free competition | State regulation and innovation | State- or municipal-owned firms, semi-private firms, private foreign firms, public authorities | Public and private actors with more emphasis on collective goals | National strategies in a global context, reasonably free trade | Distributive policies, collective services, egalitarian principles |

The Amable (2003) classification is: (1) *market-based economies* (the US and the British economies are the closest to this type); (2) *continental European capitalism* (led by Germany and France); (3) *social-democratic economies* (the Scandinavian economies); (4) *South European capitalism*; and (5) *Asian capitalism*.

*Source*: author's elaboration, adapted from Jessop (2002), Amoroso (2003), Amable (2003), and Choi Chonj Ju (2004) corporative model (forming a continental European model) and added two models (the Asian model of capitalism and the South European capitalist model). Table 5.3 summarises the main theoretical characteristics of these socio-economic models and, in parentheses, the main country leaders of each model. The table combines the work of the authors quoted above.

Following such taxonomy, and using the EBRD's six institutional variables (which are different from the strict EBRD indices discussed above), I tried to classify transition economies. The six institutional variables or dimensions are: enterprise; market and competition; trade and openness; the financial sector; the wage nexus; and social investment. On the basis of these institutional dimensions and following suggestions from the quoted varieties of capitalism literature, I identified the following five socio-economic models:

1. *Competitive capitalism.* The most important features for this model are a high level of privatisation, no/low subsidies to firms, no wage regulation and control over FDI, and social investment levels below the average for transition economies.
2. *Corporative capitalism.* The most important features for this model are a medium to high level of privatisation, wage regulation and high levels of social investment (above average in transition economies).
3. *Dirigiste capitalism.* The most important features for this model are a medium level of privatisation, above-average subsidies to firms, an above-average share of administered prices and a high level of asset shares of state-owned banks.
4. *Hybrid capitalism.* Countries among this group share different features of different types of model. They can have a high share of the private sector in terms of GDP, a high level of social protection, a high level of asset shares of state-owned banks, a low level of administered prices and subsidies to firms, wage regulation, international openness, etc. Therefore, the values of indicators here are rather unpredictable and seem to depend more on power groups, lobbies and particular stakeholders within the society. This is a similar feature to the South European models described by Amable (2003), with good examples being countries like Italy, Spain, Portugal and Greece.
5. *State capitalism.* The most important features of this model are a very low share of the private sector in terms of GDP, above-average subsidies to firms, an above-average share of administered prices, a high level of asset shares of state-owned banks and a very low level of stock market capitalisation.

Table 5.4 below shows in more detail how institutional dimensions should fit with the socio-economic models. For instance, in order to be classified as a competitive capitalist economy, a country should fit within the criteria appearing in the respective line. When an institutional variable appears in bold font, this is a necessary and theoretically required condition for country to be classified within the respective model. When it appears in italics, it is not necessary but would be a theoretically justified condition. Sometimes, some features may change across the different models.[3]

The shapes of the socio-economic models among transition economies were affected by several factors during transition. First of all, one can say that the type of transformation strategy influenced both the path of development and of institutional change through a process of cumulative changes which in the end also affected the type of socio-economic model. Table 2.1 in Chapter 2, which showed in general which kinds of macro-economic strategy transition economies adopted during the 1990s, can be recalled now.

However, the strategies implemented were important but were not a paramount issue regarding the adoption of a certain type of socio-economic model among transition economies. The type of socio-economic model is influenced by several factors, which include the policies and quality of governments; political leaders and interaction with public opinion and the media; the international mode and level of competition; foreign influence and integration into the world economy; the history and path dependency of each country; and geography (McArthur and Sachs, 2001). The past inclination during communism towards some important socio-economic features is also very important. For instance, the division of labour within COMECON (the former communist commonwealth for free trade, similar to the European Economic Communities) affected the way that FCEs are today integrating into the world economy. Other examples would be the importance of the agricultural sector in each country during communism and land nationalisation, both of which would affect today's levels of privatisation in those countries. Another example would be the level of democracy and censorship which people experienced during the communist regime in the different countries.

The table below shows the classification of transition economies among the different models following on from the taxonomy in Table 5.4.

Apart from the macro-economic features typical for each model as described above, one can observe some other interesting political

*Table 5.4* Institutional variables and varieties of capitalism in transition economies

| | Enterprise | Market and competition | | Trade and openness | | | Financial sector | | | Wage nexus | Social investment |
|---|---|---|---|---|---|---|---|---|---|---|---|
| | **Share of private sector** | **Subsidies to firms** | **Share of price administration** | **FDI control** | **Trade (import + export)** | **Tariff revenue** | **Foreign-owned banks** | **State-owned banks** | **Stock market capitalisation** | **Wage regulation** | **Gov. expend. in education and health** |
| Competitive capitalism | **Very High** (>75%) | **Below average** | *Low* | **No** | *High* | *Low* | *Low* | *Low* | *High* | **No** | **Below average** |
| | | | | | May change and vary | | | | | | |
| Corporative capitalism | **Medium-High** | *Low* | *Low* | May change and vary | | | | | | **Yes** | **Above average** |
| Dirigiste capitalism | **Medium** | **Above average** | **Above average** | May change and vary | | | | **Above average** | May change and vary | | |
| Hybrid capitalism | Mixed and unpredictable values | | | | | | | | | | |
| State capitalism | **Very low** (<30%) | **Above average** | **Above average** | May change and vary | | | | **Above average** | **Very low** | *Yes* | Above average |

*Table 5.5* Classification of socio-economic models among transition economies

| State capitalism | Hybrid capitalism | Dirigiste capitalism | Corporative capitalism | Competitive capitalism |
|---|---|---|---|---|
| Turkmenistan<br>Belarus<br>Uzbekistan | Romania<br>Bulgaria<br>Bosnia and Herzegovina with dirigiste tendency<br>Ukraine with dirigiste tendency | Azerbaijan<br>Kyrgyz Rep.<br>Serbia<br>Moldova<br>Russia<br>Tajikistan<br>Montenegro with corporative tendency | Hungary<br>Slovenia<br>Poland with hybrid tendency<br>Croatia with competitive tendency<br>Macedonia with competitive tendency<br>Czech Republic with competitive tendency | Estonia<br>Slovakia<br>Albania with dirigiste tendency<br>Armenia with dirigiste tendency<br>Georgia with dirigiste tendency<br>Kazakhstan with dirigiste tendency<br>Latvia with corporative tendency<br>Lithuania with corporative tendency |
| Average GDP growth 1989–2009 (in %): 2.8 | Average GDP growth 1989–2009 (in %): 1.9 | Average GDP growth 1989–2009 (in %): 0.4 | Average GDP growth 1989–2009 (in %): 1.1 | Average GDP growth 1989–2009 (in %): 1.5 |

*Source*: author's elaboration

elements regarding this classification. First of all, the majority of the CEECs adopted corporative and competitive models, since some of those countries are closer politically, historically and geographically to the former Austro-Hungarian Empire and Germany, while some of the others are more influenced by the Anglo-Saxon model. The latter model was in fact able to affect the path of development of several countries in Central and Eastern Europe during transformation. The hybrid model was also a target for several CEECs. One can say that this model fitted countries with a very mixed historical and political background, such as Bosnia and Herzegovina, which had been influenced by several countries and models. On the other hand, we can also find in this group countries like Romania and Bulgaria, which experienced a quite unstable transition, introducing policies and institutions without a clear transformation project. As regards the CIS, almost all of these adopted dirigiste capitalism and state capitalism models. However, a specification needed to be made for the dirigiste model. While at a theoretical level in the work on the varieties of modes of capitalism undertaken by Amoroso (2003), Jessop (2002), Rhodes (2000) and others, France can be considered a dirigiste economy, given the importance that state strategies and public institutions play in the economy among transition economies, the dirigiste model is an outcome of semi-authoritarian regimes linked to particular 'state leaders', parties, families or groups of oligarchs, which all affect the economy. Such a choice confirms the importance of history and path dependency in the building of an economic system. Tradition and the development of liberal values also have a role to play, as Beck and Laeven (2006) argue. State capitalism and dirigiste capitalism in the CIS are seen in countries where democracy, freedom and voice and accountability are found to be very limited when compared to the majority of the CEECs.

Sometimes, the classification is not so easy and smooth because countries can share different features of different models and still not be in the hybrid group, because they respect the condition that the most important feature required for classification in the model group is observed within them. In these cases, the country is included in the group in which its most important features fit best. However, a specific tendency towards another model appears beside the name of each country. In the appendix to this chapter, there is a table with all the variable values for all the countries. Table 5.6 below shows the average values of these variables.

In order to test the impact of the type of the model on economic performance, I carried out a factor analysis (see the appendix to this chapter). First of all, the factor analysis confirmed the aggregation of models made above. As the scatter figure of Factor 1 and Factor 2 shows in the appendix to this chapter, most of the CEECs are scattered in the top-right corner of the figure, with differences between the corporative model group (Hungary and Slovenia in particular) and the competitive model group (Slovakia and Estonia in particular). Most of the CIS are scattered, identifying themselves as a dirigiste model group, and Turkmenistan, Belarus and Uzbekistan identify themselves as a state capitalist model group.

*Table 5.6* Average results from aggregation of countries in models

| | State capitalism | Hybrid capitalism | Dirigiste capitalism | Corporative capitalism | Competitive capitalism | All transition economies |
|---|---|---|---|---|---|---|
| Private sector share in GDP (in %) | *33.3* | 70.6 | 65.7 | 74 | **75** | 63.7 |
| Budgetary subsidies and current transfers (% of GDP) | **8.1** | 4.8 | 3.2 | 4.3 | *2.6* | 4.6 |
| Share of administered prices in CPI (%) | **29.9** | 11.5 | *8.18* | 8.4 | 9.61 | 13.5 |
| Share of trade in GDP (%) | 99 | 88 | *85* | 102 | **108** | 98 |
| Tariff revenues (in % of imports) | 4.4 | 3.1 | **9.3** | *0.45* | 1.4 | 3.7 |
| Asset share of state-owned banks (in %) | **79.3** | 5.2 | 17.6 | 6 | *1.7* | 22 |
| Asset shares of foreign-owned banks (in %) | *8.4* | 78.1 | 38.4 | 74.4 | **79.4** | 55.7 |
| Stock market capitalisation (% of GDP) | *3.7* | 40.3 | **57.9** | 54.7 | 40 | 39.2 |

*Table 5.6* (Continued)

| | **State capitalism** | **Hybrid capitalism** | **Dirigiste capitalism** | **Corporative capitalism** | **Competitive capitalism** | **All transition economies** |
|---|---|---|---|---|---|---|
| Controls on inward direct investment | YES | YES/NO | YES/NO | YES/NO | NO | |
| Wage regulation | YES | YES/NO | YES/NO | YES | NO | |
| Government expenditure on education and heath (% of GDP): average = 8.7 | 9.7 | 8.3 | *8.1* | **11.1** | 8.6 | 9.1 |
| Competion level (1–4) | *1.6* | 2.7 | 2 | 2.7 | **2.8** | 2.3 |
| EBRD average indices (2009) | *1.76* | 3.281 | 2.646 | 3.253 | **3.437** | 3.192 |
| Average level of political rights and civil liberties 2000–6 (democracy) | *6.63* | 2.15 | 5.37 | **1.78** | 2.75 | 3.74 |

*Note*: political rights and civil liberties rank between 1 (the most free) and 7 (the least free). The lower the better
Variables with the best/highest values appear in bold underlined font. Variables with the worst/lowest values appear in italics
*Source*: Transition Report, 2009 (cf. final appendix to this book for details for each country)

The regression model with the two factors extracted is very interesting. Factor 1 (which is explained by variables which better identify a competitive capitalist model), Factor 2 (which is explained by variables which better identify a corporative capitalist model) plus democracy (the political rights and civil liberties variable)[4] and the initial condition of the countries (GDP in 1989) are the explanatory variables of the model. GDP in 2009 is the dependent variable. Factor 1 is not significant, while Factor 2, democracy and the initial conditions are all statistically significant with positive coefficients, and seem to determine a higher level of GDP per capita.[5]

*Table 5.7* Regression F1, F2, Democracy and GDP89

| **Dependent variable: GDP per capita (2008)**<br>**Method: least squares**<br>**Included observations: 28** | | | |
|---|---|---|---|
| **Variable** | **Coefficient** | **Std. Error** | **P-Value** |
| Factor 1 | −1,348.27 | 2,299.628 | 0.565 |
| Factor 2 | 1,959.25 | 937.0916 | 0.051 |
| Democracy | −2,332.032 | 1,108.715 | 0.050 |
| GDP89 | 1.615709 | 0.3780729 | 0.000 |
| Constant | 1,3781.92 | 13,781.92 | 0.003 |
| **R-squared** 0.8213 **Adjusted R-squared** 0.8213<br>Prob(F-statistic) 0.0000 | | | |

*Source*: author's elaboration

Hence, from the regression above, it can be said that the type of model has an impact on the GDP of a country, in association with initial conditions and the level of democracy. This is the first indication of a model of development which will be better explored in Part III of this book, when, it is assumed, political institutions, in association with some economic variables, lead to better levels of human development and then to economic growth.

## 5.4 Varieties of capitalism and socio-economic development

Finally, something needs to be added concerning other social indicators, such as inequality, poverty and life expectancy. First of all, economic growth has so far not eliminated poverty among transition economies (the average level in transition economies is 35 per cent against 15 per cent, on average, among the most developed economies).[6] Moreover, the level of inequality, although lower than in other regions of the world, shows an increasing upwards trend (33 per cent in transition economies against 35 per cent, on average, in the most developed economies)[7] and life expectancy is, on average, nine years below that in the most developed economies (almost 70 years in transition economies as against almost 79 years in the most developed economies). However, among transition economies, differences are considerable. In fact, as shown by average values in Table 5.8 below, dirigiste countries in general are characterised by the highest inequality and poverty levels, while corporative economies show better indicators.

EBRD indices do not seem to be significantly correlated with economic growth: the fastest growing group of countries has the lowest EBRD average indices. The type of model seems to have an impact on the type of development and on the social indicators of the country. This means for instance that countries in the corporative model group show the best values for all the social dimensions considered, such as poverty, life expectancy, pluralism, freedom and HDI. Indeed, corporative countries also had the best initial conditions, represented here by the HDI in 1990. In total, the corporative model shows the best values in ten dimensions out of the 14 considered and shows the worst indicator in only one dimension (with a score of +9 in the table below). The state capitalism model shows seven worst values and three best values, and thus gets a score of −4. The hybrid model only gets one best value (on life expectancy growth) and zero worst values, obtaining a score of +1. The competitive model gets zero worst values and zero best values, obtaining a final score of 0. Finally, and at the bottom of our classification, the dirigiste model gets six worst values and zero best values, obtaining a score of −6. On the basis of this evaluation, which takes into consideration human development, GDP and institutional dimensions, I am able to build the following ranking among transition economies, which underlines, to some extent and of course with some limits, the stage of development in transition economies after 20 years since the fall of the Berlin Wall.

This is an overall and approximate evaluation which gives equal weight to all the dimensions considered and which depends strictly on the model assigned to each country. Therefore, if one assigns a greater value to inequality, for instance, and a lesser value to GDP per capita, or vice versa, a different final picture could emerge. Obviously, different

*Table 5.8* Socio-economic indicators among transition economies by type of capitalism

| | Competitive capitalism | Corporative capitalism | Dirigiste capitalism | Hybrid capitalism | State capitalism |
|---|---|---|---|---|---|
| Poverty, 2006 (%pop $4 day) | 45.0 | <u>6.1</u> | ***54.4*** | 37.7 | 30.7 |
| Gini coefficient, 2006 | 32.1 | <u>27.5</u> | ***37.2*** | 34.2 | 35.7 |
| Voice & Accountab. 2000–5 | 0.05 | <u>0.893</u> | −0.763 | 0.437 | ***−1.157*** |
| Freedom index (avg. 2001–06) | 2.20 | <u>2.80</u> | 1.29 | 2.76 | ***1.00*** |
| Unemployment 2007 | 10.2 | ***14.5*** | 12.2 | 13.0 | <u>4.0</u> |
| GDP growth average 1989–2009 | 2.36 | 1.05 | ***0.37*** | 1.20 | <u>2.75</u> |
| GDP level 2008 (1989 = 100) | 133.3 | 116.7 | ***98.0*** | 98.3 | <u>146.5</u> |
| GDP per capita, 2008 | 10,254 | <u>17,641</u> | 4,909 | 8,766 | ***3,403*** |
| HDI 2007 | 0.814 | <u>0.869</u> | 0.761 | 0.822 | ***0.760*** |
| HDI 1990 | 0.759 | <u>0.807</u> | ***0.756*** | 0.799 | 0.785 |
| Life expectancy in years, 1995 | 70.7 | <u>73.0</u> | 68.0 | 71.0 | ***67.0*** |
| Life expectancy in years, 2007 | 70.5 | <u>73.0</u> | ***65.6*** | 71.9 | 65.7 |
| Life expectancy growth 1995–2007 | −0.24 | 0.00 | −3.60 | <u>1.36</u> | ***−2.02*** |
| EBRD average indices (2009) | 3.253 | <u>3.437</u> | 2.646 | 3.281 | ***1.763*** |

*Note*: the worst values appear in bold and italics, while the best values are underlined
The Freedom Index synthesises the level of political rights and civil liberties in a country
*Source*: World Bank, UNDP, EBRD

*Table 5.9* An overall socio-economic development rank among transition economies

| Models | Total score (+/− 14) | Standardised value[8] |
|---|---|---|
| Corporative capitalism | +9 | 1.26 |
| Hybrid capitalism | +1 | 0.14 |
| Competitive capitalism | 0 | 0 |
| State capitalism | −4 | −0.52 |
| Dirigiste capitalism | −6 | −0.7 |

*Source*: author's elaboration

results are also obtained if some countries are placed in different model groups from those given here.

## 5.5 Final comments

In this chapter I carried out an analysis of varieties of capitalism among transition economies. Using EBRD institutional variables, I classified the countries into five groups (the *competitive capitalist model*, the *corporative capitalist model*, the *dirigiste model*, the *hybrid model* and the *state capitalist model*).

The factor analysis carried out in this chapter shows that the type of socio-economic model may have an impact on GDP growth. The corporative capitalist model is associated with higher levels of GDP and of democracy (political rights and civil liberties). Moreover, I found that countries of the corporative model always show better socio-economic variables, such as inequality, poverty, voice and accountability, freedom index, life expectancy and HDI. By contrast, countries of the dirigiste model show worse indicators. In this context, it seems that the corporative model is better able to combine freedom, democracy and social rights, which is a crucial issue not only in post-communist economies, but also among advanced capitalist economies. These variables, as we will see in Part III of this book, improve the level of human development, which in turn improves economic growth.

# Appendix A5: Factor Analysis and Other Correlations

The first two factors in the table below explain more than 80 per cent of the variance. Essential variables for the explanation of Factor 1 are: private sector, foreign bank and competition, which are positively correlated, while the state bank variable is negatively correlated. These are crucial variables for a competitive capitalist model and the signs of the correlation are the expected ones. Essential variables for the explanation of Factor 2 are: trade (import + export in percentage of GDP) and public expenditure in health and education, which are both positively correlated with the factor.[9] These are crucial variables for a corporative capitalist model and the signs of the correlation are again the expected ones. A correlation matrix which also includes the two factors confirms these results.

When I extract the two factors, the scatter figure confirms the classification of models made in the previous chapter: most of the CEECs are scattered around a cloud of dots close to each other, in the top-right corner of the figure. In particular, Hungary and Slovenia have higher levels of Factor 1, which better characterises a corporative model, while Slovakia and Estonia have higher levels of Factor 1, which better characterises a competitive capitalist model. Most of the CIS are scattered close to each other, identifying the dirigiste model, and Turkmenistan, Belarus and Uzbekistan, staying in another corner of the figure, are captured best by the state capitalist model. The hybrid model brings together, Romania and Bulgaria. In general, these results are consistent with the qualitative analysis which produced the classification in Table 5.5 above.

*Table A5.1* Factor analysis

```
Factor analysis/correlation      Number of obs = 28
Method: principal factors        Retained factors = 6
Rotation: (unrotated)            Number of params = 45
```

| Factor | Eigenvalue | Difference | Proportion | Cumulative |
|---|---|---|---|---|
| Factor1 | 3.46456 | 1.79469 | 0.5644 | 0.5644 |
| Factor2 | 1.66937 | 0.87398 | 0.2720 | 0.8364 |
| Factor3 | 0.79039 | 0.36573 | 0.1288 | 0.9653 |
| Factor4 | 0.42516 | 0.15971 | 0.0693 | 1.0345 |
| Factor5 | 0.26545 | 0.14348 | 0.0432 | 1.0778 |
| Factor6 | 0.12198 | 0.20850 | 0.0199 | 1.0976 |
| Factor7 | -0.08653 | 0.02590 | -0.0141 | 1.0835 |
| Factor8 | -0.11243 | 0.05408 | -0.0183 | 1.0652 |
| Factor9 | -0.16651 | 0.06730 | -0.0271 | 1.0381 |
| Factor10 | -0.23381 | . | -0.0381 | 1.0000 |

LR test: independent vs. saturated: chi2(45) = 118.73 Prob>chi2 = 0.0000

Factor loadings (pattern matrix) and unique variances

| Variable | Factor1 | Factor2 | Factor3 | Factor2 | Factor5 | Factor6 | Uniqueness |
|---|---|---|---|---|---|---|---|
| priv_sec | 0.8304 | -0.4193 | -0.0090 | 0.1811 | 0.1450 | -0.0154 | 0.0804 |
| subs_to_firm | -0.2040 | 0.2311 | 0.4686 | 0.0368 | -0.1783 | -0.1741 | 0.6219 |
| trade | 0.2820 | 0.6331 | 0.0156 | 0.3154 | 0.0295 | -0.1376 | 0.4001 |
| import_rev | -0.4335 | -0.3355 | 0.4410 | 0.1520 | 0.2482 | -0.0310 | 0.4194 |
| state_bank | -0.8391 | 0.3999 | 0.1375 | 0.0799 | 0.0305 | 0.1368 | 0.0910 |
| foreign_bank | 0.8413 | -0.0466 | 0.1068 | 0.1020 | -0.2963 | 0.0618 | 0.1767 |
| exp_edu_heal | 0.2745 | 0.8037 | 0.0406 | -0.0941 | 0.0778 | 0.1087 | 0.2503 |
| competition | 0.8596 | 0.1873 | 0.2357 | 0.0894 | 0.1650 | 0.0989 | 0.1254 |
| stock_mkt | -0.2666 | 0.1450 | -0.5290 | 0.3073 | 0.0457 | -0.0552 | 0.5285 |
| administ_pri | -0.4107 | -0.2512 | 0.0959 | 0.3746 | -0.1614 | 0.1560 | 0.5684 |

*Source*: author's elaboration

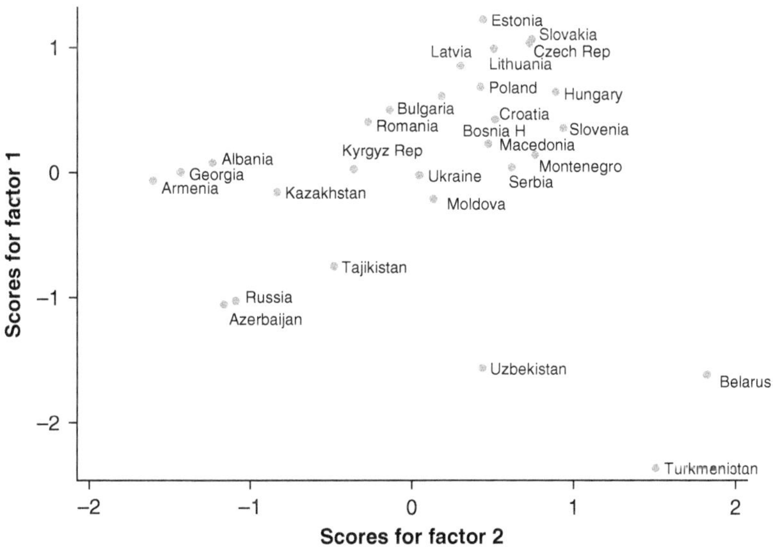


*Figure A5.1* Scatter figure for Factors 1 and 2
*Source*: author's elaboration

*Table A5.2* Correlation matrix between GDP and EBRD institutional reforms

| | growth89.09 | GDP09 | priv_sec | subs_firm | trade | import | state_b | for_ban | edu_heal | compet. | stock | adm_pr | FDI_c | Wage_R |
|---|---|---|---|---|---|---|---|---|---|---|---|---|---|---|
| GDPgrow89_09 | 1.0000 | | | | | | | | | | | | | |
| GDP09 | 0.0689 | 1.0000 | | | | | | | | | | | | |
| priv_sec | -0.2105 | 0.4216 | 1.0000 | | | | | | | | | | | |
| subs_to_firm | -0.0232 | 0.0200 | -0.3121 | 1.0000 | | | | | | | | | | |
| trade | -0.0179 | 0.4468 | 0.0476 | 0.1892 | 1.0000 | | | | | | | | | |
| import_rev | 0.0533 | -0.2126 | -0.1383 | 0.1999 | -0.2581 | 1.0000 | | | | | | | | |
| state_bakn | 0.4521 | -0.3090 | -0.8713 | 0.3021 | 0.0245 | 0.3155 | 1.0000 | | | | | | | |
| foreign_bank | -0.2634 | 0.3965 | 0.7053 | -0.0704 | 0.2358 | -0.4144 | -0.7214 | 1.0000 | | | | | | |
| ExpEduHealth | -0.0362 | 0.6563 | -0.1316 | 0.0897 | 0.5793 | -0.3952 | 0.1359 | 0.1633 | 1.0000 | | | | | |
| competition | -0.1523 | 0.7114 | 0.6887 | -0.0934 | 0.4087 | -0.2552 | -0.5888 | 0.7273 | 0.4376 | 1.0000 | | | | |
| stock_mkt | 0.2801 | -0.1733 | -0.2145 | -0.1978 | 0.1891 | -0.1329 | 0.2264 | -0.3040 | -0.0389 | -0.3207 | 1.0000 | | | |
| admini_price | 0.2654 | -0.4638 | -0.1959 | 0.0829 | -0.1941 | 0.3398 | 0.3365 | -0.1840 | -0.3517 | -0.3575 | 0.1462 | 1.0000 | | |
| FDI_control | 0.1807 | 0.0511 | -0.3437 | 0.3147 | 0.0060 | 0.4287 | 0.3899 | -0.3719 | 0.0222 | -0.2319 | -0.1786 | -0.0343 | 1.000 | |
| WageRegulat. | 0.0695 | -0.1302 | -0.5630 | 0.2895 | 0.1877 | -0.0875 | 0.4558 | -0.3812 | 0.2234 | -0.2650 | 0.2843 | -0.0503 | 0.0577 | 1.0000 |

*Note*: For a better definition of the variables in this table, see Chapter 5. These variables were used to classify countries among different types of capitalism models

It is particularly interesting to observe that neither GDP growth nor GDP in 2009 are correlated with any of the variables listed (expenditure in education and health and competition correlated with GDP levels in 2009, but not with growth)

*Source*: author's elaboration based on EBRD data

# Part III

# The Capability Approach, Social Capital and Human Development in Transition Economies

# 6
# Explaining Economic Development: Old and New Theories

## 6.1 Introduction

After briefly illustrating some of the main traditional growth theories, this chapter will examine the new trajectories of development theories relevant to the analysis I have set forth.[1] These trajectories form the basis of my development model explored in the chapters that follow. In my analysis, development is a complex process which consists of the interaction between capabilities and institutions, and goes beyond merely GDP growth. This interaction brings about human development which at a second stage brings about economic growth. Clearly, traditional growth theories such as those relating to exogenous and endogenous growth only partly explain the process of development in transition economies, and that is why a more complex analysis is required. In the thought of classical economists such as Smith, Marx and Ricardo, economic development depends mainly on the surplus quota that, as profit, flows towards capitalist entrepreneurs. Development, perceived as economic growth, would come as a consequence of the accumulation of capital. This vision of development as economic growth is also shared by neoclassical economists and Keynesians.

Starting from Schumpeter's contributions, the explanation of development moves further from the classical and neoclassical vision. Development is defined as a transition from one norm of the economic system to another norm in such a way that this transition cannot be broken down into infinitesimal steps (Schumpeter, 1932).

As I anticipated in the Introduction to this book, it is possible to distinguish two levels of development: the first one, economic growth, involves only the growth of GDP levels, while the second one is *human development*. In this second approach, the income is a *means* and not an *end* of development. Development is perceived as an expansion of people's capabilities (Sen, 1985) and involves the improvement of two fundamental variables, i.e., life expectancy and education levels, along with GDP and other social goals (UNDP, 1990). These objectives are obtained through a process of institutional change that empowers people as agents and brings about democracy and equality (UNDP, 1999). Hence, development is a process that involves institutional change (Toye, 1995) along with social, cultural and political change in a holistic way (Myrdal, 1974; Hirschman, 1981).

## 6.2 Traditional theories of economic development

For decades, economists have been challenged to explain 'how countries become rich'. Adam Smith observed that some nations are richer even if not all of the individuals in that society work, whereas other nations are extremely poor even if all of the individuals work. He attributed most of the output differences among countries to better organisation and labour division. Recently, there has been a burgeoning literature in this field, but there are incompatible implications between theories and empirical analyses about economic growth among the different approaches.

In particular, transition economies offered economists a field in which to test their theories and approaches. All these approaches still refer to economic development mainly as GDP growth. Below I will briefly explore these theories, trying to see in them the relevance for transition economies.

### 6.2.1 Harrod-Domar

The Keynesian models of Harrod (1939) and Domar (1946) suggest that the maximum possible rate of economic growth, Gn, is equal to $n + \lambda$ where n is the growth rate of a population that, in equilibrium and assuming the hypothesis of continuous full employment, is equal to the growth rate of labour force and $\lambda$ is the growth rate of productivity. In particular, based on the hypothesis of equilibrium between aggregate demand (AD) and aggregate supply (AS), $Gn = s/v$ where s is the propensity to save ($s = S/Y$ with $S = I \rightarrow s = I/Y$) and v is the capital-output ratio. However, $Gn = s/v$ is guaranteed (=Gg) only if $AD = AS$, and this happens only if the firms invest the exact amount to obtain a growth rate equal to what they expect. In other words, Gg (which should be $= Gn = s/v$) is the rate at which I (investment) and Y (output) should grow in order to maintain the equilibrium between AD and AS. It follows that no market forces exist which allow for an automatic equilibrium between AD and AS. As such, the state is called in to play its role as guarantor of full employment of productive factors, i.e., capital and labour.

Such a model was consistently used from the 1950s to the 1970s in both advanced capitalist economies and former communist countries, particularly in the latter, where public investments were made functional in order to increase the productive capacity by a forced industrialisation. This was seen as a means to push the process of economic growth. However, in several FCEs, adherence to this model caused strong inflationary pressure because the economies fell into the trap of trying to continuously maintain a high level rate of investment growth with an excess of demand over supply. In fact, the capital-output ratio (v) was very high and the rate of growth in the long run deteriorated, as was explained in Chapter 1.

### 6.2.2 Exogenous growth theory

Contrary to the Harrod-Domar model, Solow (1956) argues that the market has its own forces to create automatic equilibrium between supply and demand. As in the Harrod-Domar model, economic growth is determined by $n + \lambda$ (exogenously given population growth and technological progress) which is equal in equilibrium to the guaranteed rate of growth $Gg = s/v$. However, what guarantees that $n + \lambda = Gn = Gg = s/v$ is the hypotheses of flexibility of prices and of the substitutability of capital and labour. In fact, in the event of unemployment (i.e., in the event that the population grows faster and $Gn > Gg$), wages are supposed to decrease and capital accumulation is expected to decrease. Hence $v \downarrow$ $Gg \uparrow$ and what follows is that $Gn = Gg$. Moreover, the analysis of Solow's fundamental capital accumulation equation, with the crucial hypothesis of decreasing return of capital (and labour), shows that each country reaches a steady-state point of accumulation where $\dot{k} = 0$ and the capital-output ratio is constant: $\dot{k} = sy - (n + d)k$ whereby investment per worker (sy) increases the growth of k, while depreciation per worker (dk) limits the growth of k. n, the population growth rate (which is equal to labour growth because of the full employment hypothesis), also reduces k in the same direction as capital depreciation does. The reaching of a steady state (with $\dot{k} = 0$) allows for an absolute convergence hypothesis of growth rates: poor countries, where capital accumulation is lower, grow faster than richer countries and vice versa (beta-convergence). A conditional convergence would allow for a convergence in income levels only if s, the propensity to save, is equal among countries (sigma-convergence). The technological progress increases the growth rate of GDP and allows countries to reach the steady state sooner. However, it is considered a 'free good', hence each country can have access to it. Therefore, in the end, income convergence is always possible.

These are very important implications for the economic development of countries because the main policy rule this model rests on is that of non-interference of the state in the economy.

### 6.2.3 Endogenous growth theory

The results of Solow's model leave policy makers with little or no room for policy deliberations or initiatives, since economic growth is determined by exogenous variables (n and $\lambda$) and in the end all the countries would converge towards the same steady-state level because technological progress is a free good available to all countries.

However, the results of Solow's model did not materialise empirically and in general countries are not converging towards the same level of income or towards the same rate of growth. In order to explain the lack of convergence, at the end of the 1980s, a new theory emerged, i.e., the endogenous growth theory. The main difference between the exogenous and endogenous growth theories lies in their different treatment of technological progress. In the exogenous theory, it is assumed to be a free good, but this is not so according to the new endogenous theory (Romer, 1986; Lucas, 1988), which proposes that each country has its own path of development that depends on the technological progress the country is able to reach, given the level of organisation, social capability, institutional framework and imitation processes at play in the given territory (Abramowitz, 1986). Each country is associated with a particular function of technological progress, in the same way that Kaldor (1957; see also Kaldor and Mirrlees, 1962) was already theorising during the 1950s and 1960s, such that income convergence among countries will be excluded. In this context, skilled labour plays a leading role which, in endogenous growth models, forms a part of 'human capital' (Romer, 1986; Lucas, 1988; Barro, 1998).

### 6.2.4 Human capital contribution

Romer (1986), following the seminal works of Young (1928), Kaldor (1957) and Arrow (1962), imputed increasing economic returns to scale to the level of knowledge in the community. He assumed that an improvement in the skills of workers increases the final outcome, *ceteris paribus*, simply because skilled workers are more productive. Here, knowledge is strictly connected to school and education. Lucas (1988) directly associated human capital with 'learning by schooling' and 'learning by doing', allowing human capital to become reproducible. Physical capital, integrated into this definition of human capital, is part of a cumulative and reproducible process that avoids decreasing returns to scale.

Political institutions and public policies also play a role in the growth of human capital *per se* because they are seen as tools that support people by giving access to economic opportunities, and therefore in the end are crucial to the accumulation of knowledge (Jones and Hall, 1999). On the one hand, public policies are necessary to provide general education, training programmes and incentives for firms to invest in education and training programmes, and are likely to increase the levels of human capital with positive spill-over effects on economic growth. On the other hand, workers are more likely to achieve greater benefits in a country where political institutions, such as participation and freedom, are secure than in a country where these variables are violated. However, in order for these opportunities to be substantial, they need to be supported by social rights, giving people equal access to resources, schools, training programmes and then better jobs.

Empirically, this model was followed by, among others, Levine and Renelt (1992), Barro and Sala-i-Martin (1995) and Barro (1998), who showed that convergence between countries is conditional on improvements over time in secondary school enrolment. As a matter of fact, some studies have shown that high education levels are positively correlated with appropriate reform processes in transition economies (Goel and Budak, 2006).

## 6.3 New theories of economic development

Development is in general a complex process which, among other factors, necessarily includes institutional change, both in developed and developing countries, and which therefore cannot be explained simply by using the traditional theories described above. Empirical exercises which try to explain development simply by using traditional growth models fail to show supporting evidence (Olson *et al.*, 1998). In former communist countries, the process of development is even more complex because a systemic change is included in this process. In these countries, the relevance and the importance of appropriate institutions and of extra economic factors appear even more clearly.

*Ceteris paribus*, institutions matter more than capital. Social capital and human capital can explain more than labour and employment levels. Civil society and trust are crucial for fair economic relations, and people's opportunities and capabilities are extremely important in order to reduce poverty and inequality and to foster development.

In the following sub-sections, these statements and issues will be introduced theoretically and, in the two chapters that follow, a model which includes all these variables will be tested on transition economies.

### 6.3.1 Institutions and development

The relationship institutions → economic growth has been increasingly investigated both from a theoretical and an empirical point of view (e.g., Jones, 1981; Knack and Keefer, 1995; North and Thomas, 1981; Rodrik, 1999). Empirical research has shown that institutions, as we defined earlier following Knight's (1992: 2) definition (which considers institutions to be 'a set of social rules that structure social interactions'), and good governance in some ways matter regarding economic organisation, rising productivity and economic relationships (e.g., Knack and Keefer, 1994; Olson *et al.*, 1998; Jones and Hall 1999; Acemouglu *et al.*, 2001). Moreover, they are, according to North (1990: 3), 'the rules of the game' and can therefore help to establish relationships.

In contrast, institutions that aim only at economic growth cannot automatically bring about a process of human development in the sense of the meaning given to it by Sen with the concept of enlarging capabilities. They would instead bring about capital accumulation and at best a skilled labour force, employment and income.

Recently, Bardhan (2005) suggested that some non-income-related dimensions of development are better explained by a particular institutional index, such as participatory rights and democratic accountability, as opposed to property rights institutions. For example, according to Rodrik and Rigobon (2005), who discuss income gaps among countries, democracy and the rule of law are both good for economic performance.

However, following the classification of economic development given above, one should distinguish types of institutions and try to correlate each to the appropriate kind of development. Table 6.1, adapted from De Muro and Tridico (2008), aims to show the links and connections between institutions and development.

*Table 6.1* Institutions and types of development

| | **Economic growth** | **Human development** |
|---|---|---|
| Property rights | XXX | |
| Competition | XXX | |
| Information | XXX | |
| Trust | XX | XXX |
| Welfare institutions | | XXX |
| Voice and accountability | | XXX |
| Democracy | | XXX |
| Rule of law | XXX | X |
| Political freedoms | | XX |
| Human rights protection | | XX |
| Political participation | | XXX |
| Equal opportunities and anti-gender discrimination institutions | | XXX |
| Social opportunities | | XXX |
| Public education | | XXX |
| Transparency guarantees | XX | X |
| Protective institutions | | XX |
| Political stability | XXX | XX |
| Control of corruption | XX | X |
| Government effectiveness | X | X |
| Risk of expropriation | XXX | |
| Quality of bureaucracy | XX | X |
| Contract reinforcement | XXX | |
| Law enforcement | XX | X |
| Existence of trade unions | X | X |

*Table 6.1* (Continued)

| | | |
|---|---|---|
| Financial institutions and intermediaries | XXX | |
| Institutions providing facilities for access to credit | X | X |
| People as agents | | XXX |

*Notes*: One X underlines the possibility of a theoretical link between the relevant institutional variables and the type of development. XX stands for a strong link. XXX stands for a very strong link
*Source*: adapted from De Muro and Tridico (2008)

### 6.3.2 Capability and human development

The idea that GDP is an absolute and reliable measure of development has been widely criticised by development economists. The performance of countries in terms of GDP can be very different from basic development indicators (Morris, 1979; Noorbakhsh, 1996; Constanti and Monni, 2005). The United Nations (UN) pays very close attention to socio-economic development levels reached by countries. According to the UN, it has been clear that development does not mean growth. During the 1970s, the UN started to study a different economic development approach according to which developing countries could satisfy some 'basic needs through public policies (Streeten, 1979; Anand *et al.*, 1994). A subsequent theoretical contribution by Amartya Sen (1985) and his 'capability approach' was crucial to further investigations into development indicators. In 1990, the UNDP published its first Human Development Report where a composite human development index (HDI) was presented.

A great deal of empirical evidence shows that, both in developing and in developed economies, some countries have relatively high GDP per capita but very low indicators of socio-economic development, such as literacy, access to drinking water, infant mortality rates, life expectancy and education. This is partly due to the fact that wealth is unequally distributed. There are also cases of relatively low GDP per capita and high indicators of socio-economic development in countries where income is more equally distributed (Ray, 1998).[2]

Moreover, several problems arise with the use of GDP. First, GDP per capita is an average indicator and does not represent personal levels of income, distribution of income or access to resources. Secondly, GDP is hardly a comparable indicator among countries, since it is a weighted sum of goods and services, where the weights are prices that can vary consistently among countries. Thirdly, GDP does not include non-market transactions. In other words, average GDP is not always a good proxy for well-being.

Sen's capability approach and the subsequent HDI takes such deficiencies into account[3] and goes beyond GDP. The HDI tells us more about the real-life conditions for people: that is, health, education, access to resources, etc. People provided with human capabilities, i.e., the range of things that people can do or be in life (UNDP, 2008), will reach a more advanced stage of human development. Human development is a process that allows for an environment in which people enjoy long, healthy and creative lives (UNDP, 1990) and is considered a process that enlarges people's choices, something that is achieved by expanding human capabilities and functioning (UNDP, 1990).

Hence, the HDI is a better measure of well-being and of 'development' in its widest sense because within this composite index, GDP is only one of a number of different elements which determine the HDI, along with other elements of human life.[4]

Investment in human development is therefore crucial. Moreover, such an investment would increase both aggregate demand and the effective quality of life. A better quality of life will generate a better and more skilled labour force, with subsequent positive effects on economic growth, as shown by Barro (1998).

Institutions guide public choices and in turn these reinforce political institutions. A country in which public policies give substantial incentives for firms to accumulate human capital and for workers to learn, train and study will increase its level of knowledge, providing benefits to people in terms of capabilities and therefore to economic development (Sen, 1999). Human capital and capabilities are therefore strongly linked to institutions: in order to expand human capabilities, institutions are needed and appropriate institutional policies are necessary in order to create a skilled labour force, education and diffusion of knowledge. However, institutions need to be oriented towards providing opportunities both to the poor and to people in general.

### 6.3.3 Institutions, social capital and growth

Institutions also shape collective actions and therefore determine public choices, policies and organisation (Olson, 1982). In this context, institutions emerge as an important guide for investments in socio-economic dimensions such as health and education which have an important and positive impact on development (Tridico, 2007b). They limit what is right and what is wrong, what is appropriate and what is useless. They determine strategies and trajectories of changes. This is particularly important in countries experiencing significant transformation and affected not only by formal institutional change but also by informal rules.

As Sen (1999: 9) emphasised, 'a broad approach of this kind permits simultaneous appreciation of the vital roles, in the process of development, of many different institutions, including markets and market-related organizations, governments and local authorities, political parties and other civic institutions, educational arrangements and opportunities of open dialogue and debate (including the role of the media and other means of communication)'.

Formal and informal institutions implicitly include trust, respect for agreements and agreed rules, cooperative relations between agents, mutual confidence among the parties to an economic transaction, exchange of information and the circulation of knowledge, all of which lead to a higher level of *social capital* (Raiser, 1999; Kornai *et al.*, 2004). Increasingly, economists now focus on the relationship between social capital and economic growth. In fact, relationships of trust, loyalty, behavioural norms, cooperation, respect, certainty in economic relations and other similar factors seem to be a mirror of the intensity of economic relations, of economic exchange, of the self-reinforcement of rules and contracts, and of information and knowledge circulation. In order to perform better, an economic system needs all these elements, which can be defined as 'non-material factors'.

These 'non-material factors' also define the dimension of 'social capital', which impacts significantly and positively on human capital accumulation as well as on productivity. In fact, these factors eliminate or reduce problems due to the phenomena of adverse selection and moral hazard, lack of information, uncertainty, rent-seeking and free-riding (or opportunism). A higher level of trust may result in an increase in investment and/or higher education, an improvement in economic relations (Arrow, 1975), the overcoming of risk (Olson, 1982), the promotion of social interactions and therefore the creation of networks that allow for the flow of knowledge, the exchange of information, cooperation between agents and the creation of more productive clusters of innovation and of knowledge.[5] Therefore, the differences in these factors can create significant differences in the productivity and output of a country (Olson *et al.*, 1998).

Each society can have their own formal and informal rules, but what is important is that they provide a consistent institutional framework for a good business environment, reduce uncertainty and implement appropriate institutions and policies effectively. A consistent part of economic growth comes from the 'residual' or 'black box', which is not explained by traditional variables such as capital and labour (Solow, 1956). This residual, which is generally associated with technological progress, can be explained by the better endowment of some variables such as (formal and informal) institutions, organisation, human capital, infrastructures and above all social capital (Knack and Keefer, 1995; Olson *et al.*, 1998; Jones and Hall, 1999).

### 6.3.4 Human capital accumulation and social capital

The role of human capital with respect to an increase in the productivity and competitiveness of the productive systems is twofold: first, it is identified with the increment in productivity derived from the competencies of the workers as productive factors employed in the production processes of each firm; and, secondly, it appears as a complex series of externalities that favour the rate of innovation or technological progress within the whole system. Both these dimensions end up within the perspective of local systems, which can also be understood as regional innovation systems; these define a territory that is characterised by a set of institutions and knowledge about skilled human capital that is available to the productive system (Gunasekara, 2006). Within such a territory, the so-called *Triple Helix* model, involving cooperation between universities, firms and the state, is the main tool for the creation of networks, human capital and knowledge (Etzkowitz, 1997). In fact, at a local level, all the agents can cooperate better in order to create and disseminate innovation.

Social capital in this context stimulates cooperation processes, increases exchanges and the intensity of economic relations, stimulates the sharing of technologies and knowledge, reduces information asymmetries and reduces transaction costs to the great advantage of productivity. Moreover, both factors, that is, endogenous dynamics such as 'learning by doing' (Lucas, 1993) and the spread of innovation and knowledge due to the interaction between agents, are relevant. These factors are stimulated by geographic proximity and by different types of networks (Von Hipple, 1994; Loasby, 1999).

People investing in human capital will benefit from the jobs created by this compared to those who do not invest in human capital. Labour productivity will be lower in the latter case because skilled workers are usually more productive than unskilled workers. However, people do not always have sufficient resources to invest in advanced education. Therefore, the state and the firms must make the effort to guarantee advanced education and training to less skilled people by means of a partnership.

In this way, people will become more educated, human capital will grow and individual capabilities, i.e., opportunities, will increase as a direct consequence of the externalities coming from knowledge, with advantages for both individuals and society as a whole.

## 6.4 Economic development as a complex issue

As outlined above, explaining economic development is a complex issue because it is an outcome of the interaction of several factors, institutions and policies. Serious predictions on economic growth cannot assume that a single specific factor makes some countries richer than others. For instance, many exceptions can be raised to counter the idea that human capital is the main factor which contributes to growth: some countries such as Poland, Russia and Egypt have education levels which are very close to those in the richest economies, yet their GDP per capita is much lower. Another problem with human capital is the possibility of reverse causality between growth and education, and it is important to understand which one comes first and which causes which. Human capital is definitely an important factor for economic growth (Barro and Sala-i-Martin, 1995; Barro, 1998), but it has also been seen that differences in human capital alone can explain no more than one-fifth of the differences in living standards (Olson, 1996).

A similar argument can be put forward with regard to the relationship between technology and growth. Richer countries can afford high levels of R&D expenditure and they can enjoy positive returns and spill-over effects from this. Investment in technology is definitely correlated, both theoretically and empirically, with economic growth, but the root of the problem seems to be how countries can afford high levels of investment in technology and, at the same time, how some nations have more advanced technology than others (Yeager, 2004).

Another factor which is often considered to be very important for economic growth is natural resources (Shaban, 1987; Walker and Ryan, 1990). The USA, Norway, Germany and other richer countries possess abundant natural resources such as oil, coal and land. However, many other better or equally endowed countries such as Russia, Brazil, Nigeria, Venezuela and Saudi Arabia are not as rich, while other poorly endowed countries such as Japan, Singapore, Taiwan and Hong Kong are much richer.

The same exceptions can be found when considering trade and population density. In the first case, together with the success of some export-led countries such as Ireland and the 'Asian Tigers', the history of economies also successfully records cases of inward-oriented countries such as France and other old European Member States after the Second World War. Even the Asian Tigers, before entering the global economy, created a strong 'infant industry' and promoted import-substitution policies. From a theoretical point of view, similar contradictions can be traced between some economists who support the idea of a strong correlation between trade and growth (Galor and Mountford, 2003; Bhagwati, 2004) and others who minimise the impact of trade on growth (Krevise, 2000), arguing that in some cases negative effects such as inequality, wage discrimination and skilled and unskilled inequality seem to prevail (Nayyar, 2000). With regard to population density, today we cannot say that poverty is always associated with high density, as some economists, following Malthusian predictions, initially believed. Switzerland, Germany (and in particular the former West Germany) and newly industrialised Asian countries have a high population density, and this was not an obstacle to their economic development. In contrast, many Latin American countries such as Brazil and Mexico have a low population density, but this did not bring about development.

Hence, a comparative analysis reveals many problems and controversial aspects related to development. Economic growth does not seem to be associated with one single particular factor that is able to bring about development. No single factor is able to explain economic differences between countries. Moreover, the failure of the WC during the 1990s in several countries such as Mexico, Argentina and Russia (Stiglitz, 1998; Rodrik, 2004) also showed that there is no single economic policy formula suitable for all countries, while interaction between variables, national institutions and path dependency can better explain the recent economic success of many countries in Asia or the economic boom of some European countries after the Second World War (Rodrik, 1999).

Transition economies are, in general, economies with a middling per capita income and with an existing industrial structure. By the end of the 1980s, most transition economies were already experiencing economic stagnation due to several factors encompassing among other things economic and political issues. Development in transition economies is a complex issue which cannot only include growth eventually achieved through market economy reforms. In FCEs, the transformation from a planned economy to a market economy was mainly perceived by economists and policy makers simply as a combination of liberalisation, privatisation and stabilisation (LPS). This formula, associated with democratisation, brought about limited success in some countries such as Poland, the Czech Republic and Hungary, while in others it was less associated with democratisation, such as in the cases of Russia, Romania, Bulgaria and many other FSRs, in which it brought about failures and lower income levels than had been the case before transition. On the contrary, in China and a few other emerging economies where heterodox policies were implemented, there was no consensus on the abovementioned LPS formula, yet China's economic growth is defined as 'phenomenal' and its economic success is real (McMillan and Naughton, 1992; O'Neill *et al.*, 2005). China's success occurred without complete liberalisation, without privatisation and without democratisation (Qian, 2003). In 1988, China's GDP was half that of Russia's, but in 1998, Russia's GDP was half that of China's. Markets incentives occurred without liberalisation and secure private property rights.

China was poor, overpopulated, short of human capital and natural resources, and was constrained by an ideology which was hostile towards markets. Nevertheless, GDP growth took place and was, under such initial conditions, really surprising (Qian, 2003). GDP in China has already surpassed those of the largest European economies (Italy, France, the UK and Germany) and it is today even greater than Japan, which was the second largest economy after the USA (*The Economist*, 2010).

## 6.5 Final comments

In this chapter, some of the main traditional growth theories such as exogenous and endogenous growth theories were briefly illustrated. However, it was argued that these theories are not fully relevant in explaining economic development among transition economies. A more complex and holistic approach is needed. This approach, which will be developed in the following two chapters, mainly requires the interaction of socio-economic variables with institutions. New variables such as people's capabilities and social capital will be introduced. I assume that this interaction first brings about human development, which in turn leads to economic growth.

# 7
# Institutions, Human Development, Economic Growth[1]

## 7.1 Introduction

The main contribution of this chapter is to synthesise the interconnections between institutional change, economic growth and human development in order to see whether, at an empirical level, a relationship of causality exists between these three factors. It is mainly an empirical chapter dealing with the tests and econometric models hypothesised.

The main hypothesis can be synthesised as follows: the interaction between appropriate institutions and socio-economic variables, such as expenditure on education and health, improves the endowment of people's capabilities and leads to better human development. In turn, an improvement in human development variables, such as education levels and life expectancy, causes an acceleration process in economic growth. As such, the neoclassical paradigm is reversed and the trickle-down effect according to which economic growth brings about human development (improvements in life expectancy and education) does not apply.

## 7.2 Social costs of transition economics

When we analyse the social side of transition economies, we observe that these economies are affected by very high unemployment rates (Transition Report, 2004), a growing inequality rate (measured by Gini coefficients) and a high index of poverty (where, according to OECD, 2000, the percentage of workers among those people in poverty represents the majority). Moreover, informal economies and corruption strongly persist (Kaufmann and Kaliberda, 1995). Obviously, among transition economies, situations are highly differentiated. Among the most advanced CEECs, it is evident that the Czech Republic, Estonia, Hungary, Slovakia and Slovenia experienced a smaller recovery in GDP compared with Poland, but they have a lower poverty rate, a lower level of inequality, a lower unemployment rate, a lower level of corruption and a less informal economy. This can be partly explained by the fact that Poland, during the first part of the 1990s, adopted an extreme 'shock therapy' policy which had the effect of squeezing the economy, increasing unemployment and reducing people's purchasing power (Kolodko and Nuti, 1997).

During the transition period, many people became poorer. In 1989, about 14 million people in those countries lived on $4 a day. In the mid-1990s, this number had increased to 147 million (UNDP, 2000). Economic benefits were not well distributed and today, particularly in the FSRs, most people have a lower living standard than they had done prior to 1989. The impoverishment of people is the consequence of the economic crisis of the early and mid-1990s: a huge fall in output, very high unemployment, a reduction in real wages and a rise in income inequalities.

However, poverty increased differently among the transition economies (Beblo *et al.*, 2002; Ruminska-Zimny, 1997). Most of the poor people are concentrated in the FSRs, where the initial poverty level was already significant, whereas in the Czech Republic, Hungary, Slovakia and Slovenia, the increase in poverty was modest at around 6–9 per cent (UNICEF, 1995).[2] Among the CEECs, a high level of poverty is present in Poland, Romania and Bulgaria. The Baltic countries and the Slavic countries of the CIS also experienced a significant increase in poverty levels, while in the Asian republics of the CIS, where pre-1989 poverty was already significant, the poverty level reached the dramatic levels of around 80–90 per cent of the population. In the Caucasus, poverty is exacerbated by military conflicts and civil wars. UNICEF (1995) estimated a poverty level in Armenia and Azerbaijan of around 65 per cent, while in Georgia, wages ($5 a month) were below the minimum subsistence level of $31 a month (Ruminska-Zimny, 1997).

However, among many transition economies, it can be seen that despite the fact that some countries like Bulgaria, Latvia, Lithuania, Poland, Romania and to some extent Russia have managed to stabilise their economies, they still suffer from numerous social problems. These problems are consistent in most of the CIS. The consistent rise in poverty was caused by the collapse in GDP, a dramatic fall in real wages and an increase in inequality. After 1992, poverty stabilised at a high level but inequality continued to increase. Inequality was due to many factors such as liberalisation, privatisation and wage differentials (Cornia, 2003). The ensuing fast growth caused important wage differentials between skilled and unskilled workers (Rutkowski, 1996; Alam *et al.*, 2005).

The dynamic of the Gini coefficient shows a consistent increase in inequality in the first part of the transition in Poland (when a shock therapy policy was implemented), whereas in the second part it was more stable. The same phenomenon occurred in another 'shock therapist' country – the Czech Republic. Hungary, on the other hand, managed the transition through gradual therapy that was more socially oriented and institutionally aware.

Economic transition was very costly in social terms, particularly in the FSRs. These countries, together with the former Yugoslav countries, experienced tragic events, civil wars, crime and the worst example of a chaos economy. Moreover, in almost all the CIS, the WC paradigm was strictly implemented. Social and institutional policies, which would allow for institutional governance, the protection of weaker and poorer people and conflict management, were almost completely missing. The abrupt introduction of the market economy and the end of social policies, the welfare state and income redistribution policies caused an increase in poverty, inequality and unemployment rates (Adam, 1999).

Table 7.1 clearly shows the differences among transition economies in terms of several socio-economic variables. The most advanced transition economies are the CEEC 5+. In contrast, the FSRs (today the CIS) are the worst performing. Differences are clear not only in terms of economic performance but also in social dimensions such as inequality, poverty, life expectancy and in terms of political institutions (voice and accountability, and freedom). These variables, along with economic growth, should be taken into consideration when assessing socio-economic development.

In a very interesting article, Kovalik (2001) states that the 'best performing' transition economies are still affected by many social problems, which were eliminated or greatly reduced long ago by the older EU Member States. He refers to the increase in poverty, inequality, corruption, gender discrimination, unemployment, poverty among farmers and workers, and income divergences between regions within the same country. The worst performing transition economies are more greatly affected by these social problems, and their transformation seems to worsen such human indicators as life expectancy, education levels and living standards (Blazyca and Rapacki, 2001; Stuckler *et al.*, 2009).

*Table 7.1* Socio-economic and institutional indicators among transition economies (groups of countries)

| | CEEC 5+ | CEEC 5– | Balkans | CIS |
|---|---|---|---|---|
| Poverty level 2006 (% of population with $4 a day) | 13.8 | 27.2 | 25.2 | 52.4 |
| Gini coefficient 2006 | 30.2 | 32.2 | 33.0 | 35.0 |
| Life expectancy in years 2007 | 73.6 | 70.8 | 72.2 | 66.9 |
| Voice and accountability average 2000–5 | 1.04 | 0.84 | 0.10 | –0.94 |
| Political stability average 2000–5 | 0.78 | 0.64 | –0.49 | –0.59 |
| Freedom index 2000–6 | 3.0 | 3.0 | 2.5 | 1.4 |
| Unemployment rate 2007 (%) | 14.8 | 11.0 | 22.0 | 6.4 |

*Source*: World Bank, EBRD, UNDP

We can therefore generally state that many shadows darken the balance of that transformation, and the social costs in terms of unemployment, poverty, the reduction of well-being and increases in inequality are very significant. With this in mind, Nuti (1999: 6) stated: 'It seems therefore, and perhaps it is not surprising, that the transformation of former communist countries has passed from a central planning system to pure and simple underdevelopment, with the hope but not the certainty of a faster path towards the prosperity of advanced countries with a market economy.'

## 7.3 From institutions to development through capability

In its report on transition economies, the UNDP stated that, at the beginning of transformation in many transition economies, 'freedom has been accompanied by the loss of many *basic economic and social rights*' (UNDP, 2000: 12, emphasis added). This negatively affected people's capabilities of doing and being. Simultaneously, their economic and social freedom, in Sen's terms of 'development as freedom', worsened because many opportunities disappeared. Hence, today, in the worst performing transition economies (basically all of the CIS and a few CEECs), people acquired, in the best-case scenario, a political voice but no freedom in general terms.

The core idea maintained in this book is that those countries that have experienced an increase in human development will have sustained economic growth as a consequence of an expansion of people's capabilities. In order to reach a better level of capability endowment, both appropriate institutions and investments in specific socio-economic dimensions need to be put forward. A theoretical model underpinning such an argument would be identified by the following scheme:

*Institutions→ Capabilities & Human Development → Growth with Development*

where *institutions*, rules and social norms effectively enlarge capabilities by the way in which they structure political institutions and rights (freedom, democracy, participation) and social rights (public recourses for collective purposes). Public investments in socio-economic dimensions (such as education and health) improve people's range of choices and increase their chances of improving their living standards.

My assumption concerning political institutions is this: a country which is governed more democratically and where political institutions are oriented towards freedom, guaranteeing people participation and political rights, is a country where citizens can have some power and can lobby those who govern. Consequently, public decisions in such a country would be oriented more towards collective benefits than would be the case in a country where the level of democracy and freedom is less marked. A country that enjoys greater democracy, freedom and political rights would extend people's capabilities more easily than one where these rights are restricted. Such a restriction would cause a lower level of human capital (and of human development) and lower economic growth.

Such an assumption is represented in Figure 7.1, which describes a so-called capability curve. This curve is determined by the level of political institutions and the level of guarantees of democracy and freedom enjoyed by the people. Starting from a positive level of capability at point A, characterised by a positive endowment of capability (initially, even in the most authoritative country, people have some level of capability), the curve shows a positive trend. However, the level of political rights increases faster than the level of capabilities because, even if countries guarantee some political rights, the level of capabilities grows more slowly since it also depends on effective public policies supporting social rights (Nussbaum, 2000). Nevertheless, at an advanced stage, political

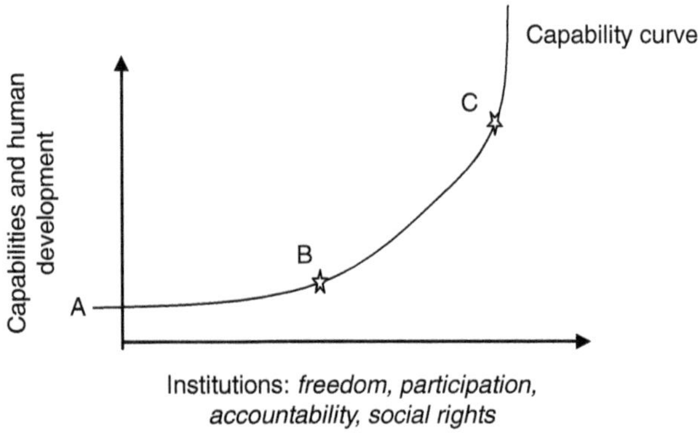


*Figure 7.1* The capability curve

pressure and democratic lobbying can stimulate those who govern into taking public decisions, which will have collective benefits in social terms (Sen, 1999). This would positively affect the trend of capabilities, which would now grow faster than political rights from point B to point C. After point C, the level of political rights would grow at a very slow rate. However, during this period, people's capabilities can increase because participation is very high and democracy is developed. The number of social rights that can be distributed by those who govern is also an important factor. Many countries among today's developed economies can be identified as being in this situation. Most developing economies fall short of point B and many transition (and emerging) economies stay between point B and point C. Point B represents a crucial one in the sense that countries that manage to overcome it can experience a process of institutional change with positive effects on their capability and hence on their development.

The graph in Figure 7.1 can be approximately tested using a regression model in which the institutions are taken as independent variables and the non-income human development variables, i.e., the education and the life expectancy indices (a proxy for capabilities), are taken as dependent variables. Capabilities, and therefore human development, are enlarged by institutions, such as political rights (freedom, democracy, participation) and social rights (public recourses for collective purposes). In the model I use, there are two political institution indicators, which represent freedom and participation respectively: the freedom index (from Freedom House) and the voice and accountability index (from the World Bank). Public investments in socio-economic dimensions such as education and health improve the range of choices for people and increase the chances of improving their living standards.[3] Expenditure on education and health is considered as the percentage of public expenditure on GDP.

However, sometimes expenditure on education alone is no longer sufficient to improve the education level in a country, because education, unlike health, is not a passive variable. Education requires the active participation of people in order to be effective, and sometimes people are limited in their actions and constrained in their opportunities. Expenditure on education therefore needs to be associated with people's accountability and participation to produce a higher education index. My hypothesis is that interaction between voice and accountability and expenditure on education, together with expenditure on health and freedom, produces effective results on human development. The equation model would then be the following:

$$HD = \alpha + \beta_1 HealthExp + \beta_2 Freedom + \beta_3 Participation \; \& \; Edu + \varepsilon$$

The dependent variable, human development (HD),[4] is an average of the education index (EI) and the life expectancy index (LEI). The regression results of a cross-country analysis among all the 28 transition economies shown in Table 7.2 are very interesting. Two models were tested. The first was where HD is regressed against expenditure on health (average 2000–5), expenditure on education (average 2000–5), the freedom index (average 2000–5) and the voice and accountability index (average 2000–5). In this model, both expenditure on education and voice and accountability are not significant. The education variable even appears to be negative. The second model included, along with expenditure on health and freedom, an interaction variable made up of expenditure on education and voice and accountability, and it excludes the two single variables (expenditure on education and the voice and accountability index). This last model is the only one which produces significant and consistent results with regard to the dependent variable.

The most interesting result of this model is the statistical significance of the variable V&A_Edu (voice and accountability*expenditure on education), which has a positive impact on HD. It means that within the model represented in Regression II, in a multivariate correlation, together with other positive values of the expenditure on health *and* freedom index variables, *interaction* (and only interaction) between expenditure on *education* and *voice and accountability* would consistently improve the explanatory power of the model. In fact, the expenditure on education and voice and accountability variables are not significant

*Table 7.2* Regression analysis for HD variables (average LEI and EI)

| **OLS model – Obs. 28<br>Dependent variable: HD (average LEI and EI) 2007** | | | |
|---|---|---|---|
| **I. Regression with education and voice and accountability** | | **II. Regression with interaction between voice and accountability and education** | |
| **Variables** | **Coeff.** | **Variables** | **Coeff.** |
| Expenditure on health | .0066548** (.0031919) | Expenditure on health | .0052873** (.0027672) |
| Freedom | 0096823* (.0030409) | Freedom | .0122228* (.0025019) |
| Expenditure on education (Edu) | −.0017852 (.0063819) | V&A_Edu | .0000709** (.0000377) |
| Voice and accountablity (V&A) | .0010574 (.0010265) | | |
| Constant | 780512* (.0182849) | Constant | .7685463* (.0093681) |
| **R-squared** 0.7792 = Adj R-squared 0.7240 | | **R-squared** 0.7940 Adj R-squared 0.8221 | |
| Mean dependent var. 0.8467 | | Mean dependent var. 0.8467 | |
| Prob(F-statistic) 0.000000 | | Prob(F-statistic) 0.000000 | |

*Source*: author's elaboration. Significance level at * = 1 per cent, ** = 5 per cent; *** = 10 per cent. Robust standard errors in parenthesis, controlled for heteroskedasticity after White tests

when they appear in the model without interaction (Regression I).[5] Expenditure on education is no longer sufficient on its own; neither is voice and accountability. Therefore, the state has not only to guarantee education through public expenditure on education, it also has to create a framework which would allow for individuals to use that education. Voice and accountability, i.e., people's participation in public life and accountability, is assumed as an indicator in such a framework, which, in interaction with expenditure on education, allows for the level of HD to increase.

In order to avoid, at least partially, endogeneity problems, I did not include GDP as a dependent variable:[6] I regress expenditure on health, freedom and the interaction variable (voice and accountability* expenditure on education) against the HD variable (i.e., an average between life expectancy and education levels) which does not include, for this purpose, the GDP index. For an interesting finding on this, see Binder and Georgiadis (2010).

## 7.4 From human development to economic growth

The literature on transition economics, apart from an analysis of poverty and social costs, has ignored human development. The human development level in transition economies is relatively high due to investments made in social dimensions by the previous regimes. Nevertheless, the transition process influenced the non-income dimensions of people, often worsening the main indicators (Ruminska-Zimny, 1997). Death rates increased and life expectancy, particularly in the CIS and in the Baltic states, declined. The second dimension of the HDI, access to education, also slowed. After 1989, public expenditure on education decreased as a consequence of a drop in GDP, and the public education system worsened.[7] The same thing occurred with public expenditure on health, which contracted in many countries because of a slump in GDP. Moreover, lack of investment and technology in this sector contributed to a reduction in the relatively high standard (with respect to the world average) of those countries during the previous regimes. Today, services and performances are negatively affected by obsolete infrastructures, hospitals, equipment, machines, etc. Very often, the partial or total privatisation of the national healthcare services contributed to creating a second-class healthcare system. People with low incomes and the losers of the transition period towards 'marketisation' cannot afford the more expensive and more advanced private healthcare services.

However, the situation is very different among CEECs and the CIS, and further detailed observations are needed. First of all, transition economies have an average level of human development, inherited from the communist era, of 0.796, which is above the world average (0.729) and is higher than all other countries, except for OECD countries (0.911). Secondly, different initial conditions among transition economies are evident in terms of human development and GDP per capita (see the appendix to this chapter for detailed data). Thirdly, countries which during transition implemented institutional policies, social policies and good governance, filling the initial *power vacuum*, increased their level of human development. Finally, countries with a higher level of human development performed better in terms of GDP growth and recovery than countries with a lower level of human development at the beginning of transition. Therefore, a higher level of human development seems to be the major cause of faster economic growth.

By contrast, countries that did not implement institutional policies of this kind did not increase their level of human development, and economic growth was neither fast enough nor sufficient for the pre-1989 level of GDP per capita to be recovered.

The model which would thus represent the idea of a process of growth deriving from human development is as follows:

$$GDPppp = \mathrm{a} + \mathrm{B}^{*}\mathrm{HD\ variables} + \mathrm{e}$$

$$\text{and more explicitly: } \mathrm{GDP} = \mathrm{a} + \mathrm{B}^{*}\mathrm{LEI} + \mathrm{B}^{*}\mathrm{EI} + \mathrm{e}$$

In other words, the per capita GDP in PPP is a function of the two non-income components of the human development index, i.e., the life expectancy and education indices, with a term of error (e).

This is a very interesting point which is confirmed by the regression model below. The exercise of the regression model was made twice: with 2002 data, after 13 years of transition, and with 2008 data, after almost 20 years of transition. In the first exercise, using an OLS method, it is found that GDP per capita (in US$ at PPP) is positively and strongly correlated with two 'pure' human development variables.[8] In the cross-section regression, the 'life expectancy index' and the 'education index' for 26 transition economies are used as independent variables for human development, and the GDP per capita (in US$ PPP)[9] is used as a dependent variable (see Tridico, 2007a for more details about data used in this first regression). The results seem to indicate a very clear correlation between the two human development variables and GDP. The former seems to determine the latter.[10]

Hence, the equation which explains GDP per capita among transition economies, according to the coefficients used in Table 7.3 below, would be:

$$GDPppp = C + \beta_1 \cdot LEI + \beta_2 \cdot EI + \varepsilon_i$$

where LEI and EI are respectively the life expectancy index and the education index, C is the constant, $\beta_1$ and $\beta_2$ are the two coefficients which appear in the table above and $\varepsilon$ is the error term. The explicit equation, with the two human development variables LEI and EI, substituted for each country, is:

$$GDPppp = -2.56 + 1.66^{*}LEI + 2.13^{*}EI + \varepsilon$$

In the second econometric exercise, I repeated the regression model with the most recent human development data concerning education and

*Table 7.3* Human development versus GDP, 2002

| **Dependent variable: GDP per capita (US$, PPP)**<br>**Method: least squares**<br>**Included observations: 26** | | | |
|---|---|---|---|
| **Variable** | **Coefficient** | **Std. Error** | **P-Value** |
| Life expectancy index | 1.661743 | 0.414746 | 0.0006* |
| Education index | 2.127335 | 0.538301 | 0.0006* |
| Constant | −2.563643 | 0.627456 | 0.0005* |
| **Adjusted R-squared 0.545264**<br>Log likelihood 26.54466<br>Durbin-Watson stat 1.193667<br>Prob(F-statistic) 0.000116 | | | |

**Significance at 1 per cent level.*
*Source*: Author's elaboration based on UNDP data

life expectancy after almost 20 years of transition. The results are even more robust than before. GDP in PPP in 2008 is explained by human development variables such as the education index and life expectancy (at 2007 values; see the appendix to this chapter for data used in this regression). Table 7.4 shows the results.

*Table 7.4* Human development versus GDP, 2008

| **Dependent variable: GDP per capita 2008 (US$, PPP)**<br>**Method: least squares**<br>**Included observations: 28** | | | |
|---|---|---|---|
| **Variable** | **Coefficient** | **Std. Error** | **P-Value** |
| Life expectancy index | 53,177.6 | 0.414746 | 0.000* |
| Education index | 127,157.2 | 0.538301 | 0.000* |
| Constant | −148,035.4 | 0.627456 | 0.000* |
| **R-squared 0.7491 Adjusted R-squared 0.7290**<br>Prob(F-statistic) = 0.0000 | | | |

**Significance at 1 per cent level.*
*Source*: Author's elaboration based on UNDP data

A simple one-way ANOVA test was carried out in order to verify whether the mean of the dependent variable (*y*) is statistically significant among different categories of the independent variable (*x*) and to measure the strength of the relationships (Kachigan, 1986: 273). In particular, we are here interested in testing whether life expectancy and education levels have some effects on GDP. The analysis of Tables 7.5 and 7.6 brings about the following output, which suggest positive results for this.

*Table 7.5* Analysis of variance, life expectancy index and GDP

| Source | SS | df | MS | F | Prob > F |
|---|---|---|---|---|---|
| Between groups | 1.0845e+09 | 27 | 41712019.7 | 1755.41 | 0.0189 |
| Within groups | 23762 | 1 | 23762 | | |
| Total | 1.0845e+09 | 28 | 40168010.1 | | |

*Table 7.6* Analysis of variance, education index and GDP

| Source | SS | df | MS | F | Prob > F |
|---|---|---|---|---|---|
| Between groups | 1.3898e+09 | 26 | 53455245.9 | 1683.14 | 0.0193 |
| Within groups | 31759.2602 | 1 | 31759.2602 | | |
| Total | 1.3899e+09 | 27 | 51476598.2 | | |

In both cases, the probability of F is significant and this strengthens the relationships between the independent variables and the GDP. Moreover, a risk of multicollarineity is excluded by the high level of tolerance (1/VIF = 0.99).

Finally, in order to further test the direction causality hypothesis, at least specifically with regard to transition economies, a Granger causality test was also carried out for both econometric exercises (Tridico, 2007a).

The results are very interesting. In particular, as Tables 7.7 and 7.8 show, the two null hypotheses *Education Index and Life Expectancy Index do not Granger cause GDP* cannot be accepted. On the contrary, the other two null hypotheses, *GDP does not Granger cause Education Index and Life Expectancy Index*, are accepted at a five per cent significance level.

These results are consistent with the findings of Binder and Georgiadis (2010), who wrote a UNDP paper showing that HDI development differs notably from that of GDP, and the HDI adjustment process is slower

*Table 7.7* Multicollarineity between the education index and the life expectancy index

```
Variable|          VIF          1/VIF
-------------------------------------
edu_index|         1.00         0.997207
life_idex|         1.00         0.997207
-------------------------------------
Mean VIF|          1.00
```

*Table 7.8* Granger causality test

| **Pairwise Granger causality tests** | | | |
|---|---|---|---|
| **Included observations: 26** | | | |
| **Null hypothesis** | **F-Statistic** | **Probability** | **Hp** |
| EDUCATION does not Granger cause GDP | 0.07391 | 0.92902 | Rejected |
| GDP does not Granger cause EDUCATION | 5.17497 | 0.01607* | Accepted |
| LIFE does not Granger cause GDP | 0.25266 | 0.77930 | Rejected |
| GDP does not Granger cause LIFE | 3.70301 | 0.04385* | Accepted |

*Asterisks denote the acceptable causality hypothesis at a 5 per cent significance level.*
*Source*: Author's elaboration

than that for GDP. Most importantly, some macro-economic policies such as international trade integration and stimulation of investment in physical capital may have an effect on GDP but not on HDI. HDI development policies should look beyond the realm of GDP development policies and should focus directly on human development variables.

The trend of the HDI during transition is very heterogeneous and varies according to the policies and institutions implemented. In Poland, for instance, the HDI in the first part of transition (1990–5) passed from 0.802 to a mere 0.816, whereas at the end of the second part of transition (in 2002) it reached 0.85. That is why in the second part of transition, appropriate institutional policies, governance mechanisms and socially-oriented policies were introduced. These policies made it possible to recover from the decline of the first part of transition, a decline that was probably caused, at least in part, by the use of a shock therapy programme. In the second part of transition, in fact, a more socially-oriented institutional programme was implemented with the introduction of the so-called 'Strategy for Poland'. In Hungary as in

Slovenia, a gradual macro-economic approach to transition was implemented from the beginning and it made the introduction of appropriate institutions and social policies possible, avoiding the power vacuum that occurred in other transition countries.

## 7.5 Growth without development in transition economies

The two exercises confirmed that, in general, only countries which experienced an increase in their HDI (that is, the Czech Republic, Hungary, Poland, Slovenia and to some extent Estonia) had sustained economic growth. These countries benefited from appropriate institutional reforms and have the best World Bank and EBRD indices. Therefore, it would seem that human development is a sufficient but not necessary condition for economic growth in transition economies. This means that there can be economic growth without human development, but if there is human development, then there will definitely be economic growth. This is confirmed by a one-by-one performance observation in terms of growth and human development below.

In the FSRs, the lack of any implementation of institutional policy was lethal. Socially-oriented policies were suddenly replaced by an economy of chaos and a free market without institutions. The withdrawal of the state from the economy caused a colossal fall in output and an explosion in unemployment levels. Social indicators immediately worsened. As a result, the relatively high HDI of those countries decreased or, at best, did not increase during the 1990s. Consequently, economic growth was negative.

The Czech Republic, Estonia, Hungary, Poland and Slovenia perform better in terms of HDI trends and, apart from Estonia,[11] did not experience a negative HDI change during transition (see Table 7.9 below). Consequently, these countries experienced faster GDP growth and reached or overtook their pre-1989 level of GDP per capita before 2000. Between 1993 and 1997, Hungary and Poland in particular adopted socially-oriented policies and institutions which made HDI growth and GDP growth possible simultaneously. However, human development was not concurrent with GDP growth for all the countries during transition. On the contrary, the empirical evidence is quite diverse and controversial, as Table 7.9 shows. First of all, when we rank countries for GDP and for HDI, we discover that the GDP rank does not correspond entirely to the HDI rank. On the basis of this, we can divide transition economies into three main groups:

*Table 7.9* HDI and GDP, 1989–2009

| | HDI rank | GDP rank | HDI-GDP rank | GDP per capita 2008 (in US$) | HDI 2007 | Average GDP growth 1989–2008 (in %) | Percentage change in HDI 1990–2007 |
|---|---|---|---|---|---|---|---|
| Slovenia | 1 | 1 | = | 27,168 | 0.920 | 2.00 | 7.60 |
| Czech Republic | 2 | 2 | = | 25,395 | 0.895 | 1.58 | 5.99 |
| Hungary | 3 | 6 | −3 | 15,326 | 0.879 | 1.19 | 8.49 |
| Poland | 4 | 9 | −5 | 13,839 | 0.872 | 2.81 | 8.24 |
| Estonia | 5 | 4 | +1 | 16,508 | 0.870 | 1.00 | 3.33* |
| Slovakia | 6 | 3 | +3 | 18,249 | 0.870 | 2.37 | 6.21 |
| Lithuania | 7 | 8 | −1 | 14,018 | 0.870 | 0.59 | 5.58 |
| Croatia | 8 | 5 | +3 | 15,552 | 0.350 | 0.55 | 5.30 |
| Latvia | 9 | 7 | +2 | 14,909 | 0.850 | 1.06 | 5.22 |
| Bulgaria | 10 | 14 | −4 | 6,561 | 0.826 | 0.60 | 3.89 |
| Serbia | 11 | 13 | −2 | 6,761 | 0.823 | −0.90 | NA |
| Montenegro | 12 | 15 | −3 | 6,509 | 0.822 | 0.05 | NA |
| Romania | 13 | 11 | +2 | 9,186 | 0.820 | 0.72 | 6.30 |
| Russia | 14 | 10 | +4 | 12,075 | 0.807 | 1.46 | −0.75 |

*Table 7.9* (Continued)

| | | | | | | | |
|---|---|---|---|---|---|---|---|
| Bosnia and Herzegovina | 15 | 18 | −3 | 4,834 | 0.807 | 6.88 (1996–2008) | 3.33* |
| Belarus | 16 | 16 | = | 6,286 | 0.800 | 2.50 | 1.90 |
| Macedonia | 17 | 19 | −2 | 4,761 | 0.800 | −0.08 | 0.88* |
| Albania | 18 | 20 | −2 | 4,066 | 0.790 | 3.65 | 11.27 |
| Ukraine | 19 | 21 | −2 | 3,937 | 0.784 | −1.59 | −1.80 |
| Kazakhstan | 20 | 12 | +8 | 8,736 | 0.770 | 1.70 | 0.39 |
| Armenia | 21 | 22 | −1 | 3,711 | 0.770 | 3.06 | 2.52 |
| Azerbaijan | 22 | 17 | +5 | 5,507 | 0.760 | 3.67 | 1.88* |
| Turkmenistan | 23 | 23 | = | 2,916 | 0.760 | 3.28 | 1.06* |
| Georgia | 24 | 24 | = | 2,845 | 0.750 | −1.46 | 1.49* |
| Uzbekistan | 25 | 26 | −1 | 1,007 | 0.720 | 2.47 | 4.65 |
| Moldova | 26 | 25 | +1 | 1,766 | 0.718 | −2.05 | −2.64 |
| Kyrgyzstan | 27 | 27 | = | 952 | 0.710 | 0.35 | 1.28* |
| Tajikistan | 28 | 28 | = | 795 | 0.690 | −0.02 | −4.27 |

* = HDI change for the period 2002–7

*Source*: UNDP, *Human Development Report* (2004) and *Transition Report* (2008)

1. The first group is made up of countries like Poland and Hungary which have a better position in terms of HDI than in terms of GDP, as Table 7.9 shows (see the 'HDI-GDP rank' column – all the countries appearing with a minus sign in this column are in this better position).
2. The second group is made up of countries such as Azerbaijan, Kazakhstan and Russia, which have a relatively better position in terms of GDP than in terms of HDI (all the countries appearing with a positive value in the 'HDI-GDP rank' column are in this worse position). This group is mainly comprised of countries which, at best, experienced growth without development.
3. The third group is made up of countries like Slovenia and the Czech Republic that have the same position in terms of HDI and of GDP.

Clearly, some of the countries of the first and the third group, like the Czech Republic, Hungary, Poland and Slovenia, can be considered to be the best performing transition economies in terms of both human development and economic growth. Some other countries in these two groups, despite their increasing trend in HDI, still have very low levels of both GDP and HDI.

Such cleavages underline the worsening position of the second group of countries in the development path during transformation. As regards this group, we can say that even if these countries grew in terms of GDP, recovering the level that they had in 1989, human development would not grow concurrently.

## 7.6 Country classification on the basis of HDI and GDP

On the basis of the analysis carried out so far, five groups of countries can be identified as follows:

1. Countries that *clearly* increased both their levels of HDI and their GDP. These are limited in number (the Czech Republic, Hungary, Slovenia, Poland and to some extent Estonia)[12] and are found where, sooner or later, socially-oriented reforms, institutional strategies, income distribution policies, conflict management institutions, social pacts and welfare supports were introduced during the 1990s. Along with these countries, one can add Albania. However, Albania, like Estonia, experienced a deeper decline of GDP at the beginning of the 1990s, started the transition from much lower levels and its GDP performance was relatively good, although a bit unstable, during

the past two decades of transition; therefore, the path of development was less consistent than that in the Czech Republic, Hungary, Poland and Slovenia. Apart from Albania, all these countries[13] now have the highest levels of both GDP and HDI (making them the top five transition economies).

2. Countries that experienced an increase in income without a simultaneous and corresponding increase in HDI (that is, Croatia, Latvia, Lithuania and Slovakia). However, these countries, in the second part of transition after 2000, improved in terms of their HDI levels as well and are now in the second group in terms of HDI levels, with a value around 0.85–0.87. In this group one has to underline the position of Slovakia which, although it has consistently overcome its 1989 GDP level (with a value today of 142), did not have the same good performance in terms of HDI in the first part of transition. Croatia, Latvia and Lithuania, which are also in this group, have just reached (Croatia) or are about to reach (Latvia and Lithuania) their pre-1989 GDP levels, but their HDI is increasing above their levels in the 1990s. All these countries were among the CEECs that experienced the worst recessions at the beginning of the 1990s.
3. A *sui generis* group is made up of Bulgaria and Romania, which have a similar value of HDI (around 0.80). Romania and Bulgaria experienced the worst recessions among the CEECs and they are considered to be the worst performing Central and Eastern European economies, with very bad indicators of institutional reforms. Moreover, although the position of Romania seems better in terms of GDP, with an income higher than that of Bulgaria, the latter is able to have a higher HDI vis-à-vis its relatively low GDP level.
4. Belarus, Turkmenistan and Uzbekistan, which are very poor countries, form a distinct group. These three countries did not experience a consistent decline in GDP at the beginning of the 1990s. However, they are basically still planned economies and do not enjoy pluralism and a high level of democracy. They are slow and inconsistent in terms of reform, but their level of GDP today is much higher than that of 1989. In my classification of varieties of capitalism, they are considered to form part of the state model of capitalism.
5. The majority of countries, including the three state capitalist countries mentioned above, experienced a reduction in HDI and a reduction in income levels, at least during the first part of transition, until 2000–5. Most of them are part of the CIS: Armenia, Azerbaijan, Georgia, Kazakhstan, Kyrgyzstan, Moldova, Russia, Tajikistan and Ukraine. Bosnia and Herzegovina, Macedonia and Serbia and

Montenegro are part of this group too, but are not part of the CIS. With few exceptions (Armenia, Azerbaijan and Kazakhstan, which now have GDP levels much higher than those of 1989, thanks to recent fast economic growth), they are the worst performing transition economies, with the lowest levels of GDP per capita of the transition economies. Their levels of GDP are still below those of 1989. They also have the lowest HDI values. Common to all these countries is the reduction in life expectancy which underlines an absolute reduction in living standards and in the well-being of people. Such a reduction also happened, to some extent, in the CEECs. Among the CIS, and therefore among all transition economies, the worst situation can be found in Georgia, Kyrgyzstan, Moldova, Russia, Tajikistan and Ukraine, where the levels of both HDI and GDP are still lower today than they were in 1989–90. The poorest country is Tajikistan ($795 per capita) which also has the lowest HDI level (0.69) and about 92 per cent of the GDP level of 1989. This is followed by Kyrgyzstan ($952 per capita), with about 94 per cent of the GDP level of 1989 and with the second lowest HDI level (0.710). Moldova is the third poorest country in terms of HDI (0.718) and the fourth lowest in terms of GDP ($1,776 per capita) after Uzbekistan ($1,007 per capita). However, Moldova has the lowest GDP level in comparison with that of 1989, at only 57 per cent. Ukraine follows Moldova in this respect with 60 per cent of the GDP level of 1989 and with a GDP per capita of $3,937. Georgia, one of the most troubled countries in political terms, has a GDP per capita of $2,845 and only 73 per cent of the GDP level that it had in 1989. All in all, the CIS are very poor countries, affected not only by a systemic recession that was deeper than in other transition economies but that was also exacerbated, in some cases, by wars and political troubles, with the highest levels of poverty and inequality among transition economies. Average GDP per capita among the CIS is $4,211, which is just about what they had 20 years ago in 1989! Russia, after a decline in GDP equal to half of its 1989 level, experienced a significant recovery and today its GDP level is 97 per cent of that of 1989. However, inequality here is the highest among transition economies (with a Gini coefficient of 42 per cent) and economic growth was not at all pro-poor. On the contrary, it was an oil-driven, 'pro-oligarch growth' and it did not produce much improvement in human development for society as a whole. I also put in this group of worst performing countries Bosnia and Herzegovina, Macedonia and Serbia and Montenegro. Although they had better initial conditions than the CIS, their political situation and the war during the 1990s drastically affected their socio-economic performance, and GDP and human development declined strongly. However, these countries still have higher GDP per capita and HDI than the average in the CIS. Nevertheless, their levels are below those of 1989.

## 7.7 Final comments

In this chapter we saw that in 2009, the average GDP in PPP among transition economies is approximately the same as it had been in 1989. In fact, the average GDP level in 2008 was close to the 1989 level considering all the transition economies together, with a level of 117. The current economic situation hit all transition economies dramatically, and at the end of 2009 their GDP levels were lower than in 2008, meaning that now the average level is much lower than 117.

However, some countries, mostly in Central Europe, performed much better than other transition economies. These are countries where a better institutional framework was created. I verified that a better institutional framework improves the level of human development, which in turn improves economic growth, as in this scheme:

Institutional framework → human development → economic growth

A better institutional framework has to be identified with a situation where relevant political, institutional and social variables interact with each other and provide people with opportunities and therefore capabilities for doing and being. These variables are: expenditure on health and education, voice and accountability, and freedom. First, it was shown that these variables increase the level of human development (without the income dimension) and then that human development causes GDP growth. The empirical observation confirmed that human development is a sufficient but not necessary condition for economic growth in transition economies. In other words, there can be economic growth without human development, but if there is human development, then there will be economic growth.

# Appendix A7: Dealing with Endogeneity: Health Expenditure and Human Development

Regression model II in Table 7.2 was as follows:

```
          Linear regression dep. Var. HD
     Number of obs = 28       Prob > F = 0.0000
                 R-squared = 0.8221
            |Coef. Rob Std. Err. P>|t|
---------------------------------------------
    Health EXPEN|  .0052873  .0022826  0.032
          VA_Edu|  .0000709  .0000381  0.078
         freedom|  .0122228  .0028701  0.000
           _cons|  .7685463  .0096776  0.000
---------------------------------------------
```

*Note*: HD is an average of the human development variables (life expectancy and education indices only)

One could consider the variable inequality to be an instrument variable for health expenditure the variable inequality.[14] As the table below shows, the instrument (inequality) used is exogenous and not weak according to the definition of Staiger and Stock (1997), with an F statistic > 7:

```
First-stage regressions IV reg.(health exp.—inequality)

                        -----------------------

Number of obs = 28
F = 10.89
Prob > F = 0.0003
R-squared = 0.6730
Adj R-squared = 0.6185
```

| Heath exp. | Coef. | Rob.Std.Err. | P>\|t\| |
|---|---|---|---|
| freedom | .3386062 | .1430865 | 0.029 |
| VA_Edu | .0051163 | .0021249 | 0.027 |
| inequal | −.1682422 | .0667797 | 0.021 |
| _cons | 7.08843 | 2.367951 | 0.008 |

```
Instrumental variables (2SLS) regress. Number of obs=28
Wald chi2(3) = 86.81
Prob > chi2 = 0.0000
R-squared = 0.7380
```

| hd | Coef. | Rob.Std.Err. | P>\|z\| |
|---|---|---|---|
| Healt Exp. | .014714 | .006135 | 0.016 |
| freedom | .0075246 | .0033318 | 0.024 |
| VA_Edu | .0000237 | .0000441 | 0.091 |
| _cons | .7598887 | .0140344 | 0.000 |

Instrumented: Healt Exp. Instrument: inequal

While multicollinearity among variables is excluded:

| Variable | VIF | 1/VIF |
|---|---|---|
| freedom | 1.36 | 0.733216 |
| inequal | 1.20 | 0.834858 |
| VA_Edu | 1.16 | 0.865590 |
| Mean VIF | 1.24 | |

Finally, the Hausman test below allowed us to believe that the null hypothesis Cov (X, u)= 0 has to be accepted because there are no significant differences between OLS and IV Reg:

| | --- Coefficients --- | | | |
|---|---|---|---|---|
| | (b)<br>iv_robust | (B)<br>ols_robust | (b-B)<br>Difference | sqrt(diag (V_b-V_B))<br>S.E. |
| Health expe | .014714 | .0052873 | .0094268 | .0056946 |
| freedom | .0075246 | .0122228 | −.0046981 | .0016922 |
| VA_Edu | .0000237 | .0000709 | −.0000472 | .0000223 |
| _cons | .7598887 | .7685463 | −.0086576 | .010164 |

```
b = consistent under Ho and Ha; obtained from ivregress
B = inconsistent under Ha, efficient under Ho; obtained from regress
Test: Ho: difference in coefficients not systematic
chi2(4) = (b-B)'[(V_b-V_B)∧(-1)](b-B)= 0.08
```

The null hypothesis is true because the Chi-square is much lower than the critical value (at a level of five per cent and with four degrees of freedom). Therefore, we accept OLS estimates since they are more efficient and we can exclude the endogeneity problem between the human development and expenditure on health variables.[15]

In addition, another test of endogeneity for expenditure on health was carried out. This is specific for small-sample analysis (Hausman *et al.*, 2005). The results are consistent with the previous result. That is, the null hypothesis (health exp. exogenous regressor) is accepted at a significance level of one per cent:

Tests of endogeneity of: health exp
H0: Regressor is exogenous

```
            Wu-Hausman F test:   4.98259 F(1,17) P-value = 0.03935
Durbin-Wu-Hausman chi-sq test: 4.98654 Chi-sq(1) P-value = 0.02555
```

# 8

# Origins of Development: Social Capital, the Middle Class and Democracy

## 8.1 Introduction

In the previous chapter, we saw that there is a causality relation between institutions and growth: an appropriate institutional framework, which is able to set up particular political institutions, bringing about first an improvement in the non-income dimensions of human development (life expectancy and education levels) and then economic growth.[1] These political institutions (freedom and voice and accountability) reflect the level of democracy in a country. The aim of this chapter is to trace the origin of both democracy and development. Democracy is defined using the concept of Dahl (1971) who refers to 'contestation' as the essential feature of democracy. Development is identified with the general progress of human beings (Ray, 1998), which can be better captured by the HDI and which does not only include income improvements.

In this chapter, the following two hypotheses are put forward to explain a process of development: (1) democratic institutions come from the middle class and social capital; and (2) a democratic society endowed with high levels of social capital and a consistent middle class generates both higher HDI and economic growth levels. In this second hypothesis, education and human capital play a crucial role. Democracy helps to distribute growth and therefore to further human development.

## 8.2 Social capital, the middle class and democracy: a virtuous cycle

Many economists argue that one of the main problems in the Russian transition is the lack of a consistent middle class (Dillon and Wykoff,

2002; Gros and Steinherr, 2004; Brancato, 2009). This seems to be an important common problem among FSRs, although it is less widespread among CEECs. Many political scientists argue in parallel that one of the main problems of transition in Russia and the FSRs is the lack of democracy (Schimmelfennig and Scholtz, 2008; Møller and Skaaning, 2009). I believe both these statements to be true. However, my argument is that these two factors, which are crucially linked, are a consequence of an appropriate institutional framework in which social capital is embedded. As such, transition in Russia and the FSRs mostly failed because such an institutional framework, which would influence the behaviour of the middle class and would in turn build democracy, was missing. Figure 8.1 helps in making clear how these variables are linked. The continuous arrows identify the direction of the initial process of development (bottom-up process), starting from: (0), the middle class and social capital, which create democratic institutions (1); then democracy, social capital and the middle class bring about human development and economic growth (2). In the second stage of the process, democracy, the middle class and social capital are reinforced by the human development and growth (3), as the dotted arrows show (top-down process).

The formation of a middle class in my approach has two origins. The first of these has to be traced back into the structural change of the economy: post-industrial society brought about a third group, between the elites and the working class, forming a distinct political actor. The second of these is social capital, which is the bearer of particular values such as trust, cooperation, civil society involvement in public affairs, the respect of rules, social networks, reputation and anti-corruption social norms. All these values characterise the institutional framework of a society and promote and set up institutions beneficial for the whole community. Thus, a middle class is not identified simply by a certain level of income but, most importantly, by a level of social capital and civil society involvement which is present first and establishes institutions capable of spinning off the process of development.

According to Moore (1966), the middle class plays a crucial role in the emergence of democracy. Democracy entails democratic political institutions (political rights and civil liberties). In particular, following Dahl (1971), a *democratic* country should have the following features: 1) the election of government officials; 2) free and fair elections; 3) an inclusive suffrage; 4) the right of all citizens to run for public office; 5) freedom of expression; 6) alternative information; and 7) associational autonomy. This definition is also followed by Freedom House (2009), which states

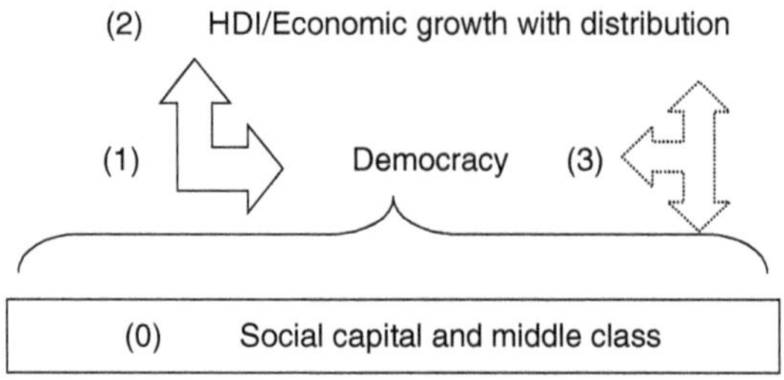


*Figure 8.1* The origins of development and democracy

that a country is considered democratic if it has free and fair political institutions. Another interesting definition of democracy was provided by Schumpeter (1943), who defined democracy as a 'method' for making decisions. This method involves the selection of leaders through competitive elections.[2]

However, democracy is not a prerequisite for economic growth. In fact, economic growth can appear without democracy and there are many examples of countries where this is the case. Nevertheless, growth with income distribution and human development, which is highly preferable, is strictly connected to democracy. Once the process of development has started, thanks to a sufficient endowment of social capital, growth with distribution reinforces the middle class, which in turn reinforces democratic institutions, as described by the direction of the dotted arrows in Figure 8.1 above. Middle-class consumption increases aggregate demand and boosts economic growth even further. In this process, the level of education increases consistently because a middle class with increasing means and income invests more and more in education, and this increases both human development and economic growth.

Hence, the idea which I aim to test in this final chapter can be represented in Figure 8.2.

The middle class is fuel for both the political system via democratisation[3] and for the economic system via mass consumption. The concept of the middle class referred to here goes beyond the Weberian definition of a socio-economic group of people in contemporary society who fall between the working class and the upper class; nor is it fully identified by Marxist terminology, where the middle class refers to either the bourgeoisie before or during capitalism, or to some

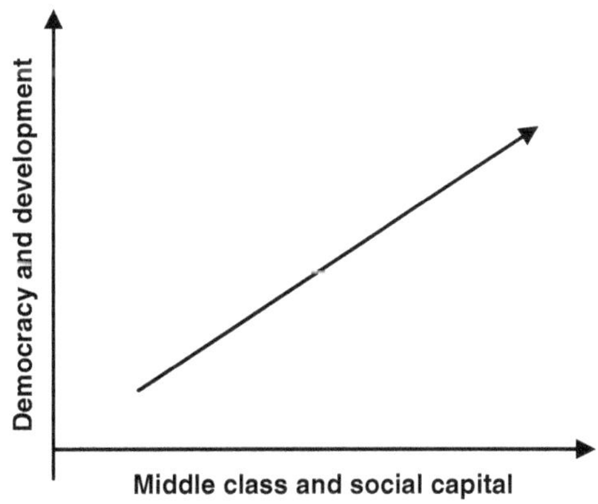


*Figure 8.2* Middle class and social capital versus democracy and human development

emergent new class within capitalism. I refer to the middle class as a group identified culturally in most contemporary Western cultures, which emphasises a set of shared values and a common sense of community, and has the means and ability to attain a dignified standard of living. However, the middle class in my view is not characterised merely by having a certain amount of discretionary income, which in any case can vary from country to country, over time and space. Most importantly, it is identified by a set of social norms and shared values oriented towards collective beliefs and respect – the middle class values education and social improvements, it possesses common sense and is able to share values, to command respect and understanding from a society, its collective institutions and community rules.

However, if one needs to estimate the magnitude of a middle class in a society, it is necessary to refer to some indicators. In order to estimate the magnitude of the strength of the middle class, I refer to poverty and inequality, assuming that the larger the values of these two variables, the weaker the middle class. As such, I measure the middle class in each economy as an interaction variable (multiplication) between two values, i.e., a poverty index (calculated as the percentage of population living with less than or equal to US$4 per day) and an inequality index (the Gini coefficient).

In my view, an economic growth that favours a middle class identifies a process of sustained development which corresponds to a process of human development. With human development, opportunities for individuals increase, health and educational systems improve, and schooling and life expectancy improve. Human development anticipates economic growth insofar as opportunities and people's capabilities are increased (Sen, 1985). In the scheme above (Figure 8.1), 'human development' and 'economic growth with distribution' are similar concepts if economic growth exhibits such particularities as opportunity and capability improvements, which bring about an increase in education, income distribution, life expectancy, etc. Unfortunately, economic growth does not always exhibit these particularities. One can have growth without development, as well as growth without democratisation. However, if a country experiences a process of human development (which also includes democratisation), economic growth will follow, as we saw in Chapter 7.

## 8.3 Social capital and trust in transition economies

Social capital in FCEs is very weak (Raiser, 1999; Raiser *et al.*, 2001; Kornai *et al.*, 2004). Putnam (1995: 67) defines social capital as 'features of social organization such as networks, norms and social trust that facilitate coordination and cooperation for mutual benefit'. Social capital refers to networks of reciprocal social relation or the glue that holds society together. In other words, the term 'social capital' is a way of defining the intangible resources of community, the shared values and trust upon which we draw in daily life (Field, 2008). As Bordieu, one of the pioneers in this field, states: 'Social capital is the sum of resources, actual or virtual, that accrue to an individual or a group by virtue of possessing durable network of more or less institutionalized relationship of mutual acquaintance ad recognition' (Bourdieu and Wacquant, 1992: 119).

Development and democracy are both underwritten by the same common factor – social capital (Anirudh, 2002; Krishna, 2002: 17). 'Social capital boosts the performance of polity and economy' (Putnam, 1993: 176) and social capital is not a product of institutional condition. Institutional performance is a result of social capital (Putnam's social capital thesis).

This is not the place to argue and test the different propositions. However, briefly, the Putnam thesis (social capital [civicness] → political and economic performance) attracted almost as much as criticism as acclaim. The most notorious opponent of the social capital thesis is probably Tarrow (1996: 394), who claims exactly the opposite: civic capacity has been variously shaped by patterns of state building and state strategy. Instead of social capital explaining institutional performance, institutions are invoked to explain social capital, following a certain 'structuralist thesis'. In the case of North-South differences in Italy, Tarrow argues that from the Norman establishment of a centralised monarchy in the twelfth century to the unified government which took over in 1861, every regime was foreign and governed by a logic and strategy of colonial exploitation. It was that logic and strategy which shaped social capital (Tarrow, 1996: 395). A similar view is put forward by Rothstein (2001), who argues that structures (i.e., institutions, politics and government) are causally prior to social relations, and social capital is a consequence of how government institutions operate rather than being the result of voluntary association. Similarly, Levi (1998) claims and attempts to demonstrate that 'Governments are a source of Social Capital'.

Conversely, Fukuyama (1995: 27) confirms Putnam's thesis. He argues that societies well supplied with social capital will be able to adopt new organisational forms more readily than those with less, as technology and markets change. However, the structuralism approach has strengthened the argument against the social capital thesis, particularly where it argues that social capital is a product of cultural and historical heritage. To some extent, this thesis is even supported by Putnam in the case of Italy. However, he rejects the structural (historical determinist) thesis in the case of the USA where, he argues, social capital has deteriorated severely in the past decade (Putnam, 2000: 27).

Another controversial issue concerning social capital is its *measurement* (Hooghe and Stolle, 2003; Field, 2008). The level of social capital, however it is measured – in terms of newspapers read, in terms of volunteer organisations, in terms of the number of non governmental and international organisations (Freedom House) or in terms of trust from the World Values Survey – is very low in transition economies as compared to Western European countries and to many other emerging economies (Lissowska, 2009). Trust between people, in governments and public institutions, and within society is strongly undermined. People fear the belief that they cannot trust each other and therefore cooperation and networking is very difficult to build. Networking and lobbying do exist, but in most of these cases they have a negative inflection. They are much more developed among dominant people, organised crime, clans and similar organisations, and include privileges, corruption, cronyism and nepotism. They favour income inequality.

The origin of lack of trust and therefore of a low level of social capital in FCEs must be found, to a great extent, in the strong censorship and persecution prevailing during the communist regime. Before that, most of the FSRs and part of Central and Eastern Europe were under the threat of Tsarist predatory governments (Brancato, 2009). In transition economies, all this created a tremendous cultural and historical heritage, with negative effects on social capital.

After the Second World War, people in Central and Eastern Europe and the FSRs were continuously threatened with being reported to the security police. Their private lives were under the control of the security police, which was continuously and dramatically searching for spies and dissidents. Even people obedient to the regime were afraid of being found guilty if they had somehow been in contact with someone supposed to be a dissident. Nobody could really know who was or was not a dissident and therefore nobody could trust anyone else. Even within the same family, there are sometimes stories of no trust and secrets between brothers and sisters, wives and husbands, children and fathers. These stories are also documented by the interesting movies and documentaries of socially aware Eastern European film directors such as Andrzej Wajda, Stanislaw Bareja, Cristian Mungiu and Jeremy Irons.

In parallel, an economy of favours was in place in FCEs with the systemic use of connections to procure favours. According to Ledeneva (1998), this was a response to the absence of the market and to the existence of a predatory state which was not operating as a good substitute for the market. With the transition to a market economy, these connections, which were no longer prohibited, promoted personal advantage, dominant position, governmental lobbying for particular interests, personal monopolies, criminally linked objectives and strategies oriented towards exploiting public resources for personal advantage. The essential element of trust is 'regular social interaction' (Putnam, 1993). These regular social interactions were missing during the Soviet era because people's behaviour was not genuine. There were mainly three kinds of behaviour:

1. behaviour guided by fear (fear of being controlled, reported, spied on, etc.);
2. behaviour subjected to and prone to being affected by the regime;
3. behaviour linked to nepotism, cronyism, the ruling classes, a 'favours economy' and a corrupted bureaucracy.

All this generated a culture of mistrust (Sztompka, 1995) which persisted during the transformation to a market economy and was frequently affected by the particular interests of oligarchs and the personal strategies of new state leaders. As such, people continued to experience uncertainty and lack of trust during the emergence of market institutions and in the process of working towards the emergence of a new democratic system.

Civil society does not develop within such an environment, while democratic control is also undermined. Civil society and social capital are two faces of the same coin; if one exists, so does the other. Both can be captured approximately by the level of trust in the society (from the World Values Survey). The lower the involvement of civil society in politics, economics and society in general, the less social mobility will occur and the lower the improvement in democracy. Indifference will prevail and in the best case scenario, one can have a society formally governed by democratic institutions (established in a top-down manner) but with a dominance of crystallised power groups and corruption. Substantially, these power groups control everything in society, delivering at best formal democracy such as voting and free expression, and no real participation and political inclusion.

The relatively better transition of most CEECs with respect to the FSRs can be explained on the basis of different levels of social capital, trust, civil society involvement and middle-class emergence, which bring about different levels of democracy and then of development. Table 8.1 below shows aggregate data trying to capture political institutions, social capital and other relevant variables in my model. I will use the data in this table to test my hypotheses in the regression exercise of section 8.7.

## 8.4 Variable definitions

Table 8.1 below shows the relevant indicators for my comparative analysis between CEECs and FSRs. Although these variables are very important in describing the institutional framework of a society, I will not use all of them in my empirical test (see section 8.7 below) because some of them are not statistically relevant in the econometric model put forward.

I have three indicators of participation, each from different sources: level of freedom (Freedom House, 2009), level of democracy (Polity IV Project, 2005) and voice and accountability (World Bank). As regards political institutions, I include political rights and civil liberties indices (from Freedom House) together with some indicators of governance such as political stability and control of corruption (from the World Bank). Social capital is a controversial variable and in the next section I will explain which variable I will use for it in my tests.

*Table 8.1* Political and economic variables: average variables for groups of countries

| | | **Advanced CEECs** | **Less advanced CEECs and Balkans** | **Average CEECs** | **FSRs** |
|---|---|---|---|---|---|
| Lev_ freedom_ avg. 2001–6 | Participation and political institutions | 3.00 | 2.75 | 2.88 | 1.41 |
| Lev_ democracy_ avg. 2000–3 | | 9.10 | 8.03 | 8.57 | −1.59 |
| Voice and accountability avg. 2000–6 | | 1.04 | 0.51 | 0.78 | −0.88 |
| Control of corruption 2008 | | 0.64 | −0.05 | 0.29 | −0.88 |
| Pol_stab. index 2000–6 | | 0.78 | 0.10 | 0.44 | −0.59 |
| Pol_rights avg. 2000–6 | | 1.00 | 1.86 | 1.43 | 5.58 |
| Civil liberties avg. 2000–6 | | | 2.23 | 1.87 | 5.03 |
| INGO avg. 2000–3 (INGO density) | Social capital | 2,769 | 1,369 | 1,907 | 776 |
| | | 583.2 | 262.1 | 362.4 | 134.7 |
| Trust 1999–2003 | | 0.218 | 0.199 | 0.204 | 0.216 |
| Edu index 2007 | Education | 0.96 | 0.91 | 0.93 | 0.92 |
| 3 lev. edu. 2005-03 | | 60.60 | 42.20 | 51.40 | 39.60 |

*Table 8.1* (Continued)

| | | Advanced CEECs | Less advanced CEECs and Balkans | Average CEECs | FSRs |
|---|---|---|---|---|---|
| HDI 2007 | Income, inequality and development | 0.887 | 0.830 | 0.859 | 0.756 |
| GDP PPP 2008 (in $) | | 19,711 | 12,196 | 15,953 | 5,816 |
| GDP growth 1989–2009 (in %) | | (1.7) | (1.2) | (1.5) | (1.1) |
| Gini coeff. 2006 | Inequality, poverty and middle class | 30 | 32.5 | 31.3 | 35 |
| Poverty 2006 | | 11.6 | 26.8 | 19.2 | 48.6 |
| Middle class indicator (Poverty*Gini) | | 350 | 861 | 595 | 1,694 |

*Note*: 3 lev. edu. = third level of education (i.e., university)
*Source*: UNDP, Freedom House, World Bank, Kaufmann *et al.*, 2007

In addition, some standard variables for income, human development, economic growth and inequality are also included and do not need definition here. The education index and the third level of education were defined in Chapter 7. Finally, I include the variable 'middle class' which, as explained before, is defined on the basis of a simple multiplication for each country between two variables, i.e., the poverty index in 2006 (US$4 a day) and the Gini coefficient of inequality (in 2006). A higher GDP per capita does not necessarily mean that all people enjoy higher income; it simply refers to the average income of the country. Households can still suffer deep inequalities and the society can still be affected by high levels of poverty, so the middle class in a very unequal country can be compressed, fragmented and less developed. This is the basis for the index of 'middle class' which I propose here, and it is possible to see significant variations among all transition economies (see the appendix to this chapter for all the variable values for each country).

### 8.4.1 Social capital measurement

As regards social capital, any quantitative measurement is very difficult and controversial. A possible measurement is the number or the density of *international non-governmental organisations* (INGOs),[4] which shows the average number (or the density per million of the population) of INGOs that have either member organisations or individual representatives in each country.[5] For many scholars, the presence of INGOs in a country is highly correlated with high levels of social capital (Putnam, 1993; Kornai *et al.*, 2004; Sabatini, 2008). Therefore, this could be a good proxy for the level of civil society involvement in public affairs, which is obviously a consequence of a high endowment of social capital and represents, to some extent, the development of a civil society.

However, there are advantages and disadvantages in using this variable as a proxy for social capital. Unlike sport, free time and non-political and hobby associations, non-governmental organisations have socio-political scope (Wollebak and Selle, 2003). Organisations of this kind function as learning schools for democracy (Stolle, 2003: 23). Associations such as non-governmental organisations (NGOs) are mirrors of a critical spirit of a society. The working classes, the average person and the middle class can organise themselves within specific socio-economic scopes in order to improve their own and others' living conditions in a sprit of solidarity. Through association, they can become the ruling class, establish new leadership and evolve, and they can achieve consensus and become the dominant majority in political scenarios. NGOs improve politicisation, with subsequent beneficial aspects for collective organisation, democracy and community. Since they are volunteer and non-profit organisations, they can be oriented purely towards collective goods and general privileges rather than towards personal privileges and particular interests. Therefore, NGOs as a representation of civil society can be a relatively good proxy for social capital endowment in a society. Volunteer associations and organisations played an important role in France between the Revolution and the second Republic in creating democratic spirit and then development (Mayer, 2003). A similar process happened within cultural and political circles during the Enlightenment in France or in Italy during the Renaissance (Agulhon, 1977).

With regard to the disadvantages, the main criticism raised against the idea of using organisations like NGOs as a proxy for civil society and then for social capital is that NGOs, although formal organisations, are not sufficiently developed in general in poor and less advanced countries. Therefore, it is methodologically incorrect to make any form of cross-country analysis using a variable which does not realistically say much about the situation of social capital in those countries (Krishna, 2002). This criticism has a strong foundation and suggests that it is impossible to use the variable in my sample.

A more genuine measurement of social capital in FCEs could be the level of trust; this can be downloaded from the World Values Survey Databank (2009). The World Values Survey has a very clear question concerning trust: 'Can most people be trusted?' I used the answers to this question[6] to measure social capital in my sample of transition economies. I believe, in fact, that the level of trust in a society goes to its very foundation and to the origins of what can be considered both the intangible good and the resources which constitute social capital.

Broadly speaking, trust within a society is a prerequisite and not a consequence of development. On the contrary, NGOs need formal institutions to become established, and formal institutions are most likely to develop in advanced societies. Therefore, an endogenous problem between development and NGOs can emerge. For these reasons, in my analysis I preferred to use the level of trust instead of the NGO as a proxy for social capital.

### 8.4.2 Participation

The level of democracy index ranks between −10 and +10[7], and combines results from political rights and civil liberties indices. A score of +10 indicates a strongly democratic state, while a score of −10 indicates a strongly autocratic state. In the analysis of the level of democracy, a fully democratic government is supposed to have three essential elements: 1) fully competitive political participation; 2) institutionalised constraints on executive power; and 3) guaranteed civil liberties to all citizens in their daily lives and in their political participation. On the other hand, a fully autocratic system sharply restricts or suppresses competitive political participation. The chief executives are chosen by an elite group and exercise power with few institutionalised constraints.

The voice and accountability index ranks between $-2.5$ and $+2.5$ (the higher the better). This is one of six World Bank governance indicators presented in 'Governance Matters VIII' (Kaufmann *et al.*, 2009); these are composite indices created from several hundred variables derived from 32 different data providers. The variables used in calculating the final indices comprise expert opinions, such as Freedom House's level of freedom indicator, surveys such as Transparency International's Corruption Perceptions Index and 'hard' data, like the percentage of government revenue generated by trade-related taxes.

The level of freedom indicator has three values: 1) not free; 2) partly free; and 3) free. It measures individual freedom or the opportunity to act spontaneously in a variety of fields outside the control of the government and other centres of potential domination. This evaluation, compiled annually by Freedom House, is a general and synthetic index that includes not only political rights and civil liberties, but also other factors. In free countries, a broad range of political rights and civil liberties are respected. Partly free countries have a mixed record on political rights and civil liberties, often accompanied by corruption, a weak rule of law and an inordinate political dominance of a ruling party, in some cases characterised by ethnic or religious strife. In not free countries, basic political rights and civil liberties are denied.

### 8.4.3 Political institutions

Political rights and civil liberties indices are variables from Freedom House. They rank between 1 (the maximum) and 7 (the minimum), the lower the better. Since these two variables are very similar in the values allocated, I used an average of the two in the model below in order to simplify it.

The civil liberties index measures freedom of expression, assembly, association and religion. To determine each country's civil liberties, researchers obtain answers to a series of survey questions using country visits and an extensive network of sources. The civil liberties questions are classified into four categories: 1) freedom of expression and belief: measures of freedom of the press, religious freedom and freedom of cultural expression; 2) association and organisational rights: measures of freedom of assembly and organisation, the ability to create trade unions and other free private organisations; 3) rule of law: this ascertains if there is an independent judiciary, protection from political terror and equal protection under the law; 4) personal autonomy and individual rights: this includes free private discussions, property rights, personal autonomy and personal freedoms.[8]

The political rights index measures the degree of freedom in the electoral process, political pluralism and participation, and the functioning of government (Freedom House, 2009). To determine each country's political rights, researchers obtain answers to a series of survey questions using country visits and an extensive network of sources.[9]

Political stability and control of corruption are two World Bank indicators of governance, ranking between −2. 5 and +2. 5. Political stability (−2. 5 low stability, +2. 5 high stability) indicates an institutional political framework in which uncertainty is reduced, property rights are ensured and protection against violence is guaranteed. Control of corruption (−2. 5 high corruption, +2. 5 low corruption) is a governance indicator which measures the 'perceptions of corruption, conventionally defined as the exercise of public power for private gain'. According to the World Bank, corruption stems from a lack of respect for the country and its institutions by both government officials and the private sector, thus representing a failure in governance. To some extent, if a country is very corrupt, it is likely that it will be endowed with low levels of social capital. The control of corruption index is comprised of indicators that also measure the transparency of governance and perceived patterns of nepotism and cronyism. The data are available online as part of the World Bank's 'Governance Matters VIII' report.

On the one hand, social capital and political institutions are closely related, while on the other hand, a strange paradox can take place. This paradox is expressed by Putnam (2000). According to him, a reduction in the main indicators of social capital in advanced economies (declining trust in government, falling voter turnout, less direct participation in political meetings, direct campaign actions, etc.), which in a country like the USA are declining, can show that richer societies experience a fall in social capital after a strong initial increasing trend, as Figure 8.3 below shows, despite the fact that formal values for political institutions such as civil liberties and political rights can remain at high levels. However, at the initial stage of development, social capital improves as well as political institutions.

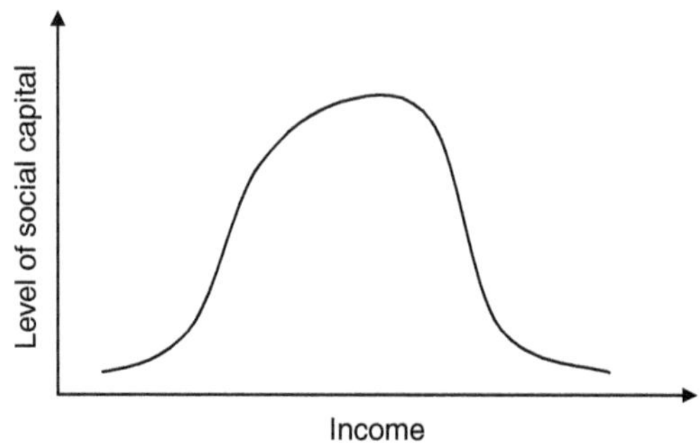


*Figure 8.3* Social capital and income

In Putnam's view, this can be seen as a decline in the civic community. People are more likely to join non-political organisations such as bowling clubs or bridge societies than any form of social organisation involving communities (Putnam, 2000).

This phenomenon is growing rapidly in ethnically and linguistically fragmented cities and in heterogeneous communities, and can have dire consequences on further economic development. If citizens are not engaged in societal affairs, they are less committed to polity and to collective goods. They are less inclined towards trust in general and have less trust in and respect for political authorities and each other. Civil society could incur a dangerous breakdown and political legitimacy could be questioned.

## 8.5 Inequality: a negative force for the middle class and social capital

Social capital decreases not only in ethnically fragmented societies like the USA today – it can also decrease in uneven societies where income distribution is worsening, where particular privileges prevail, where justice is unfair, where poverty is rapidly emerging and where dominant groups, powers and oligarchs govern. This is the case in many transition economies, which are experiencing dramatic increases in inequality (Tridico, 2010); this in turn inhibits the emergence of a strong middle class, a crucial variable for further development.

Networks and connections are well developed among small groups and dominant clans in Russia, in other FSRs and in all FCEs in general. These are negative networks and connections, the dark side of 'social capital' (Field, 2008). Networks and connections belong to the sphere of the intangible good that constitutes social capital. However, when these networks and connections decline in favour of the development of small groups that reject collective resources, privilege particular interests and are oriented towards dominant people and groups, social capital has inevitable negative consequences: there is growing mistrust, access to resources is distorted and inequality increases.

The very foundation of the problem of inequality is the concept of social welfare. According to the utilitarian approach, social welfare is the sum of individual welfare. Social welfare improvements cannot be achieved (or would not be 'Pareto efficient') by redistributing resources from one individual to another, because a 'Pareto' improvement is a situation in which it is not possible to make someone better off without making someone else worse off. On the other hand, an egalitarian approach would consider the redistribution of resources in order to avoid the situation in which one individual could become richer by taking advantage of the fact that the other is in poor health, is poorly educated or is disabled (Sen, 1973). In this latter approach, the application of the Rawls criterion would be the best policy – the aim is not individual welfare but the level of welfare in society as a whole. If one individual (A) has a lower level of welfare than another (B) and if B can be made better off by redistributing resources from A, then the Rawls criterion of justice requires that B should have sufficiently more income to make B's utility equal to that of A. In Rawlsian thinking, inequalities have to be adjusted according to two principles: 1) offices and positions must be open to everyone under conditions of *fair equality of opportunity*; and 2) they have to be of the greatest benefit to the least-advantaged members of society (Rawls, 1971: 303). The application of these criteria requires more than meritocracy. 'Fair equality of opportunity' requires not only that positions are distributed on the basis of merit but also that there is equal opportunity to all in terms of education, health, etc., to acquire the skills on the basis of which merit is assessed. The application of these principles would, in the end, produce much greater advantages for society as a whole.

Another way to look at the problem of inequality is through the lens of social peace and cohesion. Sen (1973) saw inequality as strictly linked to the concept of rebellion, and indeed the two phenomena are linked both ways, that is, inequality causes rebellion, but it may be the case that income inequality could increase after a rebellion which brings power to a specific apparatus, ruling class or social class. This has happened many times in history when, for instance, rebellions were led by army generals or by elites of nobles. In several transition economies, inequality increased after a 'rebellion' which brought oligarchs to power. In the FSRs in particular, inequality increased dramatically after the 1991 August Coup, which deposed Soviet President Mikhail Gorbachev and resulted in the dissolution of the USSR. The same thing happened in some African countries, such as Congo and Sudan: rebellions carried out by generals and warlords deposed previous authoritarian or less authoritarian regimes, but such a change brought about an increase in inequality. Nowadays, economists try to capture a causality nexus (inequality → rebellion → inequality) through the use of some modern governance indicators such as political stability. The link between political stability and inequality is demonstrated in numerous empirical works such as Alesina and Perotti (1996) and Easterly (2001), where it emerges that income inequality increases during periods of political instability.

An interesting explanation of inequality in the Americas is put forward by Sokoloff and Engerman (2000), who, in order to explain inequality in wealth, human capital and political power, suggest a historically founded institutional explanation, which lies in the initial roots of the factors of endowment of the respective colonies. In general, political institutions set up by the Spaniards and the Portuguese in Latin America were different from thosse set up by the British in North America. Moreover, the latter sent educated people and skilled workforces, along with the lords, to the New World, and these started to build their own future; conversely, the Spaniards and the Portuguese did not encourage massive migration from the motherland but sent landlords who basically exploited slaves from Africa.

One of the first cross-country studies on inequality was undertaken by Kuznets (1955). He showed that in the early stages of economic growth, income tends to be unequally distributed among individuals and the distribution of income worsens over time. In the later stages, national income starts to be more equally distributed. Hence, inequality declines in the end, after the country has accomplished the 'U'-shaped trajectory. Several later empirical studies confirmed this relationship (Chenery and Syrquin, 1975; Ahluwalia, 1976). The reason for such a relationship was attributed to structural changes, which at the beginning of the 'transition' bring about job losses and inequalities.

Nevertheless, the implicit trade-off behind the Kuznets curve (economic growth/inequality) and the idea that an increase in inequality is sometimes necessary for rapid growth has often been criticised (Atkinson, 1999). An alterative hypothesis to explain why income inequality differs between countries is put forward by Milanovic (1994), who shows that inequality decreases in richer societies because social attitudes towards it change as those societies get richer and it becomes less tolerated. Birdsall and Sabot (1994) showed, contrary to the Kuznets hypothesis, that inequality may be a constraint for growth and if inequality is lowered, a country could have a GDP per capita 8.2 per cent higher than a country with income inequality one standard deviation higher.

A similar hypothesis is suggested by Voitchovsky (2005: 273) who, however, stresses the *shape* of the distribution and suggests that inequality at the top end of the distribution is positively associated with growth, while inequality lower down the distribution is negatively related to subsequent growth. Moreover, empirical evidence in cross-country analyses, from Latin American to East Asian countries, poses the question of why Latin America has high inequality and low growth and, on the contrary, why East Asia has high growth and low inequality. Birdsall and Sabot (1994) suggest that it is a matter of policies and social attitude towards inequality. In Latin America, for a long time after the Second World War, dictators, generals and the ruling classes acted with little respect for the poorest part of society, implementing fiscal and trade policies which provided few benefits to the poor (Easterly and Rebelo, 1993). On the contrary, in East Asia, the ruling classes were more aware of social needs and implemented policies such as land reforms, public housing, public investment in rural infrastructures and public education, which had a positive effect on both growth and income distribution: better educated people can get a better job and earn more; public investment in the rural sector can bring farmer productivity and higher incomes; public housing and other social services can increase the purchasing power of people, etc.

## 8.6 Institutions for social capital improvements

One solution to prevent social capital erosion is 'deliberative democracy'. It could be introduced together with encouraging the motivation of political and social participation, as evinced by community participation and improvements in collective education. Political stability would therefore be saved, political violence, crime and fragmentation would be mitigated and social cohesion could potentially increase with the prospect of further human development.

Education and public expenditure are crucial variables in avoiding an increase in income inequality and therefore a worsening of social capital. Public expenditure which finances, among other things, a national health system with positive advantages for life expectancy should also show growth in order to reduce income inequality. In fact, following a capability approach, basic dimensions such as health and education should be guaranteed by public policies to enable people to live a long and healthy life, to become knowledgeable and to acquire a decent standard of living. If these basic capabilities are not achieved, many choices are simply not available and many opportunities will remain inaccessible (UNDP, 1999). Lack of opportunities will lead to income inequality and poverty, with further negative effects on social capital.

Very simply, if education is subject only to market rules, then higher education will be available only to children whose parents can pay market prices. Poorer parents, who in most cases are unskilled workers, cannot afford such a cost; consequently, unskilled parents will tend to have unskilled children. In this way, inequality will be 'crystallised' within the initial conditions and will not be reduced during economic growth, and at the same time social capital levels can worsen.

In Russia, where social capital and trust seem to be very low, local investors (or oligarchs) who bribe governments are investing abroad, worsening the capital account of the country's balance of payments and robbing Russian natural resources. In this perverse behaviour, it is possible to see two factors: the first is the lack of trust, by investors, in Russian institutions, while the second is the fragility of a civil society that cares very little about national interests. At the same time, these investors consume luxury imported goods, increasing the national commercial deficit and impeding, to some extent, any benefits to the country from globalisation. Such a process consistently limits social capital and hence the formation of a middle class, a process frustrated from two points of view: first, the work ethic is discouraged in an environment where the winning behaviours are lobbying and connections; and, secondly, crime and corruption favour oligarchs and people in dominant positions rather than the middle class. This process could be stopped and reversed by the application of relevant policies – anti-corruption policies, the rule of law, fair rules and appropriate individual incentives, punishments and sanctions favouring a work ethic – in order to improve social capital.

As such, on the one hand, social capital can be considered a product of cultural and historical heritage, while on the other hand, it can be improved by government policies. Realistically, however, social capital, which is tied in with social networks and trust, does not emerge overnight and its formation takes time, during which the process of development and economic growth can be inhibited. In the case of the CEECs more than the FSRs, social capital could rely on a healthier social platform consisting of: 1) a less intrusive and hierarchical state apparatus; 2) a society that is relatively more open to foreign influence; and 3) a higher level of freedom in terms of both economic activity and political participation.

All this favoured the improvement of social capital, provided individuals with more confidence in market rules after 1989 and created improved conditions for a better institutional framework where appropriate policies could be designed and implemented. Appropriate policies would be: social institutions mitigating conflicts and inequality, transparency norms and habits, democratic rules, voice and accountability reinforcement, people participation incentives and involvement in public life, the reinforcement of property rights, anti-monopoly laws, the certainty of economic relationships, public goods and socio-economic investments in education and health.

To sum up briefly, we can say that two arguments, strongly connected to one another, are relevant for the success of transition: on the one hand, the endowment of social capital, which fosters democracy and development and, on the other hand, the transformation and institutional strategy implemented in a country, which, *ceteris paribus*, makes the difference. Appropriate policies and institutions, in turn, can increase the level of trust in a society, incentivising the involvement of civil society and reinforcing social capital.

However, most transition economies, and those of the FSRs in particular, neglected these policies and incurred institutional tensions, contradictions and weakness. Most of them, as we saw earlier, implemented an uncritical package of policies inspired by the WC/shock therapy. These policies, when associated with the lack of an appropriate political economy framework and in a systemic vacuum, lower the endowment of social capital, increase egoism, threaten trust and favour anti-social behaviour and perverse attitudes such as lobbying and corruption. All these will make recession even deeper and recovery more difficult, and development will either not take place or will be uneven.

## 8.7 Bridging different approaches for a new development model

In this section, I will finally try to bridge the different approaches analysed throughout the book, and in Part III in particular, in order to synthesise and test a more analytic model of economic development.

The main idea of this book has been that economic development follows as an outcome of a complex strategy of transformation based on the simultaneous presence and interaction of some socio-economic factors and institutional variables. Education and human capital are two of the most important of these socio-economic factors, as we saw in Chapter 7. However, only when institutions provide the proper political and economic governance, thus giving the right incentives to economic agents, does an enabling process start: a positive interaction between socio-economic factors and institutional variables will then take place and development will follow. However, I have argued in this chapter that the very foundation of this process is social capital and the middle class. Countries endowed with a consistent level of social capital and with a consistent middle class will be the first to start a process of development and in a more sustainable way.

The graph below, which expands upon the scheme outlined in Figure 8.1 above, tries to illustrate the relationships and the mechanisms of development within both the institutional framework of social capital and the human capital accumulation process. It highlights the dominant role of social capital as a necessary condition for starting a process of development. A society endowed with a higher level of social capital will have higher levels of trust, tighter cooperation and more intensely positive networks. Civil society will be involved in public affairs. Incentives for economic agents will be fair in order to avoid free-riding, rent-seeking and privileges. Common social norms will be accepted. Collective values such as solidarity and equality will prevail. Society will be less fragmented and less heterogeneous. Public good will be built up and respected. Public interests will prevail over opportunism and better economic organisation will emerge. In parallel, a sustained flow of informal knowledge and the circulation of innovation and technical expertise will continue to subsist because trust, networking and cooperation are highly developed in society.

Figure 8.4 highlights the crucial role of the middle class as a vehicle able to create both the democratic political institutions and mass consumption necessary for aggregate demand and growth. A middle class is also the bearer of social institutions, collective actions and requests for public investment in health and education, which are essential for socio-economic development.

Such institutions and collective actions affect both individual opportunities (or capabilities) and improvements in education and health. Better opportunities and higher levels of education and health reinforce the middle class even more. Finally, people endowed with more opportunities will be better able to transform formal education into effective and operational human capital.

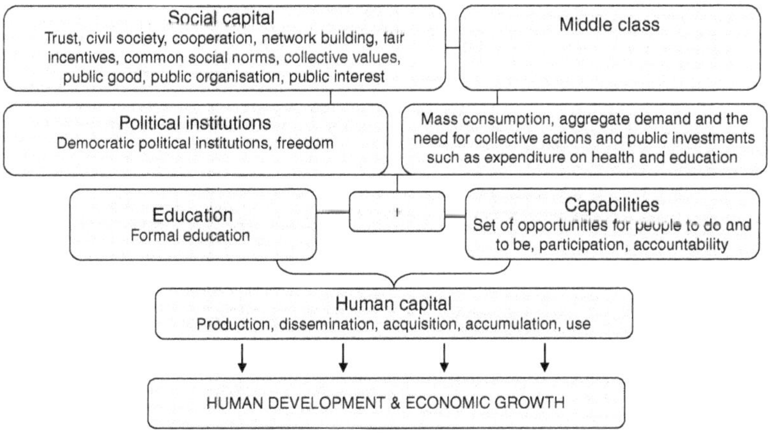


*Figure 8.4* The process of development

The attempt to bridge education and capabilities with institutions and social capital can be very fruitful and can provide a better explanation of the controversial results very often obtained by some economists when they relate human capital to economic growth. In fact, education needs to be produced first, then disseminated, then acquired and finally used. This is an evolutionary process, which requires not only investments in education and school enrolment but also: (1) the capability to exploit education; (2) cooperation, networks and trust (i.e., social capital) for knowledge diffusion; and (3) the right institutions to provide appropriate incentives for human capital accumulation.

Capabilities are also affected and enlarged by institutions (Sen, 1985). In fact, institutional policies, the consequence of prevalent norms and institutions, allow for the improvement of the basic capabilities for human development, such as leading long and healthy lives, being knowledgeable and having a decent standard of living. If basic capabilities are not achieved, many choices are simply not available and many opportunities remain inaccessible (UNDP, 1999). A better endowment of capabilities will allow people to exploit a wider range of choices and, in turn, to improve their skills. These skills are work competencies, networking, general knowledge and experience. Human capital, broadly speaking, will be better disseminated throughout society and the general level of knowledge will be higher, creating better conditions for business and for a development process. In abstract terms, the human capital accumulation can be described as follows:

$$\textit{Institutions} \rightarrow \textit{education} \rightarrow \textit{capabilities} \rightarrow \textit{human capital}$$

As we saw in Table 7.2 in the last chapter, expenditure on formal education alone, which can be represented either by education level or by education expenditure, is no longer sufficient for development. It needs to interact with voice and accountability, which represents people's participation and the active role of individuals in society – in other words, with people's capabilities. In fact, people's participation is effective when capabilities are developed. In this way, education can approach the human capital definition to some extent. Therefore, as was concluded in Chapter 7, the state not only has to guarantee education through public expenditure in education but it must also create a framework which would allow for individuals to use that education and to transform it into operational human capital.

By contrast, a society that does not have a consistent level of social capital will have a weaker institutional framework and will have more trouble building a consistent middle class able to realise the importance of education. Moreover, the transformation of formal education into effective and operational human capital would be more difficult in this case, because lower levels of social capital would inhibit the process of the circulation of knowledge.

The task now is to find evidence for this model, trying to build a function which will incorporate appropriate variables in order to verify the model. The function should be at the same time simple, in order to be easily tested, and complex, in order to represent the theoretical model above as much as possible.

The hypothesis underlying this model is that human development (which includes an education index) can be explained using three fundamental variables: social capital, a middle class and democratic political institutions, perceived as an average of the political rights and civil liberties indices. Political rights and civil liberties as well as social capital are in fact the basis of a democratisation process in a country and are considered to be the very foundation of a development process in this model. From these three variables, human development follows. The econometric model below tests this idea and tries to avoid the endogeneity problem between dependent and independent variables. I put forward the idea that the origin of human development (HDI), which now also includes GDP,[10] has to be found on the one hand in the social capital endowment that creates an appropriate institutional framework, with a middle class consciousness and a strong involvement of the civil society, and on the other hand in the political and civil liberties which empower people and increase democracy substantially. In this way, we can avoid adding education and health to the model, since they are already included in the dependent HDI variable.

As stated previously, social capital is approximated to the 'trust' variable from the World Values Survey. The PolRight_CivLib variable is an average of both the political rights and civil liberties indices, and is used in order to simplify the model. In order to avoid confusion with data interpretation, one should remember that the political rights and civil liberties indices rank between 1 (maximum) and 7 (minimum) (the lower the better). Another variable used in the regression below is 'middle class' which, as mentioned earlier, is defined on the basis of an interaction between the poverty index (2006) and the Gini coefficient of inequality (2006). In this way, I can obtain a value which tells us something about the consistency of both poverty and inequality simultaneously: the lower the 'middle class' value (poverty*Gini), the better the position of the middle class. For instance, Russia has a relatively high GDP per capita, similar to that of Croatia, Latvia, Lithuania and Poland, and higher than other FSRs. However, since Russia has the highest inequality rate among transition economies and a consistent poverty index, the GDP rank is reversed by the 'middle class' variable. The general explanation for this variable is that where inequality and poverty are higher, the middle class, having its average income compressed, is weaker and poorer.

In the regression Table 8.2 below, these three variables are used as independent variables in determining higher HDI, the dependent variable, according to the following model:

$$HDI = a + B1^{*}SocCap + B2^{*}Democracy + B3^{*}MidCl + e$$

The results are very interesting. It seems that among transition economies, HDI is determined by social capital (trust 1999–2003), middle class (poverty*Gini) and democracy. However, some endogeneity problems between democracy and human development can negatively affect the model and therefore the field is still open to further discussion and tests.[11] For this purpose, I used a instrument in the 2SLS regression, i.e., the presence of NGOs, in the table above. In regression II, the endogenous political rights and civil liberties variable is instrumented

*Table 8.2* Regression for HDI

| **Regression I: OLS model – Obs. 28 Dependent variable: HDI 2007** | | **Regression II: 2SLS model – Obs. 28 Dependent variable: HDI 2007** |
|---|---|---|
| Variables | Coeff. | Coeff. |
| Instrumental var. for democracy (NGO) | | .0268328* (.0085084) |
| PolRight_CivLib(democracy) | −.0221352* (.0035823) | |
| Social capital (trust) | .2204755** (.0960711) | .2608864** (.1197877) |
| Middle class (poverty*Gini) | −.0000246* (8.37e-06) | −.0000176** (.0000144) |
| Constant | .8710382* (.0228169) | .8698062* (.023862) |
| R-squared = 0.8606; Adj R-squared = 0.8397 | | R-squared = 0.8487 Adj R-squared = 0.8260 |
| Mean dependent var. 0.8096 | | Mean dependent var. 0.8096 |
| Prob(F-statistic) 0.000000 | | Strength of instrument first stage reg. output: F = 7.83; Second stage reg Prob > F = 0.0000 |

Significance level at * = 1 per cent, ** = 5 per cent
Standard errors in parenthesis are heteroskedasticity-robust after White test
*Note*: the negative sign of the coefficient variable of PolRight_CivLib has to be attributed to the way this variable is built with an index between 1 (maximum) and 7 (minimum) (the lower the better). Thus, the relationship with the dependent variable (HDI) *would* in fact be positive. In other words, countries which guarantee better political rights and civil liberties (i.e., that are more democratic) have higher levels of human development. The same applies to the 'middle class' variable: the higher the value of poverty*Gini, the weaker the middle class and the lower the HDI.
*Source*: author's elaboration based on data in the final appendix to this book

with the NGO variable. This instrument is not weak (F = 7.83) and not correlated with the dependent variable.[12] On the contrary, one can assume that the NGO variable is a good proxy for democracy too. The Wu-Hausman F test and the Durbin-Wu-Hausman Chi-square test confirm that the regressor PolRight_CivLib is not exogenous, so regression II (2SLS model) should be accepted instead.

Tests of endogeneity of: PolRight_CivilLib

H0: Regressor is exogenous

Wu-Hausman F test: 0.39762 F(1,19) P-value = 0.53583

Durbin-Wu-Hausman chi-sq test: 0.49196 Chi-sq(1) P-value = 0.48306 +

The results are very similar. Transition economies that enjoy better levels of social capital with a stronger and less compressed middle class, and higher levels of democracy (NGO), reach higher levels of human development which is the *end* of a process of economic development and which goes beyond the simple GDP.

Hence, the model implies that development requires democracy. However, democracy is not the only variable. Development requires a consistent middle class as well as social capital, which implies that inequality has to be low and that development policies should focus on social issues.

Interestingly enough, similar results are found by Binder and Georgiadis (2010), who argue that institutions and social norms, such as those considered in the above model, affect key development policies that are conducive to human development.

While it can be very controversial to state, in absolute terms, that democracy is a prerequisite for economic development, it can be agreed as a common consensus that after a certain income threshold, middle-income economies need democratic institutions, along with other variables, to foster development (Møller and Skaaning, 2009). In transition economies, this seems to be the case. Most transition economies are middle-income economies, which have already experienced a modernisation process through industrialisation. Therefore, the modernisation theory does not apply *tout court* to them. The modernisation theory says that countries need to advance in economic terms first of all and then democracy will follow. This theory can be applied fully to developing countries. But in FCEs, which are relatively advanced in economic terms with respect to developing countries, democracy is needed in order to foster development. This assumption is confirmed by the econometric model which also requires social capital and the middle class (with low inequality) along with democracy as necessary conditions.

Therefore, what transition economies need now in order to achieve further development is democracy, together with appropriate policies and institutions able to redistribute income and to improve important factors of development, such as education and health. In fact, as I initially showed in the model underpinned by Figure 8.1, there is also a reverse process occurring within it (a top-down process): lower inequality reinforces a middle class and investments in health and education improve social rights and people's capabilities. This in turn may positively affect social capital.

Hence, on the one hand, social capital is a product of cultural and historical heritage which establishes the level of social capital in a country over decades and centuries. On the other hand, this thesis must not be accepted as unchangeable law, and governments can do a lot to improve the level of social capital in their own countries. Appropriate policies and institutions that are implemented consistently matter in the formation of social capital.

## 8.8 Democracy and development

While it was relatively easy to establish a causality relationship between development and the independent variables (social capital, democracy, middle class), it is a more difficult task to explain democracy. It can be useful to take into account some insights on this topic drawn from the promising literature in the field of political science, which tries to explain democracy through development. This field has been well explored since the time of classical political economists and philosophers. A common belief, at least in Western society, is that economic development is associated with democracy. However, de Tocqueville and John Stuart Mill were already sceptical of this association and warned of the risk of the 'tyranny of the majority' (de Tocqueville) and of 'false democracy' (Mill). Moreover, there are many examples of countries which experienced economic development (and capitalist development) with authoritarian regimes, such as South Korea and Taiwan after the Second World War, Brazil and Chile in recent decades, and Nazi Germany and the various fascist regimes in Europe between the two World Wars, though this list is not exhauastive (Reuschemeyer *et al.*, 1992; Acemouglu *et al.*, 2006).

One of the contemporary pioneers among political scientists who tried to establish a relationship between democracy and development was Lipset (1959). Lipset pointed out two factors relevant for democracy: economic development and political legitimacy. Both these factors are associated with democracy. He argued that democratic states tend to have higher levels of socio-economic development than non-democratic ones. Moreover, he stated that the stability of a democratic system also depends on the effectiveness (an efficient bureaucracy and decision-making system) and legitimacy of the political system (maintaining the belief that existing political institutions are the most appropriate for society).

Along similar lines, Przeworski *et al.* (2008) argue that economic development does not tend to generate democracies, but that democracies are more likely to exist in richer societies. Moreover, they found that the type of political regime has no general impact on economic growth. Both these findings, which are tested through wide cross-country analyses, seem very reasonable and can also be verified among transition economies. However, in general, in transition economies, political and economic liberalisation seem to be positively correlated, whereas the relation between democracy and development remained unclear (Norgaard, 2000; Apolte, 2010).

Huntington (1991), who classified three 'waves of democratisation', considers part of the post-communist transition as being part of the third wave of democratisation (1974–91) in which he includes countries from Southern and Eastern Europe, Latin America and parts of Africa. The first wave (1828–1926) involved North America, Britain, France and some other Western European countries, while the second wave (1943–62) involved countries like India, Israel, Japan, West Germany and Italy.

FSRs remain outside the third wave of the Huntington classification, although CEECs are included. However, following the Huntington approach, it would be possible to classify further post-communist transition in the following way: the first wave of post-communist democratisation (1989–91) which concerned most of the CEECs; and the second wave (1995–2005), also known as the 'colour revolutions' which concerned the removal of autocrats such as Iliescu in Romania and Meciar in Slovakia, Serbia's Bulldozer Revolution of 2000, Georgia's Rose Revolution of 2003, Ukraine's Orange Revolution of 2004 and the Kyrgyzstan Tulip Revolution of 2005. The remaining transition economies are still untouched by consistent waves of democratisation, and in particular there are no free and fair electoral regimes. According to Freedom House, three levels of democratisation among transition economies can be identified: 1) free democracies; 2) partly free defective democracies/semi-authoritarian regimes; and 3) not free, authoritarian regimes (see the appendix to this chapter for more details).

*Table 8.3* Freedom House classification

| **Free (Democracies)** | | **Partly free (Defective democracies/ semi-authoritarian regimes)** | **Not free (Authoritarian regimes)** |
|---|---|---|---|
| Bulgaria<br>Croatia<br>Czech Republic<br>Estonia<br>Hungary<br>Latvia<br>Lithuania<br>Poland<br>Romania<br>Serbia<br>Slovakia<br>Slovenia<br>Ukraine | | Albania<br>Armenia<br>Bosnia and Herzegovina<br>Georgia<br>Kyrgykistan<br>Macedonia<br>Moldova<br>Montenegro | Azerbaijan<br>Belarus<br>Kazakhstan<br>Russia<br>Tajikistan<br>Turkmenistan<br>Uzbekistan |
| 13 countries | | 8 countries | 7 countries |
| HDI 2007 | 0.859 | 0.776 | 0.757 |
| Per capita GDP in PPP 2008 ($) | 15,284 | 5,563 | 6,795 |

*Source*: Freedom House (2009) and UNDP (2009)

Table 8.3, which shows HDI and per capita GDP associated with democratic levels, illustrates that, beyond any attempts of causality, free democracies tend to be more developed. This result in general confirms the analyses of Przeworski *et al.* (2008) and Lipset (1959). However, while 'not free' countries can have higher GDP per capita on average than 'partly free' countries, a higher HDI is always associated with democracies and semi-democracies rather than with authoritarian regimes. Reasons for these different levels of democratic performance can be explored briefly. Most of the literature in political science explains this variation using the following variables: vicinity to Western Europe, modernisation, no large-scale oil production, a strong legislature and extensive economic reforms. All of these are necessary conditions for democracy.

Møller and Skaaning (2009) found that a modernisation process is needed first and then democracy will be improved. As an indicator of modernisation, they posit an economic development threshold of about $5,300. However, as we said above, most transition economies have already overcome that income level. Way (2008) found that politicians and autocrats control oil and gas rents in countries like Azerbaijan, Kazakhstan, Russia and Turkmenistan. They use these rents to pay friends, to create political consensus and to eliminate opposition. Finally, vicinity to Western Europe and implementation of political and economic reforms are both indicated as important factors for the development of democracy (Schimmelfennig and Scholtz, 2008). The EU sets the adoption of democratic rules and practices as conditions to be fulfilled by the target countries in order to receive such rewards as financial assistance, some kind of institutional association or ultimately even membership (Schimmelfennig and Scholtz, 2008). This contributed to the more successful democratic transition of the CEECs vis-à-vis the FSRs.

Cultural and historical factors also play an important role (Brzezinski, 2001) in the development of democracy. Countries where for long periods individual liberties were frustrated by the intrusive role of the state and by the hegemony of secret police services, single-party rules and other groups, such as lobbies and oligarchs, remain behind in the development of democracy. These cultural and historical factors are closely linked to the level of social capital in the country. In fact, as I assumed from the very beginning of this chapter, in the end democracy originates first of all in social capital along with the middle class rather than in economic development. This tallies with the conclusions of Acemouglu *et al.* (2006), who found that one of the main determinants of democracy is civil society, which is obliviously related with social capital, and Moore (1966), who found the origins of democracy in the middle class.

In the model shown in Figure 8.1, democracy is a consequence of social capital and the middle class, and in turn it helps to boost the HDI. The regression model outlined in Table 8.2 uses democracy (civil liberties and political rights) as an independent variable alongside other variables. Methodologically, it would now not be fair to explain democracy with the other independent variables of Table 8.2

*Table 8.4* Development/democracy correlation

| | **PolRight_CivLib** | **HDI** |
|---|---|---|
| PolRight_CivLib | 1.0000 | |
| HDI | −0.8432 | 1.0000 |

*Source*: author's elaboration

(trust and poverty*Gini), and in fact preliminary results are not robust. However, what can be done is first of all to show the strong correlation between democracy (PolRight_CivLib) and development (HDI), as Table 8.4 above shows.

While it is important to keep in mind that in the end both democratisation and development are functions of social capital and middle class, according to the causalities of Figure 8.1, democracy can be also fostered by a good combination of social rights (public investment in health and education) and anti-corruption policies. This combination acts at a second stage, at the policy level, where there is room for policy makers to actively improve democracy (political rights and civil liberties). At this level I assume that social rights reinforce the middle class and that anti-corruption policies positively stimulate civil society and social capital. Hence, these two variables, 'control of corruption' and 'public investment in health and education', can be considered to be functional variables for social capital and the middle class respectively.

On the one hand, it would be very difficult to find causality relationships between corruption, public expenditure in education and health and democracy; however, on the other hand, one can argue that democracies are always better associated with less corruption and to some extent with education, and descriptive statistics confirm this trend. The correlation matrix and the figure below show this better.[13]

*Table 8.5* Corruption/democracy correlation

| | corrup | P.Righ_C.Liberty |
|---|---|---|
| Corruption | 1.0000 | |
| P.Righ_C.Liberty | -0.9349 | 1.0000 |

The link between corruption and democracy (political rights and civil liberties) can appear clearer because corrupted governments by definition cannot be considered free, and corrupted politicians try to reduce democratic means to eliminate any control over their actions. By contrast, the link between public investments in education and health, and democracy (which I assumed to be strong earlier in the text) needs more explanation. Investment in health and education contributes to the creation of a more educated and healthier middle class which would therefore be more able to control its government. Healthier people are not under constant threat from government health policies and are free to contest and criticise politicians. They are free from the fear

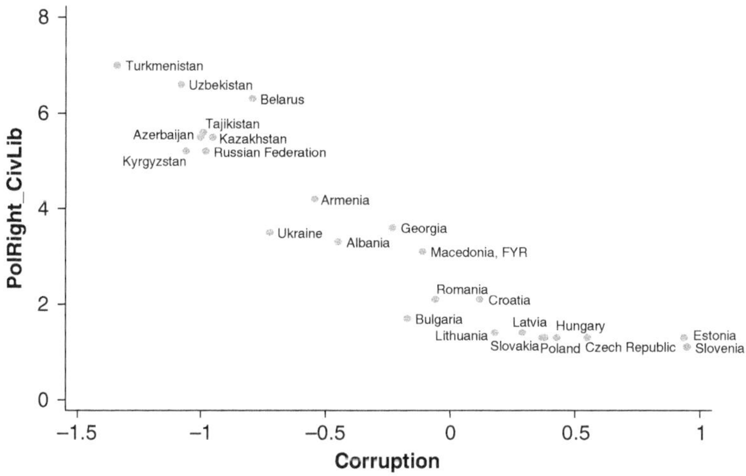


*Figure 8.5* Corruption-democracy scatter graph
*Source*: author's elaboration based on EBRD and Freedom House data

of survival and are more interested in post-materialist goods such as democracy and freedom (Inglehart, 1971).[14] At the same time, a better educated population is obviously more able to argue against bad politicians and to compete against them, having more cultural arguments and intellectual means.

All that is consistent with the general model put forward in this chapter, when I argue that democracy, as well as human development, is a consequence of social capital and the middle class. Control of corruption can also be considered a proxy for social capital, while public investment in education and health can be considered a proxy for the middle class, as was explained earlier. Corruption is one of the most important features to trace social capital. A less corrupted society has a higher endowment of social capital. At the same time, the middle class is also a bearer of social institutions, collective actions and requests for public investments in health and education. Higher investments in health and education are usually associated with a more consistent middle class.[15]

## 8.9 Final comments

The main findings of this chapter are that the process of human development is carried out by the force of a consistent middle class in association with social capital and democratic political institutions such as political rights and civil liberties. Social capital is measured using the variable 'trust' (from the World Values Survey). In parallel, education and human capital, broadly speaking, will be disseminated better in a society endowed with a higher level of social capital, and the general level of knowledge will be higher, with positive effects on development. Furthermore, a comparative analysis among the CEECs and FSRs shows that the former performed better in terms of HDI because they have a better endowment of social capital and during transformation also implemented policies better able to boost democracy and reinforce the middle class. On the contrary, in most FSRs and some CEECs, transition took place in its early stages in a sort of systemic vacuum. This vacuum favoured anti-social behaviour, perverse attitudes such as lobbying and corruption, increased egoism – which is a threat to trust – and increased inequality, and favoured personal privileges, power groups and the rent-seeking behaviour of oligarchs, with further negative effects on social capital and development. In these circumstances, democratic institutions, favoured by public investment in health and education and by better control of corruption, are discouraged too, and in fact FSRs tend not only to be poorer but also to be dominated by authoritarian regimes. This is much more evident when the HDI (rather than per capita GDP) is compared with democracy: in transition economies, a higher HDI is always associated with democracies and semi-democratic regimes rather than authoritarian ones.

# Appendix A8: Political Regimes in CEECs and FSRs

The classification made in Table 8.3 is drawn up on the basis of political rights and civil liberties indices, which in turn are constructed on the basis of such questions as the following (Political right questions, Freedom House):

- Is the head of government or other chief national authority elected through *free and fair elections*?
- Do the people have *the right to organise in different political parties* or other competitive political groupings of their choice, and is the system open to the rise and fall of these competing parties or groupings?
- Is the government *free from pervasive corruption?*
- Do cultural, ethnic, religious or other *minority groups have full political rights* and electoral opportunities?

(Civil liberties questions, Freedom House):

- Are there free and *independent media* and other forms of cultural expression?
- Is there *freedom of assembly, demonstration* and open public discussion?
- Is there *freedom for non-governmental organisations*?
- Is there *protection from political terror*, unjustified imprisonment, exile or torture for groups that either support or oppose the system? Is there freedom from war and insurgency?

*Table A8.1* Democracies

| Country | Political rights | Civil liberties | Total (average) |
|---|---|---|---|
| Czech Republic | 1 | 1 | 1 |
| Estonia | 1 | 1 | 1 |
| Hungary | 1 | 1 | 1 |
| Lithuania | 1 | 1 | 1 |
| Poland | 1 | 1 | 1 |
| Slovakia | 1 | 1 | 1 |
| Slovenia | 1 | 1 | 1 |
| Latvia | 2 | 1 | 1.5 |
| Bulgaria | 2 | 2 | 2.0 |
| Croatia | 2 | 2 | 2.0 |
| Romania | 2 | 2 | 2.0 |
| Serbia | 3 | 2 | 2.5 |
| Ukraine | 3 | 2 | 2.5 |

1 represents the most free and 7 the least free.
*Source*: Freedom House, 2009

*Table A8.2* Defective democracies/semi-authoritarian regimes

| Country | Political rights | Civil liberties | Total (averages) |
|---|---|---|---|
| Albania | 3 | 3 | 3.0 |
| Macedonia | 3 | 3 | 3.0 |
| Montenegro | 3 | 3 | 3.0 |
| Bosnia and Herzegovina | 4 | 3 | 3.5 |
| Georgia | 4 | 4 | 4.0 |
| Moldova | 4 | 4 | 4.0 |
| Kyrgyzstan | 5 | 4 | 4.5 |
| Armenia | 6 | 4 | 5.0 |

1 represents the most free and 7 the least free.
*Source*: Freedom House, 2009

*Table A8.3* Authoritarian regimes

| Country | Political rights | Civil liberties | Total (averages) |
|---|---|---|---|
| Azerbaijan | 6 | 5 | 5.5 |
| Kazakhstan | 6 | 5 | 5.5 |
| Russia | 6 | 5 | 5.5 |
| Tajikistan | 6 | 5 | 5.5 |
| Belarus | 7 | 6 | 6.5 |
| Turkmenistan | 7 | 7 | 7.0 |
| Uzbekistan | 7 | 7 | 7.0 |

1 represents the most free and 7 the least free.
*Source*: Freedom House, 2009

## Autocrats and ruling presidents

- Tajikistan: President Emomali *Rahmon* (Rakhmonov), 1994–present.
- Kazakhstan: President *Nazarbayev*, 1990–present.
- Azerbaijan: President Heydar *Aliyev*, 1993–2003 (deceased); President *Ilham Aliyev*, 2003–present.
- Kyrgyzstan: President *Akayev*, 1991–2005 (resigned); President *Bakiyev* 2005–present.
- Uzbekistan: President *Karimov*, 1991–present.
- Turkmenistan: President *Saparmurat Niyazov*, 1992–2006 (deceased); President *Berdymukhammedov*, 2006–present.
- Russia: according to Freedom House, Russia is not an electoral democracy (Freedom House, 2009). The December 2007 State Duma elections were carefully engineered by the administration, handing pro-Kremlin parties a super majority in the lower house. In the presidential election of March 2008, state dominance of the media was on full display, debate was absent and the incumbent Vladimir Putin, in power as President since 1999, was able to pass the office to his handpicked successor, Dmitry Medvedev. Putin remained as Prime Minister.

# 9
# Conclusion

This book has analysed the economic transition in the CEECs and in the FSRs. It has tried to explain why these countries had different performances during transition, what were the main institutional problems and causes of friction during transformation, and the role of institutions on economic development. It has explained why some of them grew faster than others, whether the model of capitalism that they adopted was relevant for economic development and what are, in the end, the main determinants of a process of economic development, which includes both income (GDP) and non-income dimensions (life expectancy and education levels in particular, i.e., human development).

I began by attempting to give an explanation of the widening of the gap between the East and West of Europe, which in the end brought about the economic collapse of the Soviet planned system. From a historical perspective, in 1950 some countries in the East like Poland, Hungary, Czechoslovakia and the USSR had a GDP per capita higher than Portugal, Greece and Spain, and very similar to those of Italy, Ireland and Austria. On the eve of the fall of the Berlin Wall in 1989, the situation was reversed. All the Western economies had a higher GDP per capita than those countries. After the end of the 1960s and the accomplishment of industrialisation in the FCEs, industries in the East became less competitive compared to the West due to the disappearance of the 'encompassing national interest' which enabled the industrialisation effort. Corruption, privileges, nepotism, cronyism, inefficiencies, waste, bad incentives, perverse and distorted rules, and cumbersome bureaucracy dominated societies all contributed to the loss in competitiveness (Olson, 1992). Moreover, the price administration of planning was badly managed. Above all, however, during the 1970s, FCEs missed the opportunity to embark on an innovation process because institutions and incentives were no longer appropriate and state managers had other objectives than to stimulate innovation (Berend, 2009).

The transformation strategies, initiated in FCEs between 1989 and 1991, were mainly guided by neoclassical policies. At the beginning of transition, the prevalent idea among economists and international economic organisations was ideologically driven and very market-oriented, with a minimalist state. Reforms in many transition economies mainly followed the Washington Consensus, which designed policies according to neoclassical theories, with adverse effects and poor results in many transition economies. These policies were mainly introduced using *fast strategies* – so-called 'shock therapy'. As a result, recession and systemic vacuum emerged in all transition economies. Unemployment, poverty and inequalities increased, while life expectancy and HDI levels decreased.

In 2009 average GDP in purchasing power parity among transition economies, after almost 20 years of transition, was roughly the same as it had been in 1989. The current economic crisis hit all transition economies hard. The average GDP level in 2008 was 117 (1989 level = 100). At the end of 2009 it was lower than 117, and six out of 12 FSRs (Georgia, Kyrgyzstan, Moldova, Russia, Tajikistan and Ukraine), and eight out of 16 CEECs (Bosnia and Herzegovina, Bulgaria, Croatia, Latvia, Lithuania, Montenegro, Romania and Serbia) are still below their 1989 GDP level. We can thus rephrase what Baldwin stated in 2000:[1] most of these economies lost 20 years of development. Transition in the FSRs in particular was dominated by the objectives of oligarchs, corrupted power groups and rent-seekers, who exploited the systemic vacuum, the institutional weakness and contradictions, and the lack of a genuine state control. However, most CEECs at certain points were better able to manage transition partly because they were subject to EU conditionality, which in the end allowed most of them to gain membership to the EU.

Nevertheless, the financial crisis of 2008–10 had very bad effects on the real economies in all transition countries. This has not been the main object of study of this book. However, some lessons can be drawn from this as well. Both political vulnerability and economic volatility seem to be easier to avoid in countries which, before the crisis broke, created *stronger* institutions and *better* and more appropriate integration into the global economy (Rodrik, 2008); in other words, countries that have social institutions and can rely on a domestic aggregate demand (like Poland, which is, very interestingly, one of the very few countries to experience positive growth during this international crisis at +1.3 per cent) and countries that did not adopt an extreme export-led model with an uncontrolled openness to FDI (unlike Estonia, Latvia and Lithuania, which had a fall in GDP of around −15 per cent). Among the CIS, the crisis was very severe in Armenia, Georgia, Russia and Ukraine. On average, it was worse in Eastern Europe and the Caucasus (−9 per cent) than in the rest of the CIS (+0.8 per cent) and in CEECs (−5 per cent). The three countries classified as state capitalist economies (Belarus, Turkmenistan and Uzbekistan) were even able to achieve growth consistently during the current crisis, thanks to public investment improvements and less exposure to the credit crisis. As a general assessment, the crisis was better managed where countries exhibited stronger maturity of pre-crisis institutions, external anchors and greater social cohesion.

Today there is a growing consensus on the fact that successful transition involves compromises of market mechanisms and state-supported activities, good corporate regulation and appropriate governance, grounded business environment and financial regulation (Transition Report, 2009). The 2008–10 economic crisis also brought about a resurgence of Keynesian policies, the emergence of heterodox policies and a good institutional mix able to prevent further crises and to enable better recovery (Krugman, 2008; Rodrik, 2008).

In addition, I argued that the process of transformation, which goes beyond the current crisis, must be guided by the presence and participation of the state, as well as rules and institutions that coherently discipline the economic system in the difficult phase of substitution in order to prevent a systemic vacuum and avoid social costs. Institutions, which can be formal or informal rules affecting the economic behaviour of agents, are crucial in the transformation process and in the economic development of a country. In fact, economic development should be considered a process that starts with institutional change. Such an institutional change includes a change in informal rules and power groups which would otherwise inhibit development and act as obstacles to transformation, the innovation process and knowledge diffusion. Institutional change in communist countries seems to be characterised on the one hand by abrupt rules introduced at the beginning of the transformation and on the other hand by the slow transformation of values and habits informally persistent in the relevant society. During the transition from a planned economy to a market economy, this resulted in a conflict between social groups, agents and sets of institutions. This conflict caused institutional instability and a lack of consistency in the new institutional framework. Through the *dichotomy thesis*, in Chapter 4 I explained that new institutions were built on the dichotomy between old rules (the *old ethos*) and new formal rules, and on the groups supporting each set of these rules. The inconsistencies between both seem to affect economic performance, increasing transaction costs and other institutional costs. Macro-economic stabilisation, deflationary policies, liberalisation of prices and privatisation of public assets were not sufficient conditions for economic growth. An institutional strategy was missing in almost all transition economies, and this caused recessions to deepen and stifled further economic recovery, worsening development conditions. However, some countries, in particular those in Central Europe, were able in the second half of the 1990s to introduce institutional policies and socially-oriented institutions that could promote development.

Econometric exercises carried out in Chapter 5 showed that EBRD market-oriented reforms are not significant in creating growth. In this chapter I first classified transition economies into five models (the *competitive capitalist model*, the *corporative model*, the *dirigiste model*, the *hybrid model* and the *state capitalist model*). The type of socio-economic model may have an impact on GDP. Using a factor analysis, I discovered that variables that characterise a competitive capitalist type of socio-economic model are not significant in creating economic growth, while the corporative model is associated with higher levels of GDP and with higher levels of democracy. It is also able to better combine freedom and social rights, which is a crucial issue for transition economies. In fact, countries classified as belonging to the corporative capitalist model always show better socio-economic variables, such as inequality, poverty, voice and accountability, freedom index, life expectancy and HDI – in other words, a better institutional framework. In contrast, countries classified as belonging to the dirigiste capitalist model show worse indicators.

A better institutional framework, found in the countries of the corporative model, improves the level of human development, which in turn improves economic growth, as shown in this scheme:

| Institutional framework → human development → economic growth |
|---|

A better institutional framework has to be identified with a situation where relevant political institutional and social variables interact with each other and provide people with opportunities and therefore capabilities for doing and being, as proposed by Amartya Sen (1999). These variables are: health and education expenditure, voice and accountability, and freedom. It was shown in Chapter 7 that these variables first increase the level of human development (without the income dimension) and then that human development causes GDP growth. Hence, human development emerged as a sufficient but not necessary condition for economic growth in transition economies. In other words, there can be economic growth without human development, but if there is human development, then there will be economic growth. In this context, however, further research and empirical tests would be needed in order to strengthen results, along the lines of Binder and Georgiadis (2010).

Nevertheless, at the basis of human development enlargement there is social capital and the middle class. The models tested in Chapter 8 show that social capital and the middle class are sources for both democratic institutions (political rights and civil liberties) and development (HDI).

The middle class, a distinct political actor between the elites and the working class that is extremely relevant in post-industrial society, is not only identified by a certain level of income but most importantly by a level of social capital and involvement of civil society which comes first and establishes institutions able to promote a development process. In this process, a relevant role is played by education and knowledge, which are values that are extremely important for the middle class. Moreover, education and knowledge dissemination are more available in societies endowed with higher levels of social capital.

The comparative analysis among CEECs and FSRs shows that the former performed better in terms of HDI because they had better endowment of social capital and also implemented better policies during transformation that were able to boost democracy and reinforce the middle class. Cultural and historical factors also play an important role for both development and democracy. On the contrary, at the beginning of transition, most of the FSRs and some CEECs founds themselves to be experiencing a sort of systemic vacuum which favoured oligarchs, people in dominant positions and rent-seekers, and also increased the level of corruption. The glue that holds society together, social capital, was under threat in these economies. Networking and lobbying became components of daily business, but in most cases they had a negative influence, favouring crime, clans, oligarchs, power groups and similar organisations that were bearers of particular privileges, corrupted business, cronyism and nepotism. All this increased inequality and frustrated the middle class, which became poorer and more compressed. An 'economy of favours' is in place in most FSRs, the systemic use of connections to procure favours being a recurrent feature.

Democratic institutions, which in my analysis are correlated with better control of corruption, are also discouraged in these circumstances, and in fact FSRs tend to be not only poorer but also dominated by authoritarian regimes. This is much more evident when HDI (rather than per capita GDP) is compared with democracy: in transition economies, a higher HDI is always associated with democracies and semi-democratic regimes rather than authoritarian regimes. We can therefore state that almost all FSRs have passed from planned systems to 'under-development', where democracy is defective and the level of income is lower than it was in 1989.

Briefly, some lessons can be drawn from the transition process so far. The transition towards a new system is a complex process involving values and systemic changes, and therefore needs time, proper institutions and governance ability. The analysis carried out throughout this book suggests that: 1) a country cannot have a higher HDI without social capital and a large middle class; 2) a country can have economic growth without a high HDI and without democracy; 3) if a country has a high HDI, it will have growth and in all likelihood democracy.

The transition of CEECs and the CIS has high social costs. Poverty, which emerged in all transition economies to an important degree, will not be defeated simply by economic growth. Distribution policies and a holistic institutional approach – which help to manage conflicts and reinforce social cohesion – are needed. Human development, which allows for the widening of people's choices, is possible under appropriate institutional policies which give people the capabilities of doing and being and opportunities such as access to health, education and the job market. The role of the state in creating such conditions is essential, as along with social capital, the participation and accountability of people, political rights, civil liberties and social rights. The state should provide for a well-designed educational system, health system and income opportunities. These institutional policies would allow people to improve their level of capabilities and this in turn would boost development.

# Appendix

*Table 1A* A Socio-economic variables

| | Poverty 2006 (% of population with $4 a day) | Gini 2006 | GDP ($) PPP 2008 | GDP per capita 1989 ($) | Unemployment rate 2007 | EBRD index avg. 2009 | 3rd lev. edu. 2005–7 | Health expenditure 2000–5 (% of GDP) | Education expenditure 2000–5 (% of GDP) | Life expectancy index 2007 | Education index 2007 | HDI 1990 | HDI 2007 |
|---|---|---|---|---|---|---|---|---|---|---|---|---|---|
| Albania | 47.96 | 31.09 | 5,886 | 721 | 15 | 2.844 | 19 | 2.7 | 2.8 | 0.856 | 0.886 | 0.702 | 0.79 |
| Armenia | 80.51 | 33.8 | 4,879 | 488 | 10 | 3.054 | 26 | 1.2 | 3.2 | 0.78 | 0.903 | 0.751 | 0.77 |
| Azerbaijan | 57.63 | 36.5 | 6,280 | 346 | 1 | 2.456 | 15 | 0.9 | 3.3 | 0.704 | 0.881 | NA | 0.76 |
| Belarus | 8.3 | 29.73 | 9,732 | 593 | 3 | 1.800 | 61 | 4.9 | 5.8 | 0.73 | 0.958 | 0.785 | 0.8 |
| Bosnia and Herzegovina | NA | NA | 4,834 | 818 | NA | 2.733 | | 5.2 | NA | 0.827 | 0.874 | NA | 0.807 |
| Bulgaria | 39.88 | 29.24 | 10,274 | 5,238 | 14 | 3.489 | 41 | 4.1 | 4.2 | 0.798 | 0.93 | 0.795 | 0.826 |
| Croatia | 5.59 | 29 | 14,309 | 5,193 | 14 | 3.433 | 39 | 6.5 | 4.5 | 0.842 | 0.915 | 0.806 | 0.85 |
| Czech Republic | 1 | 25.82 | 22,118 | 7,590 | 8 | 3.458 | 43 | 6.8 | 4.6 | 0.853 | 0.938 | 0.845* | 0.895 |
| Estonia | 33.15 | 36 | 18,969 | 2,760 | 10 | 3.811 | 65 | 4.1 | 5.7 | 0.771 | 0.964 | 0.817 | 0.87 |
| Georgia | 61.89 | 40.37 | 4,010 | 524 | 12 | 2.977 | 41 | 1.0 | 2.9 | 0.763 | 0.909 | NA | 0.75 |
| Hungary | 10.62 | 27 | 18,277 | 3,027 | 6 | 3.944 | 60 | 6.1 | 6.0 | 0.802 | 0.96 | 0.807 | 0.879 |
| Kazakhstan | 56.71 | 33.85 | 9,832 | 3,924 | 9 | 2.945 | 48 | 2.0 | 2.4 | 0.689 | 0.966 | 0.767 | 0.77 |
| Kyrgyzstan | 72.48 | 36 | 1,813 | 2,745 | 13 | 2.656 | 40 | 2.2 | 4.4 | 0.678 | 0.919 | NA | 0.71 |
| Latvia | 26.3 | 37.66 | 15,350 | 1,930 | 11 | 3.510 | 74 | 3.3 | 5.4 | 0.788 | 0.961 | 0.807 | 0.85 |

*Table 1A* (Continued)

| | Poverty 2006 | Gini 2006 | GDP ($) PPP 2008 | GDP per capita 1989 ($) | Unemployment rate 2007 | EBRD index avg. 2009 | 3rd lev. edu. 2005–7 | Health expenditure 2000–5 (% of GDP) | Education expenditure 2000–5 (% of GDP) | Life expectancy index 2007 | Education index 2007 | HDI 1990 | HDI 2007 |
|---|---|---|---|---|---|---|---|---|---|---|---|---|---|
| Lithuania | 36.04 | 36.01 | 15,738 | 1,310 | 12 | 3.521 | 73 | 5.0 | 5.2 | 0.795 | 0.968 | 0.823 | 0.87 |
| Macedonia | NA | NA | 7,850 | 293 | NA | 3.020 | 28 | 4.3 | 5.5 | 0.816 | 0.879 | NA | 0.8 |
| Moldova | NA | NA | 1,766 | 293 | NA | 2.833 | 29 | 4.9 | 8 | 0.727 | 0.9 | 0.736 | 0.718 |
| Montenegro | 21.95 | 38.95 | 6,509 | 1,431 | 37 | 2.678 | 3 | 6.0 | 3.4 | 0.82 | 0.891 | NA | 0.822 |
| Poland | 17.45 | 34,05 | 14,836 | 2,147 | 20 | 3.699 | 61 | 4.5 | 5.8 | 0.839 | 0.952 | 0.802 | 0.872 |
| Romania | NA | NA | 10,431 | 2,319 | NA | 3.467 | 40 | 3.3 | 3.7 | 0.786 | 0.914 | 0.771 | 0.82 |
| Russian Federation | 35.36 | 42 | 13,116 | 6,202 | 8 | 3.033 | 68 | 3.2 | 3.7 | 0.669 | 0.933 | 0.813 | 0.807 |
| Serbia | NA | NA | 6,761 | 1,773 | NA | 2.701 | 36 | 5.2 | 4.4 | 0.813 | 0.891 | NA | 0.823 |
| Slovakia | 6.69 | 25.81 | 17,730 | 3,351 | 7 | 3.610 | 36 | 5.3 | 4.4 | 0.824 | 0.928 | NA | 0.87 |
| Slovenia | 8 | 28 | 24,356 | 6,540 | 30 | 3.332 | 74 | 6.6 | 6 | 0.878 | 0.969 | 0.852* | 0.92 |
| Tajikistan | 84.71 | 32.63 | 1,610 | 216 | 2 | 2.166 | 16 | 1.4 | 4 | 0.691 | 0.896 | 0.719 | 0.69 |
| Turkmenistan | 66.88 | 40.77 | 4,300 | 298 | 5 | 1.356 | NA | 4.8 | 5.4 | 0.63 | 0.907 | NA | 0.76 |
| Ukraine | 44.68 | 28.05 | 6,212 | 480 | 9 | 2.855 | 66 | 3.6 | 6.2 | 0.712 | 0.956 | 0.798 | 0.784 |
| Uzbekistan | 16.92 | 36.72 | 2,192 | 233 | 4 | 2.135 | 15 | 2.4 | 6.2 | 0.698 | 0.89 | 0.687* | 0.72 |

* = data available for 1995
*Note*: 3rd lev. edu. = third level of education (i.e., university)
*Source*: UNDP, World Bank, EBRD, different years

*Table 2A* Main variables for classification of countries according to different types of models

| | Countries | Private sector share in GDP (%) | Budgetary subsidies and current transfers (% GDP) | Share of administered prices in CPI (%) | Share of trade in GDP (%) | Tariff revenues (% of imports) | Asset share of state-owned banks (%) | Asset share of foreign-owned banks (%) | Stock market capitalisation (% of GDP) | Controls on inward direct investment | Wage regulation | % GDP expend. edu and health | Competition level (1–4) |
|---|---|---|---|---|---|---|---|---|---|---|---|---|---|
| State capitalism | Turkmenistan | 25.0 | 1.6 | 6.7 | 98.3 | 0.5 | 93.7 | 1.1 | NA | no | yes | 10.2 | 1.00 |
| | Belarus | 30.0 | 21.2 | 30.0 | 144.4 | 10.3 | 76.5 | 19.7 | 3.0 | yes | yes | 10.3 | 2.00 |
| | Uzbekistan | 45.0 | 1.4 | 53.0 | 66.0 | 2.5 | 67.6 | 4.4 | 4.3 | yes | yes | 8.6 | 1.67 |
| Hybrid capitalism | *Bosnia and Herz. | 60.0 | 5.2 | NA | 105.5 | 5.0 | 1.9 | 93.8 | 71.8 | yes | no | NA | 2.00 |
| | *Ukraine | 65.0 | 2.9 | 8.0 | 84.1 | 3.3 | 8.0 | 39.4 | 79.2 | no | no | 9.8 | 2.33 |
| | Romania | 70.0 | 16.3 | 21.4 | 63.1 | 1.5 | 5.7 | 87.3 | 27.3 | no | yes | 7.5 | 2.67 |
| | Bulgaria | 75.0 | 1.5 | 18.6 | 123.2 | 8.0 | 2.1 | 82.3 | 51.3 | no | yes | 6.9 | 3.00 |
| Dirigiste capitalism | Azerbaijan | 75.0 | 6.5 | 7.0 | 84.2 | 13.5 | 42.4 | 7.5 | NA | no | no | 3.8 | 2.00 |
| | Kyrgyz Rep. | 75.0 | 3.2 | 17.7 | 121.8 | 3.7 | 8.7 | 58.7 | 3.0 | no | no | 7.9 | 2.00 |
| | Serbia | 60.0 | 2.5 | 9.9 | 75.3 | 4.7 | 15.8 | 75.5 | 53.7 | no | no | NA | 2.00 |
| | Moldova | 65.0 | NA | NA | 103.5 | 2.0 | 9.5 | 24.8 | 22.0 | no | yes | 12.9 | 2.33 |
| | Montenegro | 65.0 | NA | 9.2 | 106.8 | NA | 0.0 | 78.7 | 99.0 | no | no | 11.6 | 1.67 |
| | Russia | 65.0 | 3.5 | 6.7 | 43.6 | 28.7 | 40.0 | 17.0 | 112.0 | yes | no | 6.9 | 2.33 |
| | Tajikistan | 55.0 | 0.5 | 0.0 | 62.9 | 3.2 | 7.2 | 6.6 | NA | no | yes | 5.4 | 1.67 |

*Table 2A* (Continued)

| | Countries | Private sector share in GDP (%) | Budgetary subsidies and current transfers (% GDP) | Share of administered prices in CPI (%) | Share of trade in GDP (%) | Tariff revenues (% of imports) | Asset share of state-owned banks (%) | Asset share of foreign-owned banks (%) | Stock market capitalisation (% of GDP) | Controls on inward direct investment | Wage regulation | % GDP expend. edu and health | Competition level (1–4) |
|---|---|---|---|---|---|---|---|---|---|---|---|---|---|
| Corporative capitalism | Hungary | 80.0 | 2.3 | 14.6 | 133.8 | 0.1 | 7.0 | 82.6 | 32.0 | no | yes | 11.3 | 3.33 |
| | Slovenia | 70.0 | 3.3 | 13.1 | 120.2 | 0.2 | 14.4 | 28.8 | 57.2 | no | yes | 12.6 | 2.67 |
| | *Croatia | 70.0 | 2.7 | 0.0 | 67.8 | 1.3 | 4.7 | 90.4 | 119.6 | no | no | 10.8 | 2.67 |
| | *Macedonia | 70.0 | 4.0 | 1.2 | 124.2 | NA | 1.4 | 85.9 | 33.0 | yes | no | 9.7 | 2.33 |
| | *Czech Rep. | 80.0 | 9.0 | 12.0 | 136.9 | 0.2 | 2.5 | 84.4 | 32.0 | yes | no | 10.9 | 3.00 |
| | *Poland | 75.0 | 0.6 | 1.0 | 68.2 | 0.4 | 19.5 | 75.5 | 44.1 | no | no | 9.8 | 3.33 |
| Competitive capitalism | *Kazakhstan | 70.0 | 0.1 | 0.0 | 73.0 | 4.0 | 0.2 | 38.5 | 40.0 | yes | no | 5.5 | 2.00 |
| | Estonia | 80.0 | 0.6 | 23.3 | 117.1 | 0.3 | 0.0 | 98.7 | 27.0 | no | no | 10 | 3.67 |
| | Slovakia | 80.0 | 1.3 | 24.1 | 168.2 | 0.1 | 1.0 | 99.0 | 8.6 | no | no | 9.7 | 3.33 |
| | *Latvia | 70.0 | 4.5 | 12.9 | 72.8 | 0.3 | 4.2 | 63.8 | 11.0 | no | no | 9.9 | 3.00 |
| | *Lithuania | 75.0 | 0.8 | 13.5 | 123.8 | 0.4 | 0.0 | 91.7 | 25.0 | no | no | 9.8 | 3.33 |
| | *Georgia | 75.0 | 6.6 | 5.4 | 65.1 | 5.4 | 0.0 | 90.6 | 13.0 | no | no | 4.2 | 2.00 |
| | Albania | 75.0 | 0.2 | NA | 46.3 | 2.7 | 0.0 | 94.2 | NA | no | no | 5.7 | 2.00 |
| | Armenia | 75.0 | 1.0 | 8.1 | 39.9 | 2.3 | 0.0 | 49.0 | 1.0 | no | no | 4.2 | 2.33 |

*= indicate that the country does not fit the respective model exactly
*Source*: EBRD, Transition Reports, 2008 and 2009

*Table 3A* The middle class, social capital and political institutions

| Countries | Level of freedom avg. 2001–6 | Level of democracy avg. 2000–3 | Voice & account 2000–7 | Control of corruption 2000–7 | Pol. stability 2000–7 | Middle class: Poverty* Gini 2006 | INGO density 2003 | Trust (% anwering 'yes')* 1999–2003 | INGO (in numbers) 2003 | Political rights 2005–7 (2) | Civil liberties 2005–7 (2) | Average (1) and (2) |
|---|---|---|---|---|---|---|---|---|---|---|---|---|
| Albania | 2.0 | 6 | –0.04 | –0.45 | –0.69 | 1,492 | 242.6 | 24% | 778 | 3.1 | 3.4 | 3.3 |
| Armenia | 2.0 | 5 | –0.54 | –0.54 | –0.57 | 2,265 | 173.6 | 25% | 515 | 4.4 | 4.0 | 4.2 |
| Azerbaijan | 1.3 | –7 | –0.96 | –1 | –1.24 | 2,117 | 57.2 | 21% | 397 | 6.0 | 5.0 | 5.5 |
| Belarus | 1.0 | –7 | –1.49 | –0.79 | 0 | 238 | 296 | 42% | 776 | 6.5 | 6.0 | 6.3 |
| Bosnia and Herz. | NA | NA | NA | –0.32 | NA | 1,400 | 172.5 | 16% | NA | NA | NA | NA |
| Bulgaria | 3.0 | 8.75 | 0.54 | –0.17 | 0.22 | 1,170 | 80.2 | 27% | 2,138 | 1.1 | 2.3 | 1.7 |
| Croatia | 3.0 | 7 | 0.44 | 0.12 | 0.3 | 174 | 337.4 | 18% | 100 | 2.0 | 2.1 | 2.1 |
| Czech Rep. | 3.0 | 10 | 0.96 | 0.37 | 0.77 | 52 | 1,181.8 | 24% | 3,236 | 1.0 | 1.6 | 1.3 |
| Estonia | 3.0 | 6 | 1.00 | 0.94 | 0.83 | 720 | 154.4 | 23% | 1,543 | 1.0 | 1.6 | 1.3 |
| Georgia | 2.0 | 5 | –0.34 | –0.23 | –1.34 | 2,503 | 471.2 | 19% | 685 | 3.6 | 3.7 | 3.6 |
| Hungary | 3.0 | 10 | 1.11 | 0.55 | 0.82 | 297 | 360 | 22% | 3,487 | 1.0 | 1.6 | 1.3 |
| Kazakhstan | 1.0 | –5 | –1.14 | –0.95 | 0.12 | 1,929 | 33.2 | 20% | 498 | 6.0 | 5.0 | 5.5 |
| Kyrgyzstan | 1.3 | –3 | –0.98 | –1.06 | –1.04 | 2,592 | 63.2 | 17% | 267 | 5.7 | 4.7 | 5.2 |
| Latvia | 3.0 | 8 | 0.90 | 0.29 | 0.81 | 979 | 446 | 17% | 1,323 | 1.0 | 1.7 | 1.4 |
| Lithuania | 3.0 | 10 | 0.94 | 0.18 | 0.8 | 1,296 | 615.3 | 25% | 1,459 | 1.1 | 1.7 | 1.4 |

*Table 3A* (Continued)

| Countries | Level of freedom avg. 2001–6 | Level of democracy avg. 2000–3 | Voice & account 2000–7 | Control of corruption 2000–7 | Pol. stability 2000–7 | Middle class: Poverty* Gini 2006 | INGO density 2003 | Trust (% anwering 'yes')* 1999–2003 | INGO (in numbers) 2003 | Political rights 2005–7 (2) | Civil liberties 2005–7 (2) | Average (1) and (2) |
|---|---|---|---|---|---|---|---|---|---|---|---|---|
| Macedonia, FYR | 2.0 | 7.5 | –0.09 | –0.11 | NA | 1,092 | 125.4 | 14% | 683 | 3.3 | 3 | 3.1 |
| Moldova | NA | NA | NA | –0.64 | NA | 990 | 380.1 | 15% | NA | NA | NA | NA |
| Montenegro | NA | NA | NA | –0.28 | –1.07 | 660 | 169.2 | 26% | NA | NA | NA | NA |
| Poland | 3.0 | 9.5 | 1.09 | 0.38 | 0.45 | 579 | 97.6 | 19% | 3,584 | 1.0 | 1.6 | 1.3 |
| Romania | 3.0 | 8 | 0.41 | –0.06 | NA | 800 | 113.8 | 10% | 2,392 | 2.1 | 2.0 | 2.1 |
| Russian Federation | 1.5 | 7 | –0.65 | –0.98 | 0.81 | 1,470 | 22.7 | 24% | 3,087 | 5.4 | 5.0 | 5.2 |
| Serbia | NA | NA | NA | –0.16 | NA | 260 | 169.2 | 26% | NA | NA |  | NA |
| Slovakia | 3.0 | 9 | 0.97 | 0.43 | 0.72 | 181 | 411.5 | 16% | 2,084 | 1.0 | 1.6 | 1.3 |
| Slovenia | 3.0 | 10 | 1.06 | 0.95 | 1.01 | 224 | 1,122.1 | 22% | 1,996 | 1.0 | 1.3 | 1.1 |
| Tajikistan | 1.0 | –1.5 | –1.13 | –0.99 | –1.41 | 2,774 | 32.1 | 14% | 195 | 6 | 5.3 | 5.6 |
| Turkmenistan | 1.0 | –9 | –0.32 | –1.34 | –0.85 | 2,487 | 34.8 | 19% | 156 | 7.0 | 7.0 | 7.0 |
| Ukraine | 2.3 | 7 | –0.51 | –0.72 | –0.32 | 1,262 | 35.8 | 27% | 1,590 | 3.7 | 3.3 | 3.5 |
| Uzbekistan | 1.0 | –9 | –1.66 | –1.08 | –1.4 | 624 | 16.2 | 18% | 376 | 7.0 | 6.3 | 6.6 |

*: (Can most people be trusted?), World Values Survey, 2009 (www.worldvaluessurvey.org)
*Source*: World Bank, UNDP, Freedom House, 2009

*Table 4A* FDI in transition economies

| | 1997 | 1998 | 1999 | 2000 | 2001 | 2002 | 2003 | 2004 | 2005 | 2006 | 2007 | 2008 | 2009 | FDI cumulative inflow (in US$ million) 1989–2008 | FDI cumulative inflow per capita (in US$ million) 1989–2008 | FDI inflows per capita (US$) 2008 | FDI inflows (% of GDP) 2008 |
|---|---|---|---|---|---|---|---|---|---|---|---|---|---|---|---|---|---|
| | | | | | (in US$ million) | | | | | | | Estimate | Projection | | | | |
| Croatia | 348 | 842 | 1,392 | 1,105 | 1,398 | 552 | 1,927 | 732 | 1,551 | 3,212 | 4,644 | 4,098 | 2,633 | 22,613 | 5,091 | 923 | 5.9 |
| Czech Republic | 1,259 | 3,575 | 5,220 | 4,942 | 5,474 | 8,282 | 1 814 | 3,941 | 11,630 | 4,598 | 7,930 | 5,500 | NA | 71,282 | 6,954 | 537 | NA |
| Estonia | 130 | 574 | 222 | 324 | 343 | 153 | 763 | 698 | 2,249 | 673 | 1,115 | 1,044 | 50 | 9,044 | 6,749 | 779 | 4.5 |
| Hungary | 3,715 | 3,070 | 3,060 | 2,151 | 3,573 | 2,722 | 479 | 3,405 | 5,586 | 3,640 | 2,197 | 4,763 | NA | 53,320 | 5,314 | 475 | 3.1 |
| Latvia | 515 | 303 | 331 | 400 | 114 | 250 | 254 | 528 | 585 | 1,491 | 1,913 | 1,195 | 338 | 8,829 | 3,888 | 526 | 3.5 |
| Lithuania | 328 | 921 | 478 | 375 | 439 | 714 | 142 | 510 | 689 | 1,551 | 1,409 | 1,459 | 200 | 9,301 | 2,758 | 433 | 3.1 |
| Poland | 4,863 | 6,049 | 7,239 | 9,327 | 5,804 | 3,901 | 4,284 | 11,761 | 6,951 | 10,727 | 17,976 | 12,951 | 8,500 | 112,722 | 2,967 | 341 | 2.5 |
| Slovakia | 84 | 374 | 701 | 1,897 | 1,520 | 4,130 | 1,913 | 3,052 | 2,279 | 4,178 | 2,881 | 3,156 | 2,000 | 27,115 | 5,021 | 584 | 3.2 |
| Slovenia | 303 | 221 | 59 | 71 | 226 | 1,508 | –174 | 281 | –67 | –215 | –353 | 280 | –67 | 2,762.6 | 381.3 | 140.2 | 0.5 |
| Albania | 42 | 45 | 51 | 143 | 207 | 135 | 178 | 344 | 283 | 325 | 651 | 880 | 558 | 3,601 | 1,125 | 275 | 6.8 |
| Bosnia and Herzegovina | 0 | 100 | 90 | 146 | 119 | 266 | 382 | 708 | 579 | 710 | 2,023 | 1,200 | 400 | 6,323 | 1,664 | 316 | 6.5 |

*Table 4A* (Continued)

| | 1997 | 1998 | 1999 | 2000 | 2001 | 2002 | 2003 | 2004 | 2005 | 2006 | 2007 | 2008 | 2009 | FDI cumulative inflow (in US$ million) 1989–2008 | FDI cumulative inflow per capita (in US$ million) 1989–2008 | FDI inflows per capita (US$) 2008 | FDI inflows (% of GDP) 2008 |
|---|---|---|---|---|---|---|---|---|---|---|---|---|---|---|---|---|---|
| | | | | | (in US$ million) | | | | | | | Estimate | Projection | | | | |
| Bulgaria | 507 | 537 | 802 | 998 | 803 | 876 | 2,070 | 2,879 | 4,005 | 7,583 | 11,433 | 8,472 | 5,568 | 41,448 | 5,454 | 1,115 | 17.0 |
| FYR Macedonia | 30 | 128 | 32 | 175 | 441 | 105 | 117 | 322 | 94 | 424 | 700 | 612 | 300 | 3,226 | 1,613 | 306 | 6.4 |
| Montenegro | NA | NA | NA | NA | 10 | 84 | 44 | 63 | 482 | 585 | 717 | 783 | 606 | 2,769 | 4,195 | 1,186 | 18.2 |
| Romania | 1,267 | 2,079 | 1,025 | 1,051 | 1,154 | 1,080 | 2,156 | 6,368 | 6,587 | 10,957 | 9,818 | 11,000 | 5,000 | 55,894 | 2,576 | 507 | 5.5 |
| Serbia | 740 | 113 | 112 | 50 | 165 | 475 | 1,365 | 966 | 1,550 | 4,264 | 2,195 | 2,487 | 1,400 | 14,482 | 1,931 | 332 | 4.9 |
| Eastern Europe and the Caucasus | *2,412* | *2,488* | *1,664* | *1,245* | *1,415* | *2,564* | *4,461* | *5,007* | *9,273* | *6,465* | *8,259* | *13,610* | *5,596* | *61,785* | *807* | *163* | *5.4* |
| Russia | 1,681 | 1,492 | 1,102 | −463 | 216 | −72 | −1,769 | 1,662 | 119 | 10,753 | 6,800 | 20,000 | NA | 45,045 | 317 | 141 | 1.2 |
| Central Asia | *1,716* | *1,476* | *1,808* | *1,541* | *3,165* | *2,624* | *2,718* | *6,499* | *3,088* | *8,106* | *9,137* | *13,444* | *7,216* | *60,388* | *869* | *200* | *6.2* |
| **All transition countries** | **18,257** | **22,893** | **25,286** | **25,940** | **26,369** | **30,422** | **24,894** | **48,064** | **57,395** | **69,272** | **84,645** | **86,933** | **40,297** | **566,905** | **2,381** | **382** | **5.8** |

*Note*: Eastern Europe and the Caucasus: Armenia, Azrbaijan, Belarus, Georgia, Moldova and Ukraine. Central Asia: Kazakhstan, Kyrgyz Republic, Tajikistan, Turkmenista and Uzbekistan
*Source*: IMF, central banks and EBRD estimates

# Notes

## Introduction

1. These countries have both the highest investment in health and education (in percentage of GDP) and the highest levels of life expectancy and education (UNDP, 2009).
2. The Brezhnev Doctrine was illustrated by Leonid Brezhnev (First Secretary of the Communist Party of the Soviet Union from 1964 to 1982) in a speech at the Fifth Congress of the Polish United Workers' Party on 13 November 1968, when he stated: 'When forces that are hostile to socialism try to turn the development of some socialist country towards capitalism, it becomes not only a problem of the country concerned, but a common problem and concern of all socialist countries.'
3. Cf. Brinkman (1995) for a review on this perspective.
4. I partly follow the classification used in De Muro and Tridico (2008) where, however, three levels of 'development', in broad terms, were characterised.

## 1 Transition to Market: A Long and Undefined Journey

1. This term, which is often used to indicate an economic shock therapy programme, ironically has the following meaning: 'abrupt withdrawal from addictive drugs' (*Oxford English Dictionary*).
2. In addition, the crisis in South Korea, and then in other Asian countries, seemed to be caused by the sudden introduction of short-term liberalisation of capitals (see Naqvi, 1994; Stiglitz, 1998; Nayyar, 2000). Nevertheless, Asian countries are quite particular with regard to orthodoxical implementation of IMF policies. Rather, policies in Japan, South Korea and other well-performing Asian tigers seem to be quite anomalous, with extensive industrial trade protection, particular financial corporate governance and strong state interventionism.
3. As Rodrik (2004) suggests, it is obvious that if a developing country would reach the above-listed institutional aims, it would already be a developed country. Hence, not only the aims but also the means of reaching those aims are utopian for developing countries. This means that the aims are consciously too ambitious and unreachable, and that the theoretical justification of the policies is tautological.
4. Quoting Chang (2008: 16): Bad Samaritans (Western economists, politicians, policy makers, etc.) suggested wrong policies and advised transition economies not to do as they had done during their development – 'do as we say, not as we did'!
5. This is true even in countries where the systemic change was initiated by trade unions like Solidarność in Poland (for instance, the famous so-called 'paradox

of Kuron', a Polish trade unionist, who became Labour Minister and who said that he was not allowed/able to do much for the social protection of workers – see Kuron, 2004).

6. According to the EBRD (Transition Report 2001), there is no evidence of a relationship between higher interest rates and a higher flow of FDI during the 1990s.

## 2 The Great Transformation: Recession, Recovery and EU Conditionality

1. The same opinion is shared by Balcerowicz (1993), the World Bank (1996) and Dabrowski (2001).
2. Indeed, in most FSRs, a transition process did not start before the dissolution of the Soviet Empire in 1991.
3. Poland, in the taxonomy of Chapter 5, is classified as a corporative capitalist economy; Albania is classified as a competitive capitalist economy; and Azerbaijan, Tajikistan and Kyrgyzstan are classified as dirigiste economies.
4. A paradoxical case is the example of a textile firm which had the objective, fixed by the plan, to produce a certain amount of length in metres of cloth. The director of that firm, encouraged by the plan and by his production bonus, would merely be concerned with producing very long but thin pieces of cloth!
5. This has an impact even today during times of crisis: the habit of growing food in countries like Russia allows households to cope better with the recession (Gerry and Li, 2010).
6. This also underlines the pattern of FDI, which is mainly characterised by small and medium-sized firms in the Italian case.
7. PAIZ stands for *Państwowej Agencji Inwestycji Zagranicznych* in Polish (Polish Agency for Foreign Investment).
8. PAIZ and PAI (*Polskiej Agencji Informacyjnej* – Polish Agency of Information) were set up with the aim of attracting and channelling FDI in Poland.
9. Poland, Hungary, the Czech Republic, Slovenia and Estonia (hence their collective name CEEC-Luxembourg).
10. Bulgaria, Romania, Slovakia, Latvia and Lithuania (hence their collective name CEEC-Helsinki).
11. According to some econometric analyses, a catching-up scenario between the transition economies and the EU-15 in 15 years is possible, with a convergence in GDP per captia if the CEECs grow at 6 per cent and the EU-15 grow at 0 per cent. If the growth of the CEECs was 3 per cent, then it would take 30 years to catch up, assuming a 0 per cent growth rate in the EU-15. More realistically, it would take between 20 and 30 years if the CEECs grew at 4 per cent and the EU-15 at 2 per cent (Montalbano, 2002).
12. Economist Intelligence Unit (2001).

## 3 Institutional Change: Old and New Institutionalism

1. Cf. Veblen (1919).
2. When economics is compared, as within the institutional approach, to biological evolution, to its laws, rules, principles and mechanisms of natural

selection, of interaction with the external world, mutual functionality, interdependency and complexity of relationships, then any mechanic reactions of physical laws are excluded. Instead, neoclassical economics is attached to physics and to its mechanic laws and principles; where economic agents react mechanically and in a standard way, markets are in equilibrium and any form of complexity is excluded (Hodgson, 1995; Veblen, 1898).

3. NIE is also called neo-institutional economics and emerged in opposition to OIE (also called new institutionalism) which derives mainly from American institutionalism (Commons, Veblen and Mitchell), from the German Historical School and to some extent from the Scandinavian Institutional School (i.e., G. Myrdal). Today, new institutionalism has its best-known scholar in Hodgson and others such as Neale, Tools and Bush. Conventionally, new institutionalism also embraces evolutionary economics (Dosi, 1988; Lundvall, 1988; Nelson and Winter, 1996) and the Regulation School (Aglietta, 1976; Boyer and Saillard, 2002).
4. The expression 'new institutional economics' was coined by Oliver Williamson, a student of Ronald H. Coase and winner of the Nobel Prize for Economics in 2009. However, NIE as a school of thought was set up by Coase in his famous article 'The Nature of the Firm' (1937).
5. For instance, when an agent sells or buys goods from another agent, he or she acts within the sphere of collective action represented by social rules, contract laws, the institution of propriety rights, membership of an organisation, membership of a powerful family, etc. Therefore, collective action determines, directly or indirectly, all the economic relations of individuals (cf. Chamberlain, 1963: 75).
6. Cf. Alchian (1950) Demesetz (1967); North (1990); and Libecap (1998).
7. Some examples will help us to understand this better. Many African or developing countries experienced an evolution in their productive structure after the discovery of oil or diamonds. This evolution was accompanied by the emergence of new institutions, such as royalties over the resources, which were completely unknown before, or the distribution of new rights of property. Still, some countries, which experienced a significant increase in population with the arrival of pioneers and conquerors (and a consequent reduction in land fertility), at the same time experienced an important and fast privatisation process, with previously unknown concepts of new property rights and private assets, as in the case of the American Indians of the Mountains of Labrador (Demesetz, 1967). Again, 'the conquest of the West' in North America allowed for the establishment of some conventions and tacit norms between the pioneers involved in the discovery of new frontiers and new wealth (Libecap, 1998) which had never previously been used. In the same way, in Thailand and other countries of Southeast Asia, the strong increase in international trade has raised the price of rice and has also caused changes in the price of land. Consequently, land distribution changed and new property rights emerged, together with the important process of privatisation (Feeny, 1989). To sum up, the increase in the value of land, the discovery of natural resources or the changes resulting from other factors (such as international trade, technological change or the relative change of the endowment of productive factors) resulted in changes in the institutional structure.

8. The indices are: risk of expropriation; risk of repudiation of contracts by governments; quality of bureaucracy; level of corruption; law and order tradition; and international country risk. Olson *et al.* (1998) found that governance variables explain around 50 per cent of growth rate changes among countries.
9. Acemouglu *et al.* (2001) proved that different European colonisation strategies provided exogenous institutions which impacted consistently on productivity and on differences in income per capita among many developing countries.

## 4 A Model of Institutional Change in Transition Economies

1. The people adverse to changes are more willing to pay in order to protect the old framework. They can organise a representative lobby or a political party to take benefits from their current position.
2. In several CEECs, some highly nationalistic and conservative political groups and lobbies were set up during transition. In Poland, for instance, two parties arose – *Somoobrona* (Self-Defence) and *Liga Polskich Rodzin* (League of Polish Families) – both maintaining adherence to previous values, defending the interests of farmers and state-owned enterprise workers (cf. Szcerbiak, 2001). Between them they accounted for around 30 per cent of the political consensus in the 2005 election. Moreover, they are extremely anti-EU and anti-market-oriented. Along with these two parties, another one, *Prawo i Sprawiedliwość* (PiS – Law and Justice), grew consistently in recent years and after the 2005 election (for both Parliament and the presidency of the Republic) it became the dominant Polish party. The brothers Lech and Jarosław Kaczyński, the main leaders of the PiS, became respectively President of the Republic (in 2005) and Prime Minister (in 2006) (Gwiazda, 2008).
3. All CEECs have experienced such phenomena during the 1990s, though to different degrees and at differing levels of intensity. Kornai (1994) called such costs 'transformation costs' and explained the recession of the early 1990s as being caused by the dramatic change in the whole system of these countries.
4. Similarly, Solow speaks about this in Solow, 1994, p. 27.

## 5 Varieties of Capitalism and Socio-Economic Models in Transition Economies

1. EBRD indices rank between +1 and +4. These indices concern the following variables: enterprise restructuring, small- and large-scale privatisation, price liberalisation, foreign trade, competition, banking and financial institutions, and infrastructures. Hungary, Estonia, Poland and the Czech Republic have the highest indexes (cf. Figure 5.1). The World Bank indicators, elaborated by Kaufmann *et al.* (2009), reflect the statistical compilation of responses on the quality of governance given by a large number of enterprises, citizens and expert survey respondents in developed, transition and developing countries, as reported by a number of survey institutes, think-tanks, non-governmental organisations and international organisations. Indices are estimated between −2.5 and +2.5. They concern six fundamental governance dimensions: voice and accountability, political stability, government effectiveness, regulatory quality, rule of law and control of corruption.

2. China and Vietnam represent 'socialist markets' and seem to be the only two countries which embrace such a model. This represents an evolution and is a result of a reform process which first started in China in 1978 and intensified during the 1990s (Yeager, 2004). This transitional process transformed China and Vietnam from planned economies to 'socialist market economies', characterised by particular forms of property rights which allow: 1) both private and state investors to coexist, without complete liberalisation, privatisation and political pluralism; 2) integration (though modest) into the world economy; 3) government control and monitoring of domestic financial markets.
3. In this analysis, a qualitative country-by-country classification was preferred to a quantitative classification which could be drawn for instance from a factor analysis. A qualitative analysis in this case in fact allows a better matching, avoiding mistaken deriving from outliers, 'institutional jumps' based on one-year reforms, single policies or *una tantum* institutional implementation. A factor analysis will however be made thereafter (see the appendix at the end of this chapter).
4. Just to clarify: in the regression, the democracy variable (political rights and civil liberties) is negative, since this indicator ranks between 1 (the most free) and 7 (the least free). It means that the higher the level of democracy, the greater the GDP per capita.
5. There is a certain consensus among scholars regarding the fact that initial conditions were relevant for the following growth among transition economies (Nuti, 1999; Roland, 2002; Svejnar, 2002; Beck and Laeven, 2006). Democracy, which is also a variable here, will be discussed in more detail in the next two chapters. However, several authors consider it as a crucial variable for growth, indirectly via macro-economic stabilisation (Mickiewicz, 2005; Falcetti *et al.*, 2006; Kaufmann *et al.*, 2007) or directly via better institution-building (Beck and Laeven, 2006).
6. Cf. UNDP, 2006.
7. I refer here to OECD countries. However, the very high value of the Gini coefficient in the USA, i.e., 41%, should be noted (UNDP, 2006).
8. The standardised values, used to give a more immediate figure of the rank, are simply obtained by multiplying all the scores by 14 and dividing by 100 for each model.
9. The fact that trade is put among the variables which better explain a corporative capitalist model is not at all in contradiction with the empirical evidence. Countries like Germany and most of new industrialised countries in Asia are characterised by high levels of trade and would easily fit within a theoretical corporative capitalist model (see Amable, 2003; Jessop, 2002).

## 6 Explaining Economic Development: Old and New Theories

1. The literature review on economic development here is very compressed since the main objective of the book goes beyond this. For a more indepth examination, see: Boggio and Serravalli (2003); Helpman (2004); Meier and Rauch (2005); and Maddison (2008).

2. For instance, Guatemala has a GDP per capita that is higher than Sri Lanka, but inequality is much higher in Guatemala. Development indicators are much better in Sri Lanka than in Guatemala. Life expectancy (years): 72 compared with 65; infant mortality rate (per 1,000): 18 compared with 48; and adult literacy rate (per cent): 89 compared with 54 (UNDP, 1995). Examples like this are numerous and a non-perfect correlation between GDP and development indicators can be observed even in industrialised countries where there are more resources to distribute. For instance, Ireland has the highest GDP per capita after Luxembourg, yet its non-income dimension indicators, i.e., education and life expectancy, are lower than Italy or Portugal (UNDP, 2006). Saudi Arabia has a GDP per capita which is higher than many transition economies such as Poland, the Czech Republic and Hungary, but its non-income dimension indicators are lower. The USA has an income per capita which is much higher than most of the countries in the world, yet the life expectancy of black American citizens is lower than in China or in the Indian State of Kerala. As a result of all these contradictions and exceptions, the UNDP classification of HDI and GDP ranks is not at all coincidental (UNDP, 1999).
3. The UNDP HDI is a composite index ranking between 0 and 1. It is the combination of two non-income dimensions of people's lives and one income dimension. The first one is life expectancy at birth, which also reflects infant mortality. The second one is educational attainment, which is a combination of primary, secondary and tertiary educational levels and the adult literacy rate. The third element is an adjusted GDP index which reflects income per capita measured in PPP in US$ (UNDP, 1990).
4. The most authoritative paper on this theme is that by Stiglitz, Sen and Fitoussi (*Report by the Commission on the Measurement of Economic Performance and Social Progress*, available online at http://www.stiglitz-sen-fitoussi.fr/documents/rapport_anglais.pdf, date accessed 1 March 2011). See the appendix to this chapter for a classification of the different measurements of wealth.
5. The case of Italian industrial districts is a good example, which proves the direction of the relationship (↑ trust ↑ innovation ↑ human capital ↑ productivity) (Becattini, 1979). There is a growing literature focusing on social capital in transition economies, which confirms this relationship (see Raiser, 1997; Raiser *et al.*, 2001; and Kornai *et al.*, 2004).

## 7 Institutions, Human Development, Economic Growth

1. Some parts of this chapter were previously published in a journal article version in Tridico (2007a).
2. The UNICEF (1995) measure of the poverty line is equal to 60 per cent of low income. Low income was defined as a percentage between 35 and 60 per cent of the average wage in 1989. In this way, the poverty line is not measured in absolute terms but reflects the condition of the specific country. In fact, a poverty line of PPP of $4 a day (as considered by Milanovic, 1996) would be too low for the CEECs and too high for the CIS.

3. The health and education expenditure variables are the share of GDP that the state invests in education and health (World Bank, 2008). Public education and health expenditure allow an assessment of the priority a government assigns to education and the health system relative to other public investments. Education expenditure also reflects a government's commitment to invest in human capital development, while health expenditure reflects the government's commitment to invest in human development. Both these dimensions are essential for the HDI. In a sense, these variables express the orientation of countries towards social institutions, which are fundamental to a better level of capabilities.
4. The variable HD (human development) used here should not be confused with HDI (Human Development Index) which also includes along with life expectancy and education index the GDP index (per capita GDP in purchasing power parity).
5. Even when these two variables – voice and accountability and expenditure on education – are alternatively regressed alone, along with expenditure on health and freedom, against HD, they are not significant.
6. It would be easier to claim endogeneity between, for instance, health expenditure and GDP. Both are flows, and one could claim that a reverse relation applies: the higher the GDP, the higher the expenditure on health. However, since I used the HD variable, which is basically a stock variable (of years of life and years of education) and which does not include GDP, it is not easy to claim that reverse relation, and the risk of endogeneity is at least reduced. However, this is a controversial issue which would require a lot of research and several appendices in order for definite statements to be made. Unfortunately, this cannot be done here, although in the appendix to this chapter, I used basic 2SLS and IV approaches in order to partially deal with these issues.
7. In this regard, it is important to also underline that Goel and Budak (2006) show that a low level of education, captured by a low HDI, can have negative results on an important issue for transition economies, which is privatisation. They found out that small scale privatisation is positively affected, among other variables, by a higher level of education. In general, greater economic prosperity (including education, GDP and life expectancy) has a positive effect on both large-scale and small-scale privatisation (see also on these relations Stuckler *et al.*, 2009; and Gerry *et al.*, 2010b).
8. The results of this exercise were already published in Tridico, 2007a.
9. Obviously, I could not include the third component of the HDI, i.e., the GDP index, in the regression as an independent variable because there would appear to be strong collinearity between the GDP index and GDP per capita (in US$ PPP) which is used as a dependent variable.
10. As observed before, the debate about the correlation between the HDI and GDP is very lively and controversial. However, in the case of transition economies, the relationship between the HDI and GDP seems to go in the suggested direction.
11. In Estonia, the HDI decreased in the first part of transition (1989–95).
12. The Czech Republic is one of the most developed countries among transition economies in terms of both GDP and HDI levels, so its performance in terms

of the rate of growth of GDP and HDI was probably a bit lower than Hungary, Poland and Slovenia.
13. The Czech Republic, Estonia, Hungary, Poland and Slovenia.
14. Inequality is much more correlated with health expenditure and less with human development, hence it could be used as an instrument.
15. It would be ideal to carry out tests considering time-series approaches for these variables. However, such variables are sometimes unavailable for a long period of time, so these approaches could not be included.

## 8 Origins of Development: Social Capital, the Middle Class and Democracy

1. The main conclusion of Chapter 7 was that human development is a sufficient but not necessary condition for economic growth. If a county exhibits human development, economic growth will follow. However, a country can grow without human development. Obviously, human development together with economic growth is the preferred scenario.
2. Democracy also has many limits when it becomes an elite competition for power and office: 'it means only that people have the opportunity of refusing or accepting the men who are to rule them' (Schumpeter, 1943: 269).
3. 'True democratisation means more than elections. It requires the consolidation of democratic institutions and the strengthening of the democratic process, with democratic values and norms embedded in all parts of society' (UNDP, 2002: 14).
4. According to Resolution 288 of the Economic and Social Council of the United Nations, 'any international organization which is not established by intergovernmental agreement shall be considered as a non-governmental organization'.
5. Anheier, 2004.
6. The percentage of people answering 'yes'.
7. Polity IV Project (2005).
8. Freedom House notes that a country's poor rating is not necessarily a comment on the intentions of the government, but may indicate real restrictions on liberty caused by non-governmental terror.
9. Freedom House is a world leader in evaluating governments; data and methodologies are subject to rigorous internal and external reviews. The data are reproducible and the index components are clear. Ratings are assigned by a centralised team of researchers. Thus, the data are considered to be reliable.
10. In Chapter 7, human development was the dependent variable regressed against expenditure on health, the Freedom Index and an interaction variable formed by expenditure on education and voice and accountability. The human development variable is not to be confused with the HDI, which includes a GDP index (per capita GDP in PPP $) along with the life expectancy and education indices.
11. See, for instance, Binder and Georgiadis (2010), who apply a dynamic panel data approach to show the determinants of human development. The results are very similar to mine.

12. Staiger and Stock (1997) show than an instrument is not weak if F has a value that is not below 7.5.
13. Is important to recall that the variable used is control of corruption (−2.5 high corruption; +2.5 low corruption), while the political rights and civil liberties variable (for democracy) rank between 1 (the most free) and 7 (the least free). As such, in the relation above, low levels of corruption are associated with higher levels of democracy.
14. The middle class is more interested in defending post-materialist values such as education, the environment and health (Inglehart, 1971).
15. Even in countries where education and health are mostly privatised, the public expenditure in these two dimensions is still high.

## 9 Conclusion

1. Baldwin (2000) stated that most of these economies (i.e., transition economies) lost ten years of development.

# Bibliography


Abramovitz, M. 1986. 'Catching up, Forging Ahead and Falling Behind', *Journal of Economic History* XLVI(2): 385–406.

Acemoglu, D., Johnson, S. and Robinson J., (2001), 'The Colonial Origins of Comparative Development: An Empirical Investigation', *American Economic Review* 91(5): 1369–401.

——. 2006. *Economic Origins of Dictatorship and Democracy*. New York: Cambridge University Press.

Adam, J. 1999. *Social Costs of Transformation to a Market Economy in Post-Socialist Countries: The Case of Poland, the Czech Republic and Hungary*. New York: Macmillan Press.

Aglietta, M. 1976. *Regulation et crises du capitalisme*. Paris: Calmann-Levy.

Agulhon, M. 1977. *Le Cercle dans la France Bourgeoise. Etude d'une Mutation de Sociabilite*. Paris: Armand Colin.

Ahluwalia, M.S. 1976. 'Inequality, Poverty and Development', *Journal of Development Economics* 3(4): 307–42

Alam, A., Murthi, M., Yemtsov, R., Murruraga, E., Dudwick, N., Hamilton, H. and Tiongson, E. 2005. *Growth, Poverty, and Inequality: Eastern Europe and the Former Soviet Union*. Washington DC: World Bank.

Alchian, A. 1950. 'Uncertainity, Evolution and Economic Theory', *Journal of Economic Review* 58: 211–22.

Alchian, A. and Demesetz, H. 1972. 'Production, Information Costs, and Economic Organization', *American Economic Review* 62: 777–95.

Alesina, A. and Perotti, R. 1996. 'Income Distribution, Political Instability and Investment', *European Economic Review* 40: 1203–28.

Alston, L.J., Libecap, G. and Schneider, R. 1995. 'Property Rights and the Preconditions for Markets: The Case of the Amazon Frontier', *Journal of Institutional and Theoretical Economics* 151(1): 89–107.

Amable, B. 2003. *The Diversity of Modern Capitalism*. Oxford University Press.

Amoroso, B. 2003. 'Globalization and Welfare', Working Paper, University of Roskilde.

Anand, S. and Harris, C. 1994. 'Choosing a Welfare Indicator', *American Economic Review* 84: 226–31.

Andreff, W. 1998. 'Nominal and Real Convergence – At What Speed?', in J. van Braband (ed.), *Remaking Europe: The European Union and Transition Economies*. Lanham, MD: Rowman & Littlefield.

Anheier, H. (ed.) 2004. *Global Civil Society 2004/5*. Centre for the Study of Global Governance (London School of Economics). London: Sage. Available online at: http://www.lse.ac.uk/Depts/global/yearbook04chapters.htm.

Anirudh, K. 2002. *Active Social Capital: Tracing the Roots of Development and Democracy*. New York: Columbia University Press.

Antonelli, C. 2005. 'Models of Knowledge and Systems of Governance', *Journal of Institutional Economics* 1(1): 51–73.

Aoki, M. 2001. *Toward a Comparative Institutional Analysis*. Massachusetts Institute of Technology.
Apolte, T. 2010. 'Democracy and Prosperity in Two Decades of Transition', Munster University Working Papers, Discussion Paper No. 26.
Arrow, K. 1962. 'The Economic Implications of Learning by Doing', *Review of Economic Studies* 29(3): 55–173.
——. 1975. 'Gift and Exchange', in E. Phelps (ed.), *Altruism, Morality and Economic Theory*. New York: Russell Sage Foundation.
Åslund, A. 2001. 'The Myth of Output Collapse after Communism', Carnegie Endowment, Working Paper No. 18, Washington DC.
——. 2007. *How Capitalism was Built: The Transformation of Central and Eastern Europe, Russia, and Central Asia*. Cambridge University Press.
Atkinson, A. 1999. 'Is Rising Inequality Inevitable? A Critique of the Transatlantique Consensus', WIDER Annual Lectures, No. 3, Helsinki.
Balcerowicz, L. 1993. 'Common Fallacies in the Debate on the Economic Transition in Central and Eastern Europe', EBRD Working Paper No. 11.
——. 1995. *Socialism, Capitalism, Transformation*. Budapest: Central European University Press.
Baldwin, R. 2000. 'Trade and Growth: Still Disagreement about the Relationships', Economics Department, OECD Working Paper No. 264.
Bardhan, P. 2005. 'Institutions Matter, But Which Ones?', *Economics of Transition* 13(3): 499–532.
Barro, R.J. 1998. *Determinants of Economic Growth: A Cross-Country Empirical Study*. Cambridge, MA: MIT Press.
Barro, R.J. and Sala-I-Martin, X. 1995. *Economic Growth*. New York: McGraw-Hill.
Beblo, M., Golinowska, S., Lauer, C., Pietka, K. and Sowa, A. 2002. 'Poverty Dynamics in Poland: Selected Quantitative Analysis', Case Foundation No. 54/2002, Warsaw.
Becattini, G. 1979. *Scienza economica e trasformazioni sociali*. Florence: La Nuova Italia.
——. 2000. *Il distretto industriale: un nuovo modo di interpretare il cambiamento economico*. Turin: Rosemberg & Sellier.
Beck, T. and Laeven, L. 2006. 'Institution Building and Growth in Transition Economies', CEPR Discussion Paper No. 5718.
Bedi, A. and Cieslik, A. 2002. 'Wages and Wage Growth in Poland: The Role of Foreign Direct Investment', *Economics of Transition* 10(1): 1–27.
Bellandi, M. 2003. *Mercati, industrie e luoghi di piccola e grande impresa*. Bologna: Il Mulino.
Berend, I. 2006. *An Economic History of Twentieth-Century Europe*. Cambridge University Press.
——. 2009. *From the Soviet Bloc to the European Union: The Economic and Social Transformation of Central and Eastern Europe since 1973*, Cambridge University Press.
Bevan, A. and Estrin, S. 2000. 'The Determinant of Foreign Direct Investment in Transition Economies', Williamson Davidson Institute, Working Paper No. 342.
Bhagwati, J. 2004. *In Defense of Globalization*. Oxford University Press.
Binder, M. and Georgiadis, G. 2010. 'Determinants of Human Development: Insights from State-Dependent Panel Models', Human Development Research Paper 2010/24.

Birdsall, N. and Sabot, R. 1994. 'Inequality as a Constraint on Growth in Latin America', Development Policy, Newsletter on Policy Research, Inter-American Development Bank.

Blanchard, O. 1997. *The Economics of Post-Communist Transition*. New York: Oxford University Press.

Blazyca, G. and Rapacki, R. (eds). 2001. *Poland into the New Millennium*. Cheltenham: Edward Elgar.

Boggio, G. and Seravalli, L. 2003. *Lo sviluppo economico, i fatti, le teorie, le politiche* Bologna: Il Mulino.

Bosworth, B. and Collins, S. 2003. 'The Empirics of Growth: An Update', Brooking Institution, mimeo, March.

Bourdieu, P. and Wacquant, L. 1992. *An Invitation to Reflexive Sociology*. Chicago University Press.

Boycko, M., Shleifer, A. and Vishny, R. 1995. *Privatizing Russia*. Cambridge, MA: MIT Press.

Boyer, R. and Saillard, Y. (eds). 2002. *Regulation Theory: The State of the Art*. London: Routledge.

Brancato, E. 2009. *Markets versus Hierarchies: A Political Economy of Russia from the 10th Century to 2008*. Cheltenham: Edward Elgar.

Brenner, R. 2005. 'The Capitalist Economy, 1945–2000', in D. Coates (ed.), *Varieties of Capitalism, Varieties of Approaches*. Basingstoke: Palgrave Macmillan.

Brinkman, R. 1995. 'Economic Growth versus Economic Development: Toward a Conceptual Clarification', *Journal of Economic Issues* XXIX(4): 1171–88.

Brzezinski, Z. 2001. 'The Primacy of History and Culture', *Journal of Democracy* 12(4): 20–6.

Bush, P.D. 1988. 'The Theory of Institutional Change in Evolutionary Economics', in M. Tools (ed.), *Foundations of Institutional Thought*, Vol. 1. New York: Sharpe Inc.

Calvo, G. and Coricelli, F. 1993. 'Output Collapse in Eastern Europe', IMF Staff Papers 40(1).

Carlucci, F. and Cavone, F. 2004. *La Grande Europa. Allargamento, integrazione e sviluppo*. Milan: Franco Angeli.

Carter, F.W. and Turnok, D. (eds). 2002. *Environmental Problems of Eastern and Central Europe*. London: Routledge.

Chamberlain, N.W. 1963. 'The Institutional Economics of Commons', in *Institutional Economics, Lectures by J. Dorfman, C. Ayres, N. Chamberlain, S. Kuznets, R. Gordon*. Berkeley, CA: University of California Press.

Chang, H.-J. 2008. *Bad Samaritans. The Myth of Free Trade and the Secret History of Capitalism*. New York: Bloomsbury Press.

Chenery, H.B. and Syrquin, M. 1975. *Patterns of Development, 1950–1960*. Oxford University Press.

Chong-Ju, C. 2004. 'Communitarian Capitalis and the Social Market Economy: An Application to China', in J. Kidd and F. Richter (eds), *Development Models, Globalization and Economies*. Basingstoke: Palgrave Macmillan.

Clague, C. 1992. 'Introduction: The Journey to Market Economy', in C. Claugue and G. Rausser (eds), *The Emergence of Market Economies in Eastern Europe*. Cambridge, MA: Blackwell.

Clague, C. and Rausser, G. (eds). 1992. *The Emergence of Market Economies in Eastern Europe*. Cambridge, MA: Blackwell.

Coase, R. 1937. 'The Nature of the Firm', *Economica* 386–405.
——. 1960. 'The Problem of Social Cost', *Journal of Law and Economics* 3: 1–44.
——. 1984. 'The New Institutional Economics', *Journal of Institutional and Theoretical Economics* 140: 229–37.
——. 1998. 'The New Institutional of Economics', *American Economic Review* 88(2): 72–4.
Coates, D. (ed.) 2005. *Varieties of Capitalism, Varieties of Approaches*. Basingstoke: Palgrave Macmillan.
Collier, I., Roggemann, H., Scholz, O. and Tomann, H. (eds). 1999. *Welfare States in Transition. East and West*. London: Palgrave Macmillan.
Commons, J.R. 1934. *Institutional Economics*. New York: Macmillan.
Cornia, G.A. 2003. 'The Impact of Liberalisation and Globalisation on Income Inequality in Developing and Transitional Economies', CESifo Working Paper Series No. 843, CESifo Group, Munich.
Costantini, V. and Monni, S. 2005. 'Sustainable Human Development for European Countries', *Journal of Human Development* 6(3): 329–51.
Cypher, J. and Dietz, J. 2004. *The Process of Economic Development*, 2nd edn. London and New York: Routledge.
Dabrowski, M. 2001. 'Ten Years of Polish Economic Transition, 1989–1999', in M. Blejer and M. Skreb (eds), *Transition: The First Decade*. Cambridge, MA: MIT Press.
Dahl, R. 1971. *Polyarchy*. New Haven, CT: Yale University Press.
Davies, N. 2001. *Heart of Europe: The Past in Poland's Present*. Oxford University Press.
De Filippis, F. 2002. *Le vie della globalizzazione: la questione agricola nel WTO*. Rome: FrancoAngeli.
De Melo, M., Denizer, C. and Gelb, A. 1996. 'Patterns of Transition from Plan to Market', *World Bank Economic Review* 10: 397–424.
——. 2008. 'Knowledge-Based Economy and Social Exclusion: Shadow and Light in the Roman Socio-economic Model', Working Paper No. 91, Department of Economics, University Roma Tre.
De Muro, P. and Tridico, P. 2008. 'The Role of Institutions for Human Development', EAEPE 2008 Annual Conference, University Roma Tre, 6–8 November.
De Santis, R. and Vicarelli, C. 2001. 'Fattori di attrazione degli Investimenti Diretti Esteri nell'Unione Europea: il ruolo del contesto istituzionale e la competitività dell'Italia', *Rivista di Politica economica* 3: 3–32.
De Vincenti, C. 1998. 'The Transition from a Planned to a Market Economy: A Process Requiring Governance', *International Spectator* XXXIII(4): 49–62.
——. 2002. 'La Grande Trasformazione: una chiosa a Nuti', mimeo, Dipartimento di Economia Pubblica, University of La Sapienza, Rome.
Demesetz, H. 1967. 'Towards a Theory of Property Rights', *American Economic Review* 57: 347–59.
Desai, M. 1991. 'Human Development: Concept and Measurement', *European Economic Review* 35: 350–7.
Dewatripont, M. and Roland, G. 1992. 'The Virtues of Legitimacy and Gradualism in the Transition to a Market Economy', *Economic Journal*, 102: 291–300.
Dillon, P. and Wykoff, F. 2002. *Creating Capitalism: Transitions and Growth in Post-Soviet Europe*. Cheltenham: Edward Elgar.

Domar, E. 1946. *Capital Expansion, Rate of Growth and Employment*. Econometrica.

Dosi, G. 1988. 'Sources, Procedures, and Microeconomic Effects of Innovation', *Journal of Economic Literature* 26(3): 1120–71.

Dunning, J.H. 1977. 'Trade, Location of Economic Activity and MNE: A Search for an Eclectic Approach', in B. Ohlin, P. Hesselborn and P. Wijkman (eds), *International Allocation of Economic Activity*. London: Macmillan.

Easterly, W. 2001. 'The Lost Decades: Developing Countries' Stagnation in Spite of Policy Reform 1980–1998', *Journal of Economic Growth* 6: 135–45.

Easterly, W. and Rebelo, S. 1993. 'Fiscal Policy and Economic Growth. An Empirical Investigation', *Journal of Monetary Economics* 32: 417–58.

Ebert, R. 2007. 'The Successes and Failures of Economic Transition: The European Experience', *Comparative Economic Studies* 49(4): 709–11.

EBRD. 2009. Economic statistics, available at www.ebrd.com.

*The Economist*. 2010. 'The World in 2010', January.

Economist Intelligent Unit, Country Reports: Czech Republic, Poland and Hungary, 1989, 2000, 2001, 2005. London.

Etzkowitz, H. 1997. 'The Triple Helix: Academy-Industry-Government Relations and the Growth of Neo-corporatist Industrial Policy in the U.S.', in S. Campo dall'Orto (ed.), *Managing Technological Knowledge Transfer*. Brussels, EC Social Sciences COST A3, Vol. 4, EC Directorate General, Science, Research and Development.

European Commission. 1997. *Agenda 2000, Per un'Unione più forte e più ampia*, Bollettino della Ue, supplemento 5/97, Ufficio delle Pubblicazioni Ufficiali delle Comunità europee, Brussels.

——. 2002. *Rapporto Regolare 2002 sui paesi PECO*. Website of the European Commission (www.europa.eu.int).

Eurostat. 2009. Structural Indicators, online database.

Fadda, S. 1999. 'Istituzioni e sviluppo economico. Un quadro metodologico con particolare riferimento al caso del mezzogiorno', *La questione Agraria* 73.

——. 2001. 'Istituzioni economiche e economia delle istituzioni nei sistemi produttivi locali', *Argomenti*, fasc. 1.

——. 2002. 'Does the Change of Economic Institutions Require a Change in Value?', Working Paper No. 28, University of Rome III.

Falcetti, E., Lysenko, T. and Sanfey, P. 2006, 'Reforms and Growth in Transition: Re-examining the Evidence', *Journal of Comparative Economics* 34: 421–45.

Falcetti, E., Raiser, M. and Sanfey, P. 2000. 'Defying the Odds: Initial Conditions, Reforms and Growth in the First Decade of Transition', EBRD Working Paper No. 55.

Fernandez, R. and Rodrik, D. 1991. 'Resistance of Reform: Status Quo Bias in the Presence of Individual-Specific Uncertainty', *American Economic Review* 81: 1146–55.

Field, J. 2008. *Social Capital*, 2nd edn. New York: Routledge.

Foster, J.F. 1981. 'The Effect of Technology on Institutions', *Journal of Economic Issues* XV: 907–14.

Freedom House. 2009. *Freedom in the World 2009: The Annual Survey of Political Rights and Civil Liberties*. New York: Freedom House.

Friedland, R. and Alford, R.R. 1987. 'Bringing Back in: Symbols, Structure and Institutional Contradiction', paper presented at the Conference on

Institutional Change, Center for Advanced Study in Behavioral Sciences, Stanford, CA.

Fukuyama, F. 1995. *Trust: The Social Virtues and the Creation of Prosperity*. New York: Free Press.

Galor, O. and Mountford, A. 2003. 'Trade, Demographic Transition, and the Great Divergence: Why are a Third of People Indian and Chinese?', Working Paper, Brown University.

Gerry, C. and Li, C. 2010a. 'Consumption Smoothing and Vulnerability in Russia', *Applied Economics* 42(16): 1995–2007.

Gerry, C., Lee, J-K. and Mickiewicz, T. 2010a. 'Governance, Institutions and Growth: Empirical Lessons from the Post-Communist Transition', in E. Marelli and M. Signorelli (eds), *Growth and Structural Features of Transition*. Basingstoke: Palgrave Macmillan.

Gerry, C., Mickiewicz, T. and Nikoloski, Z. 2010b. 'Did Mass Privatisation Really Increase Post-Communist Male Mortality?', Economics Working Paper No. 103, UCL, London.

Giannaros, D. 2008. 'Twenty Years after the Economic Restructuring of Eastern Europe: An Economic Review', *International Business & Economics Research Journal* 7(11): 35–48.

Gil, E., Szelényi, I. and Townsley, E. 1998. *Making Capitalism without Capitalists: The New Ruling Elites in Eastern Europe*. London: Verso.

Goel, R. and Budak, J. 2006. 'Privatisation in Transition Economies: Privatisation Scale and Country Size', *Economic Systems* 30: 98–110.

Golinowska, S. 1996. *Polska bieda: Kryteria. Ocena. Przeciwdzialanie*. Warsaw: Institute of Labour and Social Affairs.

Gomulka, S. 1995. 'The IMF-Supported Programs of Poland and Russia: Principles, Errors and Results', *Journal of Comparative Economics* 20(3): 316–45.

Gorzelak, G. 1998. 'Regional Policies and Regional Capacity-Building in Poland', mimeo, Warsaw.

Groenewegen, J., Kershtholt, F. and Nagelkerke, A. 1995. 'On Integrating New and Old Institutionalism: Douglass North Building Bridges', *Journal of Economic Issues* XXIX(2): 467–75.

Gros, D. and Steinherr, A. 1995. *Winds of Change: Economic Transition in Central and Eastern Europe*. London: Longman.

——. 2004. *Economic Transition in Central and Eastern Europe. Planting the Seeds*. Cambridge University Press.

Gunasekara, C. 2006. 'Reframing the Role of Universities in the Development of Regional Innovation Systems', *Journal of Technology Transfer* 31(1): 101–13.

Gwiazda, A. 2008. 'The Parliamentary Election in Poland, October 2007', *Electoral Studies* 27: 760–4.

Hamilton, W. 1932. 'Institutions', in E. Seligman and A. Johnson (eds), *Encyclopaedia of the Social Sciences*, vol. 8, New York: Macmillan.

Hare, P. and Revesz, T. 1992. 'Hungary's Transition to a Market Economy. The Case Against a "Big-Bang"', *Economic Policy* 14: 227–64.

Harrod, R.F. 1939. 'An Essay in Dynamic Theory', *Economic Journal* 49: 14–33.

Hausman, J., Stock, J.H. and Yogo, M. 2005. 'Asymptotic Properties of the Hahn-Hausman Test for Weak Instruments', *Economics Letters* 89(3): 333–42.

Hausmann, R., Pritchett, L. and Rodrik, D. 2005. 'Growth Accelerations', *Journal of Economic Growth* 10(4): 303–29.

Hausner, J., Jessop, B. and Nielsen, N. 1995. *Strategic Choice and Path-dependency in Post-socialism: Institutional Dynamics in the Transformation Process*, Aldershot: Edward Elgar.

Helpman, E. 2004. *The Mystery of Economic Growth*. Cambridge, MA: Harvard University Press.

——. 2006. 'Trade, FDI, and the Organization of Firms', *Journal of Economic Literature* 44(3): 589–630.

Hirschman, A.O. 1981. 'The Rise and Decline of Development Economics', in A.O. Hirschman (ed.), *Essays in Trespassing: Economics to Politics and Beyond*. Cambridge University Press.

Hodgson, G. 1995. 'The Evolution of Evolutionary Economics', *Scottish Journal of Political Economy* 42(4): 469–88.

——. 1998. 'The Approach of Institutional Economics', *Journal of Economic Literature* XXXVI: 166–92.

——. 2006. 'What are Institutions?', *Journal of Economic Issues* XL(1): 1–25.

Holscher, J. and Gabrisch, H. 2006. *The Failures and Successes of Economic Transition – The European Experience*. London and New York: Palgrave Macmillan.

Hooghe, M. and Stolle, D. (eds). 2003. *Generating Social Capital. Civil Society and Institutions in Comparative Perspective*. New York: Palgrave Macmillan.

Huntington, S.P. 1991. *Democratization in the Late Twentieth Century*. Norman: University of Oklahoma Press.

Iapadre, L. 2001. 'Distretti industriali, specializzazione internazionale e quote di mercato delle esportazioni italiane', *Sviluppo Locale* 8: 7–29.

IMF. 1995. 'Gender Issues in Economic Adjustment Discussed at UN Conference on Women', *IMF Survey* (25 September): 286–8.

——. 2001a. *World Economic Outlook, May 2001: A Survey by the Staff of the International Monetary Fund*, World Economic and Financial Surveys. Washington DC: IMF.

——. 2001b. 'International Capital Markets. Developments, Prospects, and Key Policy Issues', IMF Staff Paper, Washington DC.

——. 2007. World Economic Outlook database.

——. 2009. World Economic Outlook database.

Inglehart, R. 1971. 'The Silent Revolution in Europe: Intergenerational Change in Post-Industrial Societies', *American Political Science Review* 65(4): 991–1017.

Irvin, D. and Kroszner, R. 1999. 'Interest, Institutions, and Ideology in Securing Policy Change: The Republican Conversion to Trade Liberalization after Smoot–Hanley', *Journal of Law and Economics* XLII: 643–74.

Jessop, B. 2002. *The Future of the Capitalist State*. Cambridge: Polity Press.

Jessop, B. and Sum, N.-L. 2005. *The Regulation Approach and Beyond: Putting Capitalist Economies in their Place*. Cheltenham: Edward Elgar.

Johnson, S., McMillan, J. and Woodruff, C. 1999. 'Entrepreneurs and the Ordering of Institutional Reform: Poland, Romania, Russia, the Slovak Republic and Ukraine Compared', Working Paper No. 44, London: EBRD.

Jones, C. and Hall, R. 1998. 'Why Do Some Countries Produce So Much More Output per Worker than Others?', NBER Working Paper, Stanford University.

Jones, E. 1981. *The European Miracle: Environments, Economies, and Geopolitics in the History of Europe and Asia*. New York: Cambridge University Press.

Kachigan, S. 1986. *Statistical Analysis: An Interdisciplinary Introduction to Univariate and Multivariate Methods*. New York: Radius Press.
Kaldor, N. 1957. 'A Model of Economic Growth', *Economic Journal*, 67(268): 591–624.
Kaldor, N. and Mirrlees, J.A. 1962. 'A New Model of Economic Growth', *Review of Economic Studies* 29: 174–92.
Kaufmann, D. 2007. 'Governance Matters VI: Aggregate and Individual Governance Indicators for 1996–2006', Washington DC: World Bank.
——. 2009. Governance Matters VIII: Aggregate and Individual Governance Indicators, 1996–2008', World Bank Policy Research Working Paper 4978, available online at: http://info.worldbank.org/governance/wgi/index.asp, date accessed 3 March 2011.
Kaufmann, D. and Kaliberda, A. 1995. 'Integrating the Unofficial Economy into the Dynamics of Post-Socialist Economies: A Framework of Analysis and Evidence', World Bank Working Paper. Washington DC.
Keating, M., Loughlin, J. and Deschouwer, K. 2003. *Culture, Institutions, and Economic Development: A Study of Eight European Regions*. Cheltenham: Edward Elgar.
Knack, S. and Keefer, P. 1995. 'Institutions and Economic Performance: Cross-country Tests using Alternative Institutional Measures', *Economics and Politics* 7: 207–27.
Knight, J. 1992. *Institutions and Social Conflicts*. Cambridge University Press.
Kolodko, G. 2004. 'La transizione al mercato: gradualismo o radicalismo?', *La Questione Agraria* 4: 6–30.
Kolodko, G. and Nuti, M. 1997. 'The Polish Alternative', Working Paper, UNU/WIDER.
Kornai, J. 1986. 'The Soft Budget Constraint', *Kyklos* 39(1): 3–30.
——. 1994. 'Transformational Recession: The Main Causes', *Journal of Comparative Economics* 19: 39–63.
——. 2006. 'The Great Transformation of Central Eastern Europe. Success and Disappointment', *Economics of Transition* 14(2): 207–44.
Kornai, J., Rose-Ackerman, S. and Rothstein, B. (eds). 2004. *Creating Social Trust in Post-Socialist Transition*. New York: Palgrave Macmillan.
Kovalik, T. 2001. 'The Ugly Face of Polish Success', in G. Blazyca and R. Rapacki (eds), *Poland into the New Millennium*. Cheltenham: Edward Elgar.
Kregel, J.A. and Matzner, E. 1992. 'Agenda for the Reconstruction of Central and Eastern Europe', *Challenge*: 33–40.
Krevise, I. 2000. 'Trade as a Handmaiden of Growth: Similarities between the Nineteenth and Twentieth Centuries', Working Paper, University of Pennsylvania.
Krishna, A. 2002. *Active Social Capital: Tracing the Roots of Development and Democracy*. New York: Columbia University Press.
Krugman, P. 1998. 'The Role of Geography in Development', Annual World Bank Conference on Development Economics, Washington DC, April.
——. 2008. *The Return of Depression Economics and the Crisis of 2008*. New York and London: W.W. Norton.
Kuron, J. 2004. *Rzeczpospolita dla moich wnuków*. Warsaw: Wydawnictwo Rosner i Wspólnicy.

Kuznets, S. 1955. 'Economic Growth And Income Inequality', *American Economic Review* 45(1): 1–28.

——. 1965. *Economic Growth and Structure: Selected Essays*. New York: W.W. Norton.

Lane, D. and Myant, M. 2007. *Varieties of Capitalism in Post-Communist Countries*. New York: Palgrave Macmillan.

Lavigne, M. 1999. *The Economics of Transition, From Social Market Economy to Market Economy*. Houndmills: Macmillan.

Ledeneva, A.V. 1998. *Russia's Economy of Favours: Blat, Networking and Informal Exchange*. Cambridge University Press.

Levi, M. 1998. 'A State of Trust', in V. Braithwaite and M. Levi (eds), *Trust and Governance*. New York: Russell Sage Foundation.

Levin, B. 1993. 'One Who Got it Right', *National Interest*, Spring.

Levine, R. and Renelt, D. 1992. 'Sensitivity Analysis of Cross-Country Growth Regression', *American Economic Review* 82: 942–63.

Libecap, G. 1998. 'The New Institutional Economics and Economic Development', Working Paper No. 4, International Centre for Economic Research, Turin.

Lin, J.Y. 2005. 'Viability, Economic Transition and Reflection on Neoclassical Economics', *Kyklos* 58(2): 239–64.

Linz, J. and Stefan, A. 1996. *Problems of Democratic Transition and Consolidation: Southern Europe, South America, and Post-Communist Europe*. Baltimore, MD: Johns Hopkins University Press.

Lipset, S.M. 1959. 'Some Social Requisites of Democracy: Economic Development and Political Legitimacy', *American Political Science Review* 53(1): 69–105.

Lipton, D. and Sachs, J. 1990. 'Creating a Market Economy in Eastern Europe: The Case of Poland', *Brookings Papers on Economic Activity* 1: 75–133.

Lissowska, M. 2001. 'Institutional Change in Transition Countries – Constraints and Path Dependency (on the Example of some Real Estate Property Aspects)', Warsaw School of Economics.

——. 2009. 'The Deficit of Social Capital in Post-transition Economies', Warsaw School of Economics, mimeo.

Litwack, J. and Qian, Y. 1998, 'Balanced or Unbalanced Development: Special Economic Zones as Catalysts for Transition', *Journal of Comparative Economics* 26(1): 1–25.

Loasby, B. 1999. *Knowledge, Institutions and Evolution in Economics*. London: Routledge.

——. 2001. 'Time, Knowledge and Evolutionary Dynamics: Why Connections Matter', *Journal of Evolutionary Economics* 11: 393–412.

Lockwood, W.W. 1954. *The Economic Development of Japan: Growth and Structural Change, 1868–1938*. Princeton University Press.

Lucas R.E. 1988. 'On the Mechanism of Economic Development', *Journal of Monetary Economics* 22: 3–42.

——. 1993. 'Making a Miracle, *Econometrica* 61: 251–7.

Lundvall, B.A. 1988. 'Innovation as an Interactive Process: From User-Producer Interaction to the National System of Innovation', in D. Giovanni, C. Freeman, R. Nelson, G. Silverberg and L. Soete (eds), *Technical Change and Economic Theory*. London: Pinter Publishers.

Mabogunje, A.L. 1989. *The Development Process. A Spatial Perspective*, 2nd edn. London: Unwin Hyman.

MacBean, A. (ed.). 2000. *Trade and Transition*. London: Frank Cass.

Maddison, A. 1995. *Le Forze dello Sviluppo Capitalistico, un confronto di lungo periodo*. Milan: Giuffrè Editore.

——. 2008. *L'economia mondiale dall'anno 1 al 2030: un profilo quantitativo e macroeconomico*, Milan: Pantarei.

Malinowsky, B. 1960. *A Scientific Theory of Culture*. New York: Oxford University Press.

Manzocchi, S. and Beatrice, P. 2001a. 'Allargamento a est dell'Ue: gli effetti sul mercato dei beni', Working Paper, University of Perugia and Centro Studio Confindustria, Perugia-Rome, 2001.

——. 2001b. 'L'allargamento a est dell'Ue, l'impatto sugli IDE', Working Paper, University of Perugia and Centro Studio Confindustria, Perugia-Rome, 2001.

Marelli, E. and Signorelli, M. (eds). 2010. *Growth and Structural Features of Transition*. London: Palgrave Macmillan.

Markowski, S. and Jackson, S. 1993. 'The Attractiveness of Poland to Foreign Direct Investors', Polish Policy Research Group, Warsaw University, Working Paper No. 24.

Marx, K. 1867. *Capital*. Moscow: Progress.

Marx, K. and Engels, F. 1848. *The Communist Manifesto*. International Publishing.

Matzner, E. 1993. 'Policies, Institutions and Employment Performance', in M. Tool (ed.), *Institutional Economics: Theory, Method, Policy*. Dordrecht: Kluver Academic Publishers.

Mauro, P. 1995. 'Corruption and Growth', *Quarterly Journal of Economics* 10(3): 681–712.

——. 2000. 'Stock Returns and Output Growth in Emerging and Advanced Economies', IMF Working Paper, No. 89, Washington DC.

Mayer, N. 2003. 'Democracy in France: Do Associations Matter?', in M. Hooghe and D. Stolle (eds), *Generating Social Capital. Civil Society and Institutions in Comparative Perspective*. New York: Palgrave Macmillan.

Mayhew, A. 1998. *Recreating Europe, The European Union's Policy towards Central and Eastern Europe*. Cambridge University Press.

McArthur, J. and Sachs, J. 2001. 'Institutions and Geography: Comments on Acemoglu, Johnson and Robinson (2000)', Working Paper No. 8114, NBER.

McMillan, J. and Naughton, B. 1992. 'How to Reform a Planned Economy: Lessons from China', *Oxford Review of Economic Policy* 8: 130–43.

Meier, G. and Rauch, J. 2005. *Leading Issues in Economic Development*, 8th edn. Oxford University Press.

Mickiewicz, T. 2005. *Economic Transition in Central Europe and Commonwealth of Independent States*. New York and London: Palgrave Macmillan.

Milanovic, B. 1994. 'Determinants of Cross-country Income Inequality: An Augmented Kuznets Hypothesis', Policy Research Working Paper Series, No. 1246.

——. 1996. 'Income, Inequality and Poverty during the Transition', World Bank, Research Paper Series, No. 11.

Mitchell, W. 1950. 'The Prospects of Economics', in *The Backward Art of Spending Money and Other Essays*. Cambridge, MA: Harvard University Press.

Møller, J. and Skaaning, S.-E. 2009. 'The Three Worlds of Post-Communism: Revisiting Deep and Proximate Explanations', *Democratization* 16(2): 298–322.
Montalbano, P. 2002. 'Analisi dei Flussi Potenziali di Interscambio Commerciale nel Mercato Comune Paneuropeo', CIDEM Working Paper No. 1, University of La Sapienza, Rome.
Moore, B. 1966. *The Social Origins of Dictatorship and Democracy: Lord and Peasant in the Making of the Modern World.* Boston: Beacon Press.
Morris, D.M. 1979. *Measuring the Condition of the World's Poor: The Physical Quality of Life Index.* New York: Pergamon Press.
Mundell, R.A. 1997. 'The Great Contractions in Transition Economies', in M.I. Blejer and M. Skreb (eds), *Macro-economic Stabilisation in Transition Economies.* Cambridge University Press.
Murrel, P. 1992. 'Evolution in Economics and in the Economic Reform of the Centrally Planned Economies', in C. Claugue and G. Rausser (eds), *The Emergence of Market Economies in Eastern Europe.* Cambridge, MA: Blackwell.
Myant, M. and Drahokoupil, J. 2010. *Transition Economies: Political Economy in Russia, Eastern Europe, and Central Asia.* Hoboken, NJ: Wiley-Blackwell.
Myrdal, G. 1974. 'What is Development?', *Journal of Economic Issues* VIII: 729–36.
Nagy, A. 1994. 'Transition and Institutional Change', *Structural Change and Economic Dynamics* 5(2): 315–27.
Naqvi, S. 1995. 'The Nature of Economic Development', *World Development* 23: 543–56.
Nayyar, D. 2000. 'Globalizzazione e strategie per lo sviluppo', *Politica Internazionale* 1–2.
Neale, W.C. 1988. 'Institutions', in M. Tools (ed.), *Foundations of Institutional Thought,* Vol. 1. New York: Sharpe Inc.
Nelson, R.R. and Winter, S.G. 1996. *An Evolutionary Theory of Economic Change.* Cambridge, MA: Belknap Press.
——. 1973. 'Toward an Evolutionary Theories of Economic Capabilities', *American Economic Review* 84: 440–9.
Noorbakhsh, F. 1996. 'Some Reflections on UNDP's Human Development Index', CDS occasional paper, No. 17, University of Glasgow.
Norgaard, O. 2000. *Economic Institutions and Democratic Reform. A Comparative Analysis of Post-Communist Countries.* Cheltenham: Edward Elgar.
North, D.C. 1981. *Structure and Change in Economic History.* New York: W.W. Norton.
——. 1990. *Institutions, Institutional Change and Economic Performance.* Cambridge University Press.
North, D.C. and Thomas, R. 1981. *The Rise of the Western World: A New Economic History.* Cambridge University Press.
Nugent, J.B. and Lin, J.Y. 1995. 'Institutions and Economic Development', in H. Chenery, T.N. Srinivasan and J. Behrman (eds), *Handbook of Development Economics.* Amsterdam: North-Holland.
Nussbaum, M. 2000. *Women and Human Development: The Capabilities Approach.* New York: Cambridge University Press.
Nuti, D.M. 1984. 'Economic Crisis in Eastern Europe: Prospects and Repercussions', EUI Working Paper No. 26, Florence, July.
——. 1986. 'Hidden and Repressed Inflation in Soviet-Type Economies: Definitions, Measurements and Stabilisation', *Contributions to Political Economy* 5: 37–82.

——. 1999. '1989 1999: la grande trasformazione dell'Europa centrorientale', *Europa/Europe* 8(4): 59–70.

——. 2001. 'I Sistemi Economici Post-Comunisti, ovvero, 2001 Odissea nella Transizione', paper presented at the 2001 SIE Annual Conference, Rome.

——. 2009. 'Venti anni dopo: ragioni, processi, risultati della transizione post-socialista', XVIIth Scientific Conference, Growth and Development Patterns: The Role of Institutions in a Comparative Perspective, University of Perugia, 25–27 June.

O'Brien, R. and Williams, M. 2007. *Global Political Economy. Evolution and Dynamics*. Basingstoke: Palgrave Macmillan.

O'Neill, J., Wilson, D., Purushothaman, R. and Stupnytska, A. 2005. 'How Solid are the BRICs?', Goldman Sachs Global Economics Paper No. 134.

OECD. 2000. *Economic Surveys, Poland 1999–2000*, Paris.

——. 2004. *Understanding Economic Growth*. Basingstoke: Palgrave Macmillan.

Ohlin, B., Hesselborn, P. and Wijkman, P. (eds). 1977. *International Allocation of Economic Actvity*. London: Macmillan.

Olson, M. 1965. *The Logic of Collective Action: Public Goods and the Theory of Groups*. Cambridge, MA: Harvard University Press.

——. 1982. *The Rise and Decline of Nations: The Political Economy of Economic Growth, Stagflation and Social Rigidities*. New York: Yale University Press.

——. 1992. 'The Hidden Path to a Successful Economy', in C. Claugue and G. Rausser (eds), *The Emergence of Market Economies in Eastern Europe*. Cambridge, MA: Blackwell.

——. 1996a. 'Distinguished Lecture on Economics in Government: Big Bills Left on the Sidewalk: "Why Some Nations are Rich, and Others Poor?"', *Journal of Economic Perspectives* 10(2): 3–24.

——. 1996b. *Capitalism, Socialism and Dictatorship*. Cambridge, MA: Harvard University Press.

Olson, M., Sarna, N. and Swamy, A. 1998. 'Governance and Growth: A Simple Hypothesis Explaining Cross-country Differences in Productivity Growth', Center for Institutional Reform and the Informal Sector, Working Paper No. 218, University of Maryland at College Park.

Ostrom, E. 2005. *Understanding Institutional Diversity*. Princeton University Press.

——. 2007. 'Challenges and Growth: The Development of the Interdisciplinary Field of Institutional Analysis', *Journal of Institutional Economics* 3(3): 239–64.

Pejovich, S. 1999. 'The Effects of the Interaction of Formal and Informal Institutions on Social Stability and Economic Development', *Journal of Market & Morality* 2: 164–81.

Penrose, E.T. 1952. 'Biological Analogies in the Theory of the Firm', *American Economic Review* 42: 804–19.

Perkins, H.D, Radelet, S. and Lindauer, D.L. 2006. *Economics of Development*, 6th edn. New York: W.W. Norton.

Pitelis, C. 1996. 'Seven Reasons Why "Beyond" Transaction Costs Economics to Thesmoeconomics', in J. Groenewegen (ed.), *Transaction Cost Economics and Beyond*. London: Routledge.

Polany, K. 2001. *The Great Transformation*. Boston: Beacon Press.

Polity IV Project. 2005. 'Political Regime Characteristics and Transitions', College Park: University of Maryland, http://www.bsos.umd.edu/cidcm/inscr/polity/index.htm, date accessed 3 March 2011.

Pomeranz, K. 2000. *The Great Divergence*. Princeton University Press.

Popov, V. 2007. 'Shock Therapy versus Gradualism Reconsidered: Lessons from Transition Economies after 15 Years of Reforms', *Comparative Economic Studies* 49(1): 1–31.
Portes, R. 1993. 'Economic Transformation in Central Europe: A Progress Report', London: CEPR.
Powell, W. and Di Maggio, P. (eds). 1991. *The New Insitutionalism in Organizational Analysis*. Chicago University Press.
Prausello, F. 2003. *The Economics of Enlargement*. Milan: Franco Angeli.
Pryor, F.L. 2006. 'Economic Systems of Developing Nations', *Comparative Economic Studies* 48(1): 77–99.
Przeworski, A., Alvarez, M., Cheibub, J.A. and Limongi, F. 2008. *Democracy and Development. Political Institutions and Material Well-Being in the World, 1950–1990*. New York: Cambridge University Press.
Putnam, R. 1993. *Making Democracy Work*. Princeton University Press.
——. 1995. 'Bowling Alone: America's Declining Social Capital', *Journal of Democracy*: 65–78.
——. 2000. *Bowling Alone: The Collapse and Revival of American Community*. New York: Simon & Schuster.
Raiser, M. 1997. 'Informal Institutions, Social Capital and Economic Transition: Reflections on a Neglected Dimension', EBRD Working Paper No. 25, London.
——. 1999. 'Trust in Transition', EBRD Working Paper No. 39, London.
Raiser, M., Haerpfer, C., Nowotny, T. and Wallace, C. 2001. 'Social Capital in Transition: A First Look at the Evidence', EBRD Working Paper No. 62, London.
Ranis, G., Stewart, F. and Ramirez, A. 2000. 'Economic Growth and Human Development', *World Development* (28)2: 197–219.
Rawls, J. 1971. *A Theory of Justice*. Cambridge, MA: Harvard University Press.
Ray, D. 1998. *Development Economics*. Princeton University Press.
Reuschemeyer, D., Stephens, E.H. and Stephens, J.D. 1992. *Capitalist Development and Democracy*. Cambridge: Polity Press.
Rhodes, M. 2000. 'Employment Policy. Between Efficacy and Experimentation', Working Paper, European University Institute, Florence.
Rodrik, D. 1994. 'Foreign Trade in Eastern Europe's Transition: Early Results', in O. Blanchard, K. Froot and J. Sachs (eds), *The Transition in Eastern Europe*, Vol. 2. NBER and Chicago University Press.
——. 1995. 'Political Economy of Trade Policy', in G. Grossman and K. Rogoff (eds), *Handbook of International Economics*, vol. III. New York: Elsevier Science.
——. 1999. *Making Openness Work*. Baltimore, MD: Johns Hopkins University Press.
——. 2003. 'Growth Strategies', NBER Working Paper No. 10566, National Bureau of Economic Research, Inc.
——. 2004. *Rethinking Growth Policies in the Developing World*. Cambridge, MA: Harvard University Press.
——. 2008. *One Economics, Many Recipes: Globalization, Institutions, and Economic Growth*, New York and London: W.W. Norton.
Rodrik, D. and Rigobon, R. 2005. 'Rule of Law, Democracy, Openness and Income. Estimating the Interrelationships', *Economics of Transition* 13(3): 533–64.

Roland, G. 1994. 'The Role of Political Constraints in Transition Strategies', *Economics of Transition* 2(1): 27–41.

——. 1996. 'Political Economy Issues of Ownership Transformation in Eastern Europe', in M. Aoki and H.K. Kim (eds), *Corporate Governance in Transitional Economies: Insider Control and the Role of Banks*. Washington DC: World Bank, EDI Development Studies.

——. 2002. 'The Political Economy of Transition', *Journal of Economic Perspectives* 16: 29–50.

Roland, G. and Verdier, T. 1994. 'Privatization in Eastern Europe: Irreversibility and Critical Mass Effects', *Journal of Public Economics* 54: 161–83.

Romer, P. 1986. 'Increasing Returns and Long-Run Growth', *Journal of Political Economy* 94(5): 1002–37.

Rose, R. 2009. *Understanding Post-Communist Transformation. A Bottom-Up Approach*. London: Routledge.

Rostow, W.W. 1960. *The Stages of Economic Growth*. Cambridge University Press.

Rothstein, B. 2001. 'Sweden: Social Capital in the Social Democratic State', in R.D. Putnam (ed.), *The Dynamics of Social Capital*. Oxford University Press.

Ruminska-Zimny, E. 1997. 'Human Poverty in Transition Economies', Regional Overview for HDR.

Rutkowski, J. 1996. 'Changes in the Wage Structure During Economic Transition in Central and Eastern Europe', World Bank Technical Paper No. 340.

Sabatini, F. 2008. 'Social Capital and the Quality of Economic Development', *Kyklos* 61(3): 466–99.

Sachs, J. 1991. 'Accelerating Privatisation in Eastern Europe: The Case of Poland', *World Bank Economic Review* 6: 15–31.

——. 1996. 'The Transition at Mid-decade', *American Economic Review (AEA Papers and Proceedings)* 86: 128–33.

Sala-i-Martin, X. 1996. 'The Classical Approach to Convergence Analysis', *Economic Journal* 106(437): 1019–36.

Sarajevs, V. 2003. 'Convergence of European Transition Economies and the EU: What Do the Data Show?', Bofit Discussion Paper No. 13.

Schimmelfennig, F. and Scholtz, H. 2008. 'EU Democracy Promotion in the European Neighbourhood. Political Conditionality, Economic Development and Transnational Exchange', *European Union Politics* 9(2): 187–215.

Schmidt, K. 1998. 'The Political Economy of Mass Privatization and the Risk of Expropriation', *European Economic Review* 44(2): 393–421.

Schneider, F. and Enste, D. 2000. 'Shadow Economies: Size, Causes and Consequences', *Journal of Economic Literature* 38: 77–114.

Schotter, A. 1981. *The Economic Theory of Social Institutions*. Cambridge University Press.

Schumpeter J.A. 1928. 'The Instability of Capitalism', *Economic Journal* 38: 361–86.

——. 1932. 'Development', Festschrift offered to Emil Lederer in honour of his 50th birthday on 22 July 1932, text available at www.schumpeter.info.

——. 1943. *Capitalism, Socialism and Democracy*. London: Unwin University Books.

Scott, W.R. 1987. 'The Adolescence of Institutional Theory', *Administrative Science Quarterly* 32: 493–511.

Sen, A. 1973. *On Economic Inequality*. Oxford: Clarendon Press.

——. 1985. 'A Sociological Approach to the Measurement of Poverty: A Reply to Prof. Peter Townsend', *Oxford Economic Papers* 37: 669–76.

——. 1999. *Development as Freedom*. New York: Oxford University Press.

Serguey, B. and Yavlinsky, G. 2000. *Incentives and Institutions: The Transition to a Market Economy in Russia*. Princeton University Press.

Shaban, R.A. 1987. 'Testing between Competing Models of Sharecropping', *Journal of Political Economy* 95: 893–920.

Shleifer, A. and Treisman, D. 1999. *Without a Map. Political Tactics and Economic Reform in Russia*. Cambridge, MA: MIT Press.

Simatupang, B. 1994. *The Polish Economic Crisis, Background Causes and Aftermath*. London and New York: Routledge.

Sokoloff, K. and Engerman, S. 2000. 'History Lessons. Institutions, Factor Endowments, and Paths of Development in the New World', *Journal of Economic Perspectives* 14: 217–32.

Solow, R.M. 1956. 'A Contribution to the Theory of Economic Growth', *Quarterly Journal of Economics* 70: 65–94.

——. 1994. *Il mercato del lavoro come Istituzione sociale*. Bologna: Il Mulino.

Staehr, K. 2005. 'Reforms and Economic Growth in Transition Economies: Complementarity, Sequencing and Speed', *European Journal of Comparative Economics* 2(2): 177–202.

Staiger, D. and Stock, J.H. 1997. 'Instrumental Variables Regression with Weak Instruments', *Econometrica* 65: 557–86.

Stiglitz, J. 1998. 'More Instrument and Broader Goals: Moving Toward the Post-Washington Consensus', WIDER Annual Lecture.

Stiglitz, J., Sen, A. and Fitoussi, P. 2010. 'Report by the Commission on the Measurement of Economic Performance and Social Progress', http://www.stiglitz-sen-fitoussi.fr/documents/rapport_anglais.pdf, date accessed 3 March 2011.

Stolle, D. 2003. 'The Source of Social Capital', in M. Hooghe and D. Stolle (eds), *Generating Social Capital. Civil Society and Institutions in Comparative Perspective*. New York: Palgrave Macmillan.

Streeten, P. 1979. 'From Growth to Basic Needs, Premises and Promises', *Journal of Policy Modelling* 1(1): 136–46.

——. 1994. 'Human Development: Means and Ends', *American Economic Review*, 84(2): 232–7.

Stuckler, D., King, L. and McKee, M. 2009. 'Mass Privatisation and the Post-Communist Mortality Crisis: A Cross-National Analysis', *Lancet* 373(9661): 399–407.

Sugden, R. 1989. 'Spontaneous Order', *Journal of Economic Perspective* 3(4): 85–97.

——. 1998. 'Normative Expectations: The Simultaneous Evolution of Institutions and Norms', in L. Putterman and A. Ben-Ner (eds), *Economics, Values and Organization*. Cambridge University Press.

Summers, L. 1992. 'The Next Decade in Central and Eastern Europe', in C. Claugue and G. Rausser (eds), *The Emergence of Market Economies in Eastern Europe*. Cambridge, MA: Blackwell.

——. 2003. 'Goodkin Lectures', Kennedy School of Governement, Harvard University.

Svejnar, J. 1989. 'A Framework for the Economic Transformation of Czechoslovakia', *PlanEcon Report* 5(52): 1–18.

——. 2002. 'Assistance to the Transition Economies. Were There Alternatives?' William Davidson Institute Working Paper, University of Michigan.

Szczerbiak, A. 2001. 'Europe as a Re-aligning Issue in Polish Politics?: Evidence from the October 2000 Presidential Election', Working Paper No. 48, Sussex European Institute.

Szelényi, I. 2009. 'Global Socialisms and Post-Socialisms', SOYUZ Annual Symposium, Department of Anthropology, Yale University, 24–25 April.

Sztompka, P. 1995. 'Vertrauen: Die fehlende Ressource in der Postkommunistischen Gesellschaft', in B. Nedelmann (ed.), *Politische Institutionen im Wandel*. Opladen. Westdeutscher Verlag.

Tarrow, S. 1996. 'Making Social Science Work Across Space and Time', *American Political Science Review* 90: 389–97.

Tools, M. (ed.). 1988. *Foundations of Institutional Thought*, 2 vols. New York: Sharpe Inc.

Toye, J. 1995. 'The New Institutional Economics and its Implications for Development Theory', in J. Harris, J. Unter and C. Lewis (eds), *The New Institutional Economics and Third World Development*. London: Routledge.

Transition Reports 2001, 2004, 2005, 2006, 2009. London: EBRD.

Tridico, P. 2004. 'Institutional Change and Economic Performance in Transition Economies: The Case of Poland', PhD thesis, University Roma Tre.

——. 2006. 'Institutional Change and Governance Indexes in Transition Economies: The Case of Poland', *European Journal of Comparative Economics* 3(2): 197–238.

——. 2007a. 'Institutions, Human Development and Economic Growth in Transition Economies', *European Journal of Development Research* 19(4): 569–93.

——. 2007b. 'Rozwoj spoleczny i wzrost gospodarczy w gospodarkach w okresie transformacji: rola instytucji', *Zarzadzanie Publiczne* 1(1): 27–53.

——. 2008. 'Uneven Regional Development in Transition Economies: The Role of Institutions', *Emergo* 13(1): 33–49.

Tridico, P. 2010. 'Growth, Inequality and Poverty in Emerging and Transition Economies', *Review of Transition Studies* 16(4): 979–1001.

Tullock, G. 1998. 'The Fundamentals of Rent-Seeking', in A. Owens (ed.), *The Locke Luminary* 1(2) (Winter): Part 2.

UN, 2009. *The Millennium Development Goals*, New York.

UNCDAT, 2009. Statistical Yearbook, online database.

UNDP, *Human Development Report*, 1990, 1995, 1999, 2000, 2004, 2006, 2009.

——. 2000. *Beyond Transition. Ten Years After the Fall of the Berlin Wall*. New York.

UNICEF. 1995. *Poverty, Children and Policy: Responses for Brighter Future*. Regional Monitoring Report No. 3. Florence: UNICEF ICDC.

Uvalic, M. 2010. *Serbia's Transition. Towards a Better Future*, New York: Palgrave Macmillan.

Veblen, T. 1898. 'Why is Economics Not an Evolutionary Science?', *Quarterly Journal of Economics* 12(3): 373–97.

——. 1919. *The Place of Science in Modern Civilization*. New York: Viking Press.

Voitchovsky, S. 2005. 'Does the Profile of Income Inequality Matter for Economic Growth? Distinguishing between the Effects of Inequality in Different Parts of the Income Distribution', *Journal of Economic Growth* 10: 273–96.

Von Hipple, E. 1994. 'Sicky Information and the Locus of Problem Solving: Implications for Innovation', *Management Science* 40: 429–39.

Van Zon, H. 1994. 'The Lack of Cohesion as the Crucial Problem for Post-socialist Societies', *AI & Society* 8(2): 151–63.

Walker, T.S. and Ryan, J.G. 1990. *Village and Household Economies in India's Semi-arid Tropics*. Baltimore, MD: Johns Hopkins University Press.

Way, L. 2008. 'The Real Causes of the Color Revolutions', *Journal of Democracy* 19(3): 55–69.

Wei, S.-J. 1997. 'Gradualism versus Big Bang: Speed and Sustainability of Reforms', *Canadian Journal of Economics* 30(4): 1234–47.

Weitzman, M.L. 1993. 'How Not to Privatize', in Mario Baldassarri, Luigi Paganetto and Edmund Phelps (eds), *Privatization Processes in Eastern Europe*. New York: St Martin's Press.

Weresa, M. 1999. 'Foreign Direct Investments and Trade Patterns: Theory and Evidence from Poland', paper presented to the 'Poland and the Transformation in Europe: The Role of FDI' workshop, School of Slavonic and East European Studies, University of London, November.

Williamson, J. 1990. 'What Washington Means by Policy Reform', in J. Williamson (ed.), *Latin American Adjustment: How Much Has Happened?* Washington DC: Institute for International Economics.

Williamson, O.E. 1981. 'The Economics of Organisation: The Transaction Cost Approach', *American Journal of Sociology* 87(3): 548–77.

——. 1985. *The Economic Institutions of Capitalism. Firm, Markets, Relational Contracting*. New York: Free Press.

——. 1998. 'The Institutions of Governance', *America Economic Review* 88(2): 75–9.

Wilson, E.O. 1975. *Sociobiology: The New Synthesis*. Cambridge, MA: Harward University Press.

Wollebak, D. and Selle, P. 2003. 'The Importance of Passive Membership for Social Capital Formation', in M. Hooghe and D. Stolle (eds), *Generating Social Capital. Civil Society and Institutions in Comparative Perspective*. New York: Palgrave Macmillan.

World Bank. 1996. *World Development Report: From Plan to Market*. Oxford University Press.

——. 1998a, *Global Economic Prospects 1998/99: Beyond Financial Crisis*. Washington DC: World Bank.

——. 1998b. *East Asia: The Road to Recovery*, Washington DC: World Bank.

——. 2000. *World Development Report 2000/2001*. Oxford University Press.

——. 2009. Millennium Development Goals, online database.

World Values Survey Databank. 2009. http://www.worldvaluessurvey.org, date accessed 3 March 2011.

Yavlinsky, G., Fedorov, B., Shatalin, S., Pekatrov, N., Aleksashenko S., Vavilon, A., Grigoriev, L., Zadornov, M., Machits, V., Mikhailov, A. and Yasin, E. 1991. *500 Days: Transition to the Market*. New York: St Martin's Press.

Yeager, J.T. 2004. *Institutions, Transition Economies and Economic Development*. Boulder, CO: Westview Press.

Young, A. 1928. 'Increasing Returns and Economic Progress', *Economic Journal* 38: 527–42.

# Index

www.ingramcontent.com/pod-product-compliance
Ingram Content Group UK Ltd.
Pitfield, Milton Keynes, MK11 3LW, UK
UKHW021015050925
462611UK00012B/1274
* 9 7 8 1 3 4 9 3 1 6 5 5 7 *